Politics, Society, and Democracy

Essays in Honor of Juan J. Linz

*H. E. Chehabi, Richard Gunther, Scott Mainwaring,
Alfred Stepan, and Arturo Valenzuela, Series Editors*

Politics, Society, and Democracy: The Case of Spain,
edited by Richard Gunther

Politics, Society, and Democracy: Comparative Studies,
edited by H. E. Chehabi and Alfred Stepan

Politics, Society, and Democracy: Latin America,
edited by Scott Mainwaring and Arturo Valenzuela

Politics, Society, and Democracy

Latin America

EDITED BY

Scott Mainwaring
and Arturo Valenzuela

WestviewPress

A Division of HarperCollins*Publishers*

Essays in Honor of Juan J. Linz

Copyright © 1998 by Westview Press, A Division of HarperCollins Publishers, Inc. An earlier version of Chapter 6, "The Crisis of Presidentialism in Latin America," by Arturo Valenzuela, appeared in *Journal of Democracy*, Vol. 4, No. 4 (Oct. 1993). Reprinted with permission.

Published in 1998 in the United States of America by Westview Press, 5500 Central Avenue, Boulder, Colorado 80301-2877, and in the United Kingdom by Westview Press, 12 Hid's Copse Road, Cumnor Hill, Oxford OX2 9JJ

Library of Congress Cataloging-in-Publication Data
Politics, society, and democracy. Latin America / edited by Scott
    Mainwaring and Arturo Valenzuela.
        p.   cm. — (Essays in honor of Juan J. Linz)
    Includes bibliographical references (p.   ) and index.
    ISBN 0-8133-8548-2 (HC)
    1. Latin America—Politics and government.   2. Authoritarianism—
Latin America.   3. Executive power—Latin America.   4. Democracy—
Latin America.   I. Mainwaring, Scott, 1954–   . II. Valenzuela,
Arturo, 1944–   . III. Series.
JL960.P655   1998
320.982—dc21   97-33166
                                                                                    CIP

10   9   8   7   6   5   4   3   2   1

Contents

Acknowledgments

The series editors wish to acknowledge the generous support for this project granted by the Program for Cultural Cooperation between Spain's Ministry of Culture and the United States' Universities. Without that financial assistance this enormous project would have been difficult, if not impossible, to complete successfully.

The editors of this volume would also like to thank the following persons for their assistance: Esperanza Palma and John Rieger for translating Carlos Huneeus's chapter, originally written in Spanish; Carol Stuart for copyediting and preparing the book for publication; Caroline Domingo for copyediting; and Karl Yambert and Barbara Ellington of Westview Press for their attention and assistance.

Acknowledgments

About the Editors and Contributors

Miguel Angel Centeno is Assistant Professor of Sociology at Princeton University. He received his Ph.D. from Yale University. Recent publications include *Democracy within Reason* (2nd ed., 1997), *Toward a New Cuba* (1997), and *The Politics of Expertise in Latin America* (1997). He is currently working on a book on war and the state in Latin America, an article from which will be published in the *American Journal of Sociology*.

Michael Coppedge is a Faculty Fellow at the Kellogg Institute for International Studies of the University of Notre Dame and Associate Professor in the Department of Government. His book, *Strong Parties and Lame Ducks: Presidential Partyarchy and Factionalism in Venezuela* (Stanford University Press, 1994), analyzes institutional problems underlying the crisis of Venezuelan democracy. His current research seeks to explain cleavages, fragmentation, and volatility in eleven 20th-century Latin American party systems. Coppedge wrote his 1988 dissertation at Yale University under the direction of Juan Linz and has taught at the Nitze School of Advanced International Studies (SAIS) of the Johns Hopkins University, Princeton, Yale, and Georgetown.

Susan Eckstein is Professor of Sociology at Boston University. She is the author of *Back from the Future: Cuba under Castro* (1994), *The Poverty of Revolution: the State and Urban Poor in Mexico* (1977, 1988), and *The Impact of Revolution: A Comparative Analysis of Mexico and Bolivia* (1976), as well as editor of *Power and Popular Protest: Latin American Social Movements* and author of approximately four dozen articles on Latin American politics, economics, and society. She is President of the Latin American Studies Association (1997–1998).

Jonathan Hartlyn is Associate Professor of Political Science at the University of North Carolina at Chapel Hill. He is interested in comparative issues of democratization and development in Latin America. His publications include *The Politics of Coalition Rule in Colombia* (1988) and "Democracy in Latin America since 1930," with Arturo Valenzuela, in Leslie Bethell, ed., *The Cambridge History of Latin America*, vol. VI, part II (1994). He is completing a book on the struggle for democratic politics in the Dominican Republic.

Carlos Huneeus is Director of CERC and Professor of Political Science at the Pontificia Universidad Católica de Chile. Educated in England and Germany (M.A., Essex University; Ph.D., Heidelberg University), he is the author of several books including *La Unión de Centro Democrático y la transición a la democracia en España* (Madrid, 1985) and *Los chilenos y la política* (Santiago, 1987).

Joseph L. Love is Director of Latin American Studies and Professor of History at the University of Illinois at Urbana-Champaign. His special interests are the economic and political history of Brazil, including the interplay of regions, and the history of Latin American economic thought and policy. He is the author of *Rio Grande do Sul and Brazilian Regionalism* (1971), *São Paulo in the Brazilian Federation* (1980), and *Crafting the Third World: Theorizing Underdevelopment in Rumania and Brazil* (1996), all published by Stanford University Press.

Scott Mainwaring is the Conley Professor of Government and International Studies at the University of Notre Dame. His latest books are *Building Democratic Institutions: Party Systems in Latin America* (coedited, Stanford University Press, 1995), *Presidentialism and Democracy in Latin America* (coedited, Cambridge University Press, 1997), and *The Party System and Democratization in Brazil* (Stanford University Press, forthcoming).

Matthew Soberg Shugart is Associate Professor of Political Science at the Graduate School of International Relations and Pacific Studies at the University of California, San Diego. He is coauthor of *Seats and Votes* (Yale, 1989) and *Presidents and Assemblies* (Cambridge, 1992); coeditor of *Presidentialism and Democracy in Latin America* (Cambridge, 1997) and *Executive Decree Authority* (Cambridge, in press); and the author of several journal articles on electoral systems, electoral reform, and presidentialism. His current research focuses on policymaking processes in new democracies.

Arturo Valenzuela is Professor of Government and Director of the Center for Latin American Studies at Georgetown University. A specialist on regime transitions, democratic breakdown, and democratic consolidation, he has written widely on Chilean politics. During the first Clinton Administration, he served as Deputy Assistant Secretary for Inter-American Affairs in the United States Department of State.

Samuel Valenzuela is Professor of Sociology and Fellow of the Kellogg Institute at the University of Notre Dame. He was formerly on the faculty at Yale and Harvard Universities, and has been a Visiting Fellow and Senior Associate Fellow at St. Antony's College, Oxford University. He has held fellowships from the National Endowment for Humanities and the John Simon Guggenheim Foundation. He is the author of *Democratización vía reforma: La expansión del sufragio en Chile* and (with Erika Maza Valenzuela) of *Religion, Class and Gender: Constructing Electoral Institutions and Party Politics in Chile* (forthcoming). He has co-edited several books and written forty (excluding translations and reprints) articles for books and journals on the intersection between labor and politics, the origins of democracies in the nineteenth century, democratization out of contemporary authoritarian regimes, and social change.

1

Introduction: Juan Linz and the Study of Latin American Politics

Scott Mainwaring*

In December 1991, on the occasion of Juan Linz's 65th birthday, his friends, students, and admirers gathered in New York City to honor one of the world's great social scientists and teachers. This volume is one in a series of three—the others include one on Spain and one of comparative studies—that were organized around that celebration.[1]

For those who are only familiar with Linz's scholarly writings and not with him as a teacher, there might initially seem to be little reason to organize a volume on Latin America. Relatively little of Linz's voluminous written work has focused directly on Latin America; the vast majority of his empirical work has concentrated on Spain. Linz has never done much empirical research in Latin America, and only once has he been a member of the Latin American Studies Association. Yet despite this, Linz has had a major impact on political science and political sociology in Latin America, both through his writings and as a teacher. Indeed, although Linz would not call himself a Latin Americanist, very few scholars have had comparable impact on the study of Latin American politics.

In this introductory essay, I briefly highlight some major themes on which Linz has deeply contributed to the analysis of Latin American politics and society. I attempt to shed light on why someone who has

* I am grateful to Manuel Alcántara, Michael Coppedge, Susan Eckstein, Carlos Huneeus, Juan Linz, J. Samuel Valenzuela, and Alex Wilde for helpful comments.

not worked primarily on Latin America has had a decisive influence on the study of Latin American politics. I do not deal with all of Linz's themes, mostly because this volume does not include essays on all of them.

Authoritarian and Totalitarian Regimes

In his work on Spain and in his comparative studies, Linz developed a number of themes that resonated deeply among scholars working on Latin America. First was his characterization of authoritarian regimes as a regime type with distinctive characteristics and dynamics, as distinct from democratic and totalitarian regimes. This conceptualization of authoritarianism first appeared in a seminal article, "An Authoritarian Regime: Spain," originally published in 1964. Linz defined authoritarian regimes as "political systems with limited, not responsible, political pluralism; without elaborate and guiding ideology (but with distinctive mentalities); without intensive nor extensive political mobilization (except some points in their development); and in which a leader (or occasionally a small group) exercises power within formally ill-defined limits but actually quite predictable ones."[2]

Before Linz, nobody had clearly defined what was distinctive about authoritarianism. Authoritarianism had been treated as a residual category, distinct from democracy and totalitarianism, but not as a category to explore in its own right. For Linz, authoritarian regimes had three defining features vis-à-vis both democratic and totalitarian regimes. First, in contrast to totalitarian regimes, which attempt to impose a monopolistic political system, authoritarian regimes allow for limited political pluralism. In contrast to democratic regimes, the pluralism is restricted and often not legitimate. Second, whereas totalitarian regimes create and rely on well defined ideologies, authoritarian systems employ less codified mentalities.[3] Third, totalitarian systems mobilize the population, which is expected to actively support the regime; authoritarian regimes tolerate and often prefer apathy or passive acceptance. Democratic regimes allow for ample participation but generally do not mobilize the population from above.

This seminal contribution had a significant impact in thinking about authoritarian regimes. Then in a 236 page article published in 1975, Linz developed his analysis of totalitarian, sultanistic (personalistic patrimonial systems), and authoritarian regimes. He presented a typology of seven different kinds of authoritarian regimes: bureaucratic-military authoritarian regimes; organic statism, mobilizational authoritarian regimes in postdemocratic societies; competitive regimes with racial exclusions (such as South Africa until 1994); pretotalitarian regimes, and post-totalitarian authoritarian regimes.[4] This typology excluded highly personalized, weakly institutionalized patrimonial regimes, which Linz called sultanistic, from authoritarian regimes—a distinction his earlier work on authoritarianism had not introduced. In his latest book, Linz also considered post-totalitarian regimes as separate from the authoritarian category.[5]

Linz's works helped spawn reflections about authoritarianism in Latin America, including about the "new authoritarianism" of the 1970s. Some important contributions on authoritarianism in Latin America were influenced by Linz.[6] Linz wrote only one piece specifically on authoritarianism in Latin America: his contribution to Alfred Stepan's edited book, *Authoritarian Brazil: Origins, Policies, and Future,* argued that the Brazilian authoritarian regime was not well institutionalized— that it therefore should be called an authoritarian situation rather than a regime. The problem of leadership succession from one military president to the next created serious friction; the military's initial ideology of restoring democracy constrained the extent to which it could create an enduring regime; the regime had no clear legitimacy formula; and prospects for creating a hegemonic party akin to the Mexican Partido Revolucionario Institucional (PRI) were remote.[7] Although Linz was not an expert on Brazil—indeed, he claims that he had only spent perhaps 12 days in Brazil, some of them on the beach in Copacabana—his profound understanding of authoritarian regimes and his comparative breadth enabled him to develop some arguments that proved correct, and that Brazilians and Brazilianists had not understood.

Exactly as Linz had anticipated (though he did not predict the timing), one year after the publication of Stepan's book, the military regime began the slow, gradual process of political liberalization that ultimately led to a transition to civilian government in 1985. One of the masterminds of the liberalization project, General Golbery de Couto e Silva, had read Linz's analysis and was convinced that he was correct that the authoritarian regime was not well institutionalized or legitimate and had few chances of becoming so.[8] Linz's paper reinforced Golbery's conviction that the Brazilian regime should liberalize. In this way, Linz's analysis may have contributed to the military's decision to initiate the process of political liberalization. When Linz wrote the article, the military regime had an aura of impenetrability; few scholars anticipated the regime opening. Years later, Bolivar Lamounier, one of Brazil's outstanding political scientists, argued that Linz better than anyone had understood crucial aspects of the Brazilian military regime.[9] In retrospect, Linz's chapter stands out not only for its percipient character, but also for its theoretical contribution to our understanding of what fosters and impedes the institutionalization of authoritarian regimes. It proved to be one of the most enduring contributions in one of the best books published on Latin American politics in the 1970s.

Three papers in this volume reflect Linz's concern with authoritarian and totalitarian regimes. Miguel Angel Centeno's "The Failure of Presidential Authoritarianism: Transition in Mexico," embodies many of the concerns that have guided Juan Linz's career. In an effort to both improve our understanding of the Mexican case and illustrate the fertility of Linz's thought, this essay offers a categorization for the PRI regime and an analysis of the consequences of extreme presidentialism. Although the Mexican system meets some of the requirements of Linz's definition of democracy, Mexico is obviously not a democracy. At least until 1994 and especially at the local level, elections have been neither free nor fair. The systematic victories of the PRI discouraged the organization of opposition forces and generated voter apathy. The rights associated with democracy have also been restricted through informal and unofficial means. It seems best, then, to conceive of Mexico as a special kind of authoritarian regime that does not clearly fit any of Linz's categories. Centeno argues that we should locate it somewhere between the mobilizational-authoritarian and the bureaucratic-military subtypes. This regime has eroded in recent years, and a form of "delegative authoritarianism" came to replace a more inclusive authoritarianism. Centeno claims that this regime erosion has its roots in the centralization of power and constitutional rigidities associated with presidentialism. As the office of the presidency enlarges its control, the stakes of electoral competition rise, political interactions become more conflictual, and policy articulation and implementation become more difficult. Paradoxically, the no reelection clause, a constitutional provision aimed at moderating the effects of the personalization of power, is the most infelicitous institutional feature of Mexican presidentialism. It discourages policy continuity, stimulates authoritarian control, favors the development of patronage networks, and discourages politicians from cultivating electoral bases outside the state bureaucracy. For Centeno, the elections of 1994 constitute a milestone in Mexico's route towards pluralism and democracy. He argues that in order to make the state apparatus more responsive to society's demands and needs, the reelection of incumbent presidents should be permitted.

Susan Eckstein's chapter, "Communist States as Ideocracies?: Lessons from Cuba," acknowledges Linz's seminal contributions to understanding authoritarian and totalitarian regimes. Eckstein focuses on two aspects of Linz's characterization of totalitarian regimes: the role of ideology and state/society relations. She argues that Cuban communism was less ideologically driven than regimes in Linz's totalitarian category. Examining the process of ideological rectification in the late 1980s, she argues that communist states are not homogeneous, self-contained, ideologically driven compacts. The rectification campaign is an especially appropriate case study because if totalitarian regimes are not ideologically driven during their most ideological moments, then they are less ideological than Linz's ideal type suggests. This rectification campaign involved a clampdown on market strategies tolerated earlier in the decade, a return to collective forms of organizing production and labor, and a call for volunteer labor to help out the revolution. However, many aspects of the rectification campaign cannot be understood through examining ideology: the reduction of subsidies or the pursuit of Western economic ties, for example. For Eckstein, these policies represented an effort to address the fiscal crisis affecting the Cuban state at that time. She affirms that we should focus less on ideology and more on the constraints imposed by the international context, the resistance strategies of civil society, and the conflicts of interests within the state bureaucracy itself. While challenging some aspects of Linz's characterization of totalitarian regimes, the analysis is in the historically grounded tradition that Linz considers so important.

In light of Eckstein's criticisms, it is interesting to note that in his recent book with Alfred Stepan, Linz refined his typology of nondemocratic regimes. He now considers post-totalitarian regimes as a distinct category that differs from both totalitarian and authoritarian regimes in crucial ways. The details of these differences need not concern us here; what does matter is that the new typology of nondemocratic regimes constitutes an innovation that would seemingly address Eckstein's criticisms.

In "The Pinochet Regime: A Comparative Analysis with the Franco Regime," Carlos Huneeus applies Linz's model of authoritarian regimes to compare the Pinochet regime in Chile with the case that began Linz's fruitful line of inquiry, the Franco regime in Spain. He focuses on three central aspects of Linz's model: the degree of personalization or institutionalization of the authoritarian regime, including the position of the dictator and the military in the political system; the use of coercion and its connection to limited pluralism and limited synchronization; and mechanisms, based primarily on economic interests, for the cooptation and political integration of civilian groups into the regime. As Huneeus argues, Linz's penetrating insight into the attributes of authoritarian regimes offers important tools for understanding both of these regimes. At the same time, there were important differences between the two regimes that arose from each country's unique trajectory of political development and the different strategies used by Franco and Pinochet to achieve and consolidate power. As Huneeus argues, a historically-grounded comparison based on Linz's model of authoritarianism that highlights each regime's uniqueness in specific areas can be a useful analytical instrument for understanding both the authoritarian period and its enduring legacy under democratization.

Democratic Breakdowns

In 1973, Linz and Alfred Stepan organized a conference at Yale on the breakdown of democratic regimes. Out of this conference grew their outstanding four volume set, *The Breakdown of Democratic Regimes*. The first volume was Linz's overview, *The Breakdown of Democratic Regimes: Crisis, Breakdown, and Reequilibration*. One volume was on Europe, one on Chile, and one on the rest of Latin America. With distinguished collaborators and the intellectual leadership of Linz and Stepan, this project became an enduring contribution to the study of democracy.

Linz's contributions on this theme had a significant impact on the study of Latin American politics, both because of the subject matter and his theoretical approach to it. Many books and articles had already been written on the democratic breakdowns that afflicted Argentina, Bolivia, Brazil, Chile, Peru, and Uruguay in the 1960s and 1970s.[10] However, *The Breakdown of Democratic Regimes* even today stands as a landmark contribution.

At a time when structural analyses of politics were in vogue among Latin Americanists and in political science in general, Linz emphasized the fact that democratic breakdowns were not inevitable. Whereas dependency theory and other structural approaches saw political outcomes as determined by structural factors, Linz always emphasized the underdetermination of most political events by structures. Thus, democratic breakdowns occurred because actors made decisive miscalculations or bad decisions that, rather than inviting compromise and negotiation, had a polarizing impact. Effective or ineffective leadership, and values and behavior that were not reducible to structural situations, were decisive in leading to breakdown or in enabling democratic leaders to avoid it and achieve what Linz called democratic reequilibration.

Linz wrote that in the structural approaches to regime stability and breakdown, "social scientists...tend to emphasize the structural characteristics of societies—socioeconomic infrastrucures that act as a constraining condition, limiting the choices of political actors. They focus on the underlying social conflicts, particularly class conflicts, that in their view make the stability of liberal democratic institutions unlikely, if not impossible....In our view, one cannot ignore the actions of either those who are more or less interested in the maintenance of an open democratic political systems or those who, placing other values higher, are unwilling to defend it or even ready to overthrow it. These are the actions that constitute the true dynamics of the political process. ...[A]ctors have certain choices that can increase or decrease the probability of the persistence and stability of a regime...We shall focus on those more strictly political variables that tend to be neglected in many other approaches to the problem of stable democracy, because in our view political processes actually precipitate the ultimate breakdown."[11] Linz helped reorient the study of Latin American politics by calling attention to the underdetermination of regime breakdowns (and most regime changes) by structural factors. In his view, leadership and the attitudes of actors made a decisive difference. He brought to the social sciences a keen awareness of the importance of history.

For Linz, democratic regimes break down or survive primarily on the basis of political legitimacy, not social or economic results. This claim, too, challenged the structuralist thinking that was dominant in Latin America at that time. Following in Max Weber's footsteps, Linz sees legitimacy as a central category for understanding political regimes. "[L]egitimacy is the belief that in spite of shortcomings and failures, the existing political institutions are better than any others that might be established, and that they therefore can demand obedience. ...[T]he legitimacy of a democratic regime rests on the belief in the right of those legally elevated to authority to issue certain types of commands, to expect obedience, and to enforce them, if necessary, by the use of force....That belief does not require agreement with the content of the norm or support for a particular government, but it does require acceptance of its binding character and its right to issue commands until changed by the procedures of the regime."[12]

Linz is aware of the importance of social structures. His Ph.D. dissertation and some of his subsequent work on party systems analyzed the social roots of politics. But the main thrust of his work on politics has been to emphasize that actors and institutions matter, and that their behavior is not determined by structures.

Linz defined a democracy as a political regime that offered "legal freedom to formulate and advocate political alternatives with the concomitant rights to free association, free speech, and other basic freedoms of person; free and nonviolent competition among leaders with periodic validation of their claim to rule; inclusion of all effective political offices in the democratic process; and provision for the participation of all members of the political community, whatever their political preferences."[13] In today's debate about democracy, procedural definitions overwhelmingly prevail, but this was not the case when *The*

Breakdown of Democratic Regimes was published. Many scholars and actors on the left regarded Linz's set of democratic procedures as formalities and felt that true democracy required greater socioeconomic equality. They were inclined to define democracy not merely in terms of political procedures, but also outcomes. Linz felt that this conflation was a conceptual mistake that confused two separate dimensions.

Linz argued that maximalist positions, i.e., the efforts to attain radical social change, could endanger democracy. This position challenged the thinking on the left, which, to the extent that it cared about liberal democracy, believed that radical change would enhance it, and which failed to pay sufficient attention to the tradeoffs that Linz highlighted. By the 1980s, most analysts agreed with Linz's position.

After 1978, Linz's theoretical perspective made greater inroads in the study of Latin American politics, partly because his students made important contributions that emphasized concrete actors, leadership, and institutions. Whereas he had stood out against the mainstream in scholarship on Latin America in the 1970s, by the 1980s, the mainstream in the Latin American politics field moved toward Linz.

That Linz's perspective has gained ground in the study of Latin American politics does not suggest that it is uniformly accepted. Some prominent scholars have criticized Linz for understating the importance of structural factors in political life. Rueschemeyer, Stephens, and Stephens, for example, argue that Linz's emphasis on process and agency "are direct results of the short time horizon [he chose] and the case selection. Had he compared breakdown cases with those in which democracy survived and/or selected a longer time horizon,...structural differences would have appeared as much more important in the analysis."[14] My point here is not to assess whether Linz's analysis is correct in every respect, but rather to indicate some of the ways in which he has influenced the study of Latin American politics and society.

Democracy

Linz's work on democracy, transitions to democracy, and democratic consolidation also influenced analyses of Latin American politics. Linz has constantly stressed the need to avoid seeing democracy as a panacea. "We should never oversell what democracy can achieve, since ultimately the success of a society depends on its economy, its cultural and scientific achievements, and its values and moral climate. These are attributes that governments can enhance, but that escape their capacity to control directly. Nor should we undersell democracy's possible virtues: freedom and some accountability to the citizens."[15]

In most of Latin America, political scientists and sociologists undersold the virtues of democracy in the 1960s and 1970s, which many on the left dismissed as bourgeois formalism. By the 1980s, however, most scholars agreed with the broad contours of Linz's analysis.[16] This new valorization of democracy reflects in part the dismal political experience of living under authoritarianism in the aftermath of the coups of those decades. However, ideas have an independent impact, and it would be simplistic to assume that the new valorization of democracy inexorably resulted from concrete experiences lived under dictatorships. To attribute this shift in values to any single person would be folly, but to deny Linz's impact in reflections about democracy, its virtues, and its limitations would be equally short sighted.

Linz's work on authoritarianism already contained the seeds of his interest in the erosion of authoritarian regimes and transitions to democracy. One of his early contributions on transitions to democracy compared the Spanish and Portuguese cases, distinguishing between the *reforma pactada–ruptura pactada* of the latter and the *ruptura* by *golpe* of the latter. This contribution began a lengthy debate that soon filtered into discussions on Latin America about how to compare transitions and whether different modes of transition matter. Although Linz's distinction was simple, it has held up well over time, not only for analyzing the Spanish and Portuguese cases, but more generally.[17]

Consistent with their emphasis on the indeterminacy of politics and the importance of leadership and attitudes, Linz and Alfred Stepan argued for the importance of what they called political crafting of democratic consolidation. "More than is commonly deemed to be the case, we think that the difference between political survival or breakdown [of democracies] is...a question of 'political crafting.'" They then identified elements of political crafting that had facilitated democratic consolidation in Europe that were of relevance for the Latin American cases. Again challenging prevailing wisdom and developing themes that both had elaborated in *The Breakdown of Democratic Regimes*, Linz and Stepan argued that democratic legitimacy was not necessarily highly dependent on economic performance. "[T]he political perception of desired alternatives has a greater impact on the survival of democratic regimes than economic and social problems per se."[18] At the time, the economic crises prevailing in most Latin American countries had generated pessimism regarding prospects for democratic consolidation.[19] Over time, however, Linz's thinking about the importance of specifically political factors in democratic consolidation has exercised widespread—though not uncontested—influence.[20]

Like his work on democratic breakdowns, Linz's analysis of democratic consolidation has emphasized the importance of political leadership.[21] He has consistently argued that consolidation is not simple or foreordained, even with propitious circumstances such as the Spanish. "It is now becoming fashionable to see the Spanish consolidation as being almost overdetermined due to its supportive socioeconomic and geopolitical context. We believe that such an unexamined opinion not only leads to a serious misinterpretation of the actual process of democratic consolidation in Spain, but contributes to the dangerous lack of theoretical attention to relationships between democratic transition, stateness, and electoral sequence."[22] He credits King Juan Carlos and Prime Minister Adolfo Suárez for helping to reduce the chances of an authoritarian regression and consolidating democracy. Conversely, democratic consolidation is possible even under difficult conditions.

As another example of how political decisions and institutions matter, Linz and Stepan argued that holding national elections before regional or local elections helped defuse a potentially dangerous problem of divided national allegiances in Spain after Franco's death. By focusing attention and loyalties first at the national level, political leaders helped facilitate the construction of national parties and identities. The reverse sequence, holding local or regional elections first, exacerbated divided national loyalties in Yugoslavia and the former Soviet Union by creating incentives for politicians to first emphasize regional identities. In collaboration with Yossi Shain, Linz has also analyzed the role of interim governments, between the authoritarian and democratic periods, in shaping regime change.

Along with Larry Diamond and Seymour Martin Lipset, Linz coordinated a large study on democracy in developing countries. It remains the largest comparative analysis of this subject, with lengthy volumes on Africa, Asia, and Latin America. The three project coordinators and editors fashioned cohesive volumes and brought together excellent collaborators. The chapters dealt with the countries' entire experience with democracy and with the myriad social, cultural, political, and economic conditions that foster or impede it. Along with Diamond, Linz coauthored the introduction to the volume on Latin America. Their introduction conveys familiar Linzian themes such as the importance of value orientations of the main political actors and the importance of an effective leadership committed to democracy.[23]

Linz's characteristic concern with attention to actors' choices and behavior influenced the major writings on transitions to democracy in Latin America (and elsewhere). This issue became a growth industry for some time, and one heavily influenced by Linz. Many contributions to the influential four volume opus, *Transitions from Authoritarian Rule:*

Prospects for Democracy, adopted essentially Linzian lines of analysis. In the concluding volume, which framed the project as a whole, Guillermo O'Donnell and Philippe Schmitter emphasized the indeterminacy of regime changes from authoritarianism, and the fact that actors' behavior could not be inferred from their structural position. As Nancy Bermeo has argued, *Transitions from Authoritarian Rule* serves as a reflection of the degree to which Linzian style analysis had come to prevail in Latin America.[24]

The chapter by Jonathan Hartlyn, "Political Continuities, Missed Opportunities and Institutional Rigidities: Another Look at Democratic Transitions in Latin America," addresses Linz's concern with transitions to democracy. One of the most significant contributions of the initial studies on democratization is the association between the mode in which transitions take place and the quality of subsequent democratic evolution. The basic distinction between pacted transitions and transitions by regime collapse, which closely follows Linz's distinction, risks exaggerating the importance of transitions in a country's social and institutional history. Hartlyn argues that misplaced emphasis on the mode of transition may result in overlooking "missed opportunities" that a transition represents, and that the institutional rigidities that are the true legacy of transition periods may easily be miscast. To avoid these pitfalls, Hartlyn disaggregates the notion of "mode of transition" into three components: 1) the nature of the authoritarian regime, existing sociopolitical forces, the international context, and other structural factors; 2) the new institutions generated by the transition process itself; and 3) the opportunities for consolidation opened up by the transition. Hartlyn argues that different modes of transition may not necessarily have opposing consequences, as the comparison of the Argentine and Brazilian cases shows, and that similar modes of transition may have different effects, as the cases of Venezuela and Colombia demonstrate. Hartlyn calls for greater attention to the complex interplay of these factors in order to understand continuities and discontinuities in the Latin American political processes.

Presidentialism and Parliamentarism

In 1985, Linz wrote a paper entitled "Democracy: Presidential or Parliamentary: Does It Make a Difference?," which claimed that presidentialism is less likely than parliamentary government to promote democratic consolidation. This paper circulated widely in unpublished form in English until 1990, when a shortened version appeared in the

Journal of Democracy. The final English language version appeared in 1994.[25]

Linz bases his argument about the superiority of parliamentary systems partially on the observation that few long established democracies have presidential systems of government. He maintains that the superior historical performance of parliamentary democracies stems from intrinsic defects of presidential regimes. In presidential systems, the president and assembly have competing claims to legitimacy. Since both the president and legislature "derive their power from the vote of the people in a free competition among well-defined alternatives, a conflict is always latent and sometimes likely to erupt dramatically; there is no democratic principle to resolve it."[26] Linz argues that parliamentarism obviates this problem because the executive is not independent of the assembly.

The fixed term of the president's office introduces a rigidity that is less favorable to democracy than the flexibility offered by parliamentary systems, where governments depend on the ongoing confidence of the assembly. There is no easy way to resolve the impasse if a president becomes immobilized because of lack of congressional support. Linz argues that presidentialism "introduces a strong element of zero-sum game into democratic politics with rules that tend toward a 'winner-take-all' outcome." In contrast, in parliamentary systems, "Power-sharing and coalition-forming are fairly common, and incumbents are accordingly attentive to the demands and interests of even the smaller parties."[27]

Linz argues that the style of presidential politics is less propitious for democracy than the style of parliamentary politics. The president's sense of being the representative of the entire nation may lead him or her to be intolerant of the opposition. Finally, Linz claims that political outsiders are more likely to win the chief executive office in presidential systems, with potentially destabilizing effects. Individuals elected by direct popular vote are less dependent on and less beholden to political parties. Such individuals are more likely to govern in a populist, anti-institutionalist fashion.

Prior to Linz, it had been decades since comparative presidentialism had been at the center of academic debate. Linz's essay sparked great interest in Latin America, both among academics and policy makers. The paper was published in Argentina in 1988, Chile in 1990, and Brazil in 1991 (as well as in Hungary, Italy, and Mongolia).[28] It sparked a broad debate about the liabilities of presidential government.

Probably no other work of Linz's ever drew so much attention in Latin America. In the 1980s in South America, a fresh concern with political institutions emerged. Linz's work simultaneously furthered this concern and found a receptive audience because of it. Most academics who wrote on the subject agreed with Linz that presidentialism was a defective regime type that hindered prospects for stable democracy. Some, however, disagreed with some of Linz's core claims. Lipset, for example, suggested that the problem in Latin America is not presidentialism, but political culture. Horowitz argued that Linz had overstated the defects of presidentialism and neglected some problems of parliamentary systems. Shugart and Carey, and Mainwaring and Shugart claimed that presidentialism has certain virtues as well as the defects Linz had pointed to. They also argued that some of the apparent advantage of parliamentarism has stemmed from where it has been implemented: frequently in countries where economic and social conditions are favorable to democracy regardless of institutional arrangements.[29]

Linz's work on presidentialism had repercussions well beyond the academic world. In Argentina, in 1985 President Alfonsín appointed a commission, the Committee for Democratic Consolidation (Consejo para la Consolidación de la Democracia), to study constitutional reform. Carlos Nino, head of the committee, was a friend and colleague who had been influenced by Linz's view of presidentialism. The committee recommended a switch to semipresidential government, but it never had great impact.[30] In Brazil, the members of the constitutional assembly of 1987–1988 seriously considered implementing a semipresidential government, with a powerful prime minister. Presidentialism ultimately prevailed, but with such lingering doubts that the constituent assembly voted to have a referendum on the issue in 1993, at which time the popular vote consecrated the decision on behalf of presidentialism. Another of Linz's friends, Bolivar Lamounier, was one of the most influential Brazilian advocates of parliamentarism. In Bolivia, the constitutional assembly of 1994 also considered a semipresidential system but ultimately retained that country's distinctive hybrid presidential regime. Linz went to Brazil and Bolivia several times to give input into these debates. Ultimately, no country moved away from presidentialism. If one wanted a short explanation of why the pro-parliamentary movement fell short, it would be that, not surprisingly, the logic of political interests triumphed over dispassionate analysis. Still, Linz's work had helped generate a fertile debate about regime types throughout several Latin American countries, and he did influence the Bolivian constitution.

Arturo Valenzuela's chapter on the crisis of presidential democracy in this volume is reflective of the work that Linz stimulated on presidentialism. Following Linz, Valenzuela argues that presidential systems have no ready-made solution to the paralyzing problem caused by minority congressional support for a president. Presidential systems offer few incentives for opposition leaders to cooperate. Most of the time, supporting the president's policies accrues only to the president's advantage. The writers of Latin American constitutions adopted the presidential system from the United States, but Latin American societies failed to develop most of the features that secured the success of U.S. presidentialism, especially a strong two-party system. In Latin America, the combination of deep societal divisions and proportional represent-ation resulted in fragmented party systems — a situation that renders the construction of majority parties very unlikely. All Latin American constitutions drafted in the 1980s introduced runoff elections for presidential races in an effort to remedy the problem of minority presidentialism. This strategy has favored the construction of shortlived and fictitious majorities and, stimulating the multiplication of presi-dential candidates in the first round, further encourages party system fragmentation. The typical reaction to legislative/executive impasse has been to increase presidential prerogatives, but expanded presidential power has aggravated conflict and transformed many governmental crises into threats to regime survival. As both the relevant literature and the failure of several authoritarian experiments indicate, a change of the nature of the party system is not a feasible solution to the problem. Valenzuela argues that partial reforms within the context of president-ialism do not offer a longterm answer either. A context of societal divi-sion and party fragmentation like that of Latin America requires an institutional context that encourages the formation of coalitions. Valenzuela asserts that the logical option is to move towards parliamentary government.

The chapter by Scott Mainwaring and Matthew Shugart also addresses Linz's work on presidentialism. Although Mainwaring and Shugart agree with several of Linz's criticisms of presidentialism, they argue that presidentialism is less oriented towards winner-takes-all results than are Westminster parliamentary systems. They believe that the superior record of parliamentary systems has rested partly on where parliamentary government has been implemented and claim that presidentialism has some advantages that partially offset its drawbacks. These advantages can be maximized by paying careful attention to differences among presidential systems. Finally, they argue that switching from presidentialism to parliamentarism could exacerbate problems of governability in countries with undisciplined parties. In their view, even if Linz is correct that parliamentary government is more conducive to stable democracy, a great deal rests on what kind of parliamentarism and presidentialism are implemented.

Voting Behavior, Public Opinion, and Party Systems

Linz's work on voting behavior, public opinion, and on party systems dates back to his graduate student days at Columbia University, when he coauthored an article on this subject and wrote a 900 page Ph.D. dissertation on the West German party system.[31] The dissertation provided one of the most indepth studies ever of survey data. Ever since, he has continued to use and encourage the use of public opinion surveys and elite surveys. Many of his publications on Spain make ample use of surveys,[32] as does his recent coauthored *Problems of Democratic Transition and Consolidation*. He was one of the founders of the Spanish public opinion firm, DATA, which engages in both political and commercial surveys. He served as President of the World Association for Public Opinion Research.

Linz helped invigorate the study of public opinion in Latin America, where this tradition was limited prior to the 1980s. He helped create a network of public opinion researchers in Argentina, Brazil, Chile, and Uruguay, advising them and encouraging them to repeat the same question in different countries. This original network began to meet in Santiago and Buenos Aires in the mid-1980s. Linz was one of the drafters of the original questionnaire of the European Values Study and many surveys on politics during the Spanish transition, and he helped familiarize the participants of the southern cone network with these experiences. He also helped devise the questionnaire. This earlier network then spawned an even larger one, the Latinobarometro, directed by Marta Lagos, which is carrying out the most important comparative project ever on public opinion in Latin America. Linz is on the International Advisory Board of the Latinobarometro Corporation.[33] His student, Luis Eduardo González, created one of the major public opinion firms in Uruguay.

After doing his dissertation on the West German party system, Linz later published extensively on the Spanish party system.[34] In his writings on party systems, Linz has underscored the value of doing careful empirical work and the utility of elite and mass surveys.

Although Linz has never published on party systems in Latin America, he directed dissertations that dealt extensively with party systems in Venezuela (Michael Coppedge) and Uruguay (Charles Gillespie and Luis Eduardo González). Characteristically, these dissertations employed either structured interviews with political elites or public opinion surveys. He also advised students who did research on business elites in Brazil—Leigh Payne, Wendy Barker, and Harry Makler, who conducted elite surveys.

Michael Coppedge's analysis of the evolution of party systems in Latin America in this volume deals with this side of Linz's work. In the aftermath of independence almost all of the new nations of Latin America were divided by the same cleavage: liberals versus conservatives. Today, significant differences can be registered among Latin American party systems in terms of the importance of class cleavages, the weight of pluralist or hegemonic tendencies, and the degree of institutionalization of the political parties. This chapter explains why contemporary Latin American party systems are so diverse in spite of their common point of departure in the nineteenth century. Coppedge provides a brief comparative political history of eleven countries of the region to support the claim that the most important differences among Latin American party systems are explained by the nature of the political order (if any) that was achieved before the expansion of political participation and by the timing of this expansion. Inspired in Linz's analysis of the Spanish party system, Coppedge's study describes the evolution of party systems characterized by radical discontinuities and lagging social development. Coppedge argues that the principal distinction to be made among the party systems of Latin America is between established and chaotic systems (Brazil, Bolivia, Ecuador and Peru). Among established systems, Coppedge identifies three classes: one in which interelite conflict resulted in the clear hegemony of the liberal side (Argentina, México and Venezuela), a second one in which liberals and conservatives were more evenly matched and the cleavage between them thus more resilient (Colombia and Uruguay), and finally a class in which conflicts were peacefully handled before mass participation began (Chile and Costa Rica).

Federalism and Regionalism

Another old Linzian theme that is resurfacing in his current research is federalism and regionalism. Linz's work on regionalism in Spain is a classic. Writing with Amando de Miguel, Linz argued for the importance of careful intranation comparisons. Such comparisons expand the universe of cases, and they hold many key variables constant, with the attendant advantages of comparing most similar cases. After making this broad argument on the benefits of intranation comparisons, Linz and de Miguel underscored and analyzed the vast differences among the regions of Spain. Published in 1966, this contribution remains one of the most sophisticated statements on behalf of the advantages of intranation comparisons.[35]

This particular Linzian theme did not have a major impact among political scientists who worked on Latin America, but it did influence

Joseph L. Love, a Columbia University doctoral student of his who went on to write excellent political and social histories of the states of São Paulo and Rio Grande do Sul in Brazil. Love's collaborators, Robert Levine and John Wirth, simultaneously produced similar books on Pernambuco and Minas Gerais. Thus it is appropriate that we include a contribution by Love that reprises his work on regionalism and federalism in Brazil.

In his chapter, "Regionalism and Federalism in Brazil, 1889–1937," Love acknowledges the impact that "The Eight Spains" and other works by Linz had on his thought and those of his colleagues who have studied Brazilian federalism. Love's article is an overview of regionalism and federalism during the first half-century of Brazil's Republican regime. In contrast to the centralizing trend evident in several Latin American countries during the time period under consideration (1889–1937), the Brazilian coup d'état of 1889 led to the consolidation of a Republican regime with a decentralized political structure that granted sweeping fiscal and other powers to Brazilian states. In his analysis of the most important, longstanding, and contradictory effects of federalism and regionalism, Love emphasizes both political and economic developments. He highlights the shift in power from the Northeast to the Southeast that accompanied the displacement of sugar by coffee as the country's principle export crop; the fiscal and political advantages that accrued to three states (São Paulo, Minas Gerais and Rio Grande do Sul) that had the economic strength, political clout, and police forces to stand up to the federal government; conflict among the leading states and between the states and the federal government; repeated federal interventions in the 17 less powerful "satellite states," often to unseat corrupt leaders; and the role of political parties that were formally "national" in scope but representative of a single state. Although Getúlio Vargas proclaimed the end of federalism after the presidential coup of 1937, he was unable to do more than blunt the fiscal decentralization of the Republican regime. Hence, the significance of this period is not only historical; its legacy continues to exert its influence to the present day.

Linz's Theoretical and Methodological Approach

Linz brought certain theoretical and methodological lenses to the study of politics that challenged dominant thinking in the 1960s and 1970s. His work is grounded in a careful study of history and considerable knowledge of many different cases. Illustrative of his concern with careful empirical knowledge is his many writings on the history of

Spanish society and politics. Linz once spent a semester teaching history at Stanford University, and he deals with his themes with the empirical care of a historian. One cannot build theory or even middle range generalizations on the basis of faulty or limited knowledge of history. Although his prolific writings on Spanish history are not well known to social scientists who write on Latin America, they constitute an important share of his overall opus, and they reflect the deep commitment to understanding historical processes.

Linz has always advocated comparisons, but has felt that effective comparisons must be based on a deep knowledge of the cases. His own comparisons have generally initially been inspired by the Spanish case, though his knowledge of the political histories of different countries is truly encyclopedic. He has a high regard for careful empirical work, even while seeking to build broader theoretical themes. Linz has been criticized for his preference for work based on careful knowledge of the facts over grand theory. He himself openly acknowledges this predilection: He prefers middle range theory to abstruse grand generalization as was in vogue in comparative politics in the United States in the 1960s during the heyday of structural functionalism. Linz has written wide ranging analyses of themes that are still of broad theoretical import: democratic breakdown, presidentialism, democratic transition and consolidation, etc. He has also constructed Weberian style taxonomies based on immense historical erudition. His work pays careful attention to actors and institutions.

J. Samuel Valenzuela's chapter argues that reflections on the comparative method have not matched the development that comparative studies have acquired. He argues that Linz has been a model in how one should undertake comparative analysis. Drawing illustrations from Linz's work, this chapter presents a protocol determining how to set up comparisons without falling into common error-inducing pitfalls. Valenzuela notes the commonalties and differences among comparative, statistical, and case studies. Like case studies, comparative analyses conceive of their object as a complex configuration of a large number of elements. Unlike case studies, macro comparisons try to build up explanations that account for crossnational variations. Statistical approaches are also aimed at explaining variation but do not rely on a deep acquaintance with the cases to the extent that macrocomparisons do. The relative appropriateness of these approaches depends on the research question. Assuming that the research question has been clearly defined and its answer requires the use of macro comparisons, Valenzuela proposes the following guidelines in order to avoid the most common methodological errors: 1) analyses should be anchored in clear definitions; 2) the universe of cases should be neatly delimited; 3) typologies should be made explicit and devised on the basis of variants of the phenomenon; 4) comparisons should include at least as many cases as variations shown by the phenomenon and, if possible, twice that number; 5) the number of cases should be kept low enough as to match the abilities of the researcher(s) to undertake thorough analyses; 6) research designs should be avoided that examine cases with sharply disparate outcomes when it is possible to compare similar cases; 7) conclusions derived from the analysis of similar cases should be checked looking at those that have different outcomes. The logic underlying this protocol tries to overcome the insufficiencies of John Stuart Mill's methods. The final section of the paper presents its general attributes and discusses its advantages. Because it addresses these overarching questions of how to engage in comparative analysis, Valenzuela's chapter makes an ideal concluding chapter.

Linz as Teacher

So far I have focused mostly on the ways Linz's scholarship reshaped the study of Latin American politics. However powerful Linz's scholarship is, his influence in Latin America would not have extended as far were it not for his equally remarkable talent and generosity as a teacher and mentor.

I met Linz in 1974 when I was a junior at Yale. That fall, I took Linz's seminar on authoritarian and totalitarian regimes. Every week, Linz spoke uninterruptedly for the whole two hours while captivating everyone's interest. It was as if there were an unspoken understanding among the students that interruptions would have cut short the time that we had to glean information and analysis from one of the world's great scholars. Frequently, students got together after the seminar to discuss the lectures. Many aspects of the course were memorable: Linz arriving in class every week with a brief case exploding with books on the most varied political regimes; Linz chain smoking; the lengthiest syllabus I've ever seen, with the greatest comparative breadth; and above all, the lectures.

Linz's lack of pretentiousness is as noteworthy as his intellect is powerful. He is willing to engage anybody who takes ideas seriously and works hard. After taking his seminar, in January 1975 I went to Argentina for seven months to undertake some research. At one point, I wrote Linz soliciting advice. A couple of weeks later, I had a four page, single spaced reply, full of insights and helpful suggestions. How many individuals of his renown would have taken the time to reply in detailed fashion to an undergraduate?

When I came back to the United States in 1982 after doing my dissertation field work in Brazil, I immediately saw Linz to get his feedback on my first chapter. Although I had long since left Yale, he obliged me and provided detailed criticisms. He cares deeply about the world of ideas and is willing to go to great lengths to nurture others who share this passion.

My story is far from unique. Linz has had a profound impact on students of many nationalities and both sexes. Susan Eckstein, who studied with Linz at Columbia at a time when there were few women in the profession, notes that he was "gender blind. He took everyone seriously."[36] As a teacher, Linz knows no ideological boundaries. At Columbia in the heyday of student radicalism, Linz taught a young Marxist, Albert Szymanski, who later dedicated a book to "the National Liberation Front of South Vietnam and to Juan Linz."[37]

Teaching at Columbia University in the 1960s, Linz helped train a generation of scholars who became prominent in Latin American politics, sociology, and history: Ralph Della Cava, Susan Eckstein, Kenneth Paul Erickson, Joseph Love, Harry Makler, Susan Kaufman Purcell, Peter Smith, Alfred Stepan, Arturo Valenzuela, Alexander Wilde. Linz has long been as devoted to his students as he is to his own scholarship, and his generosity as a mentor became widely known while he was at Columbia. He was the primary advisor to countless students who wrote on Latin America.

Linz moved to Yale in 1969. There he taught Miguel Angel Centeno, Catharine Conaghan, Michael Coppedge, Charles Gillespie, Luis Eduardo González, Jonathan Hartlyn, Evelyn Huber, Daniel Levine, Alonso Lujambio, María José Moyano, Guillermo O'Donnell, Leigh Payne, Brian Smith, and John D. Stephens, among others. Lúcia Avelar and Bolivar Lamounier, among others, did post-docs at Yale to work with Linz. He nurtured and influenced junior faculty members such as Alfred Stepan, with whom he formed one of the great tandems in the history of comparative politics, and J. Samuel Valenzuela. After Stepan's departure in 1983, Yale did not have a senior Latin Americanist in political science or sociology, so Linz again became the primary director of most students working on Latin America. Linz has directed some fifty theses dealing with 29 countries in 4 continents. Although Linz never wrote on the Latin American church, he taught several students who made major contributions in this area: Daniel Levine, Brian Smith, Alexander Wilde.[38]

Although much of his career has been spent in the United States, Linz has always spent considerable time in Spain, where he also fostered the development of countless graduate students, including some who worked on Latin America. And he has "adopted" countless young scholars who wrote him seeking advice, without formally being his student. Many of these "adopted students" developed enduring personal as well as intellectual admiration for Linz. For example, Carlos Huneeus went to the University of Essex to study in the aftermath of the Chilean coup. There he wrote Linz about his interest in studying the breakdown of democracy. Linz's response initiated a long friendship. The two corresponded while Huneeus was a student at Heidelberg, and they saw each other in Madrid, New Haven, and Santiago. In Spain, Linz encouraged Manuel Alcántara, Spain's pioneering figure in promoting the study of Latin American politics.

Throughout his distinguished career, Linz has maintained a refreshing indifference to conventional academic standards of success. One revealing indication of this attitude has been his tendency to circulate papers widely and for a long time before publication, and then frequently to publish them in a potentially obscure book because of a commitment to a friend. Yet the sheer force of his ideas lifted some such volumes into prominence. Even those students who have not replicated this indifference to convention admire it.

This book is a tribute to Juan Linz by some of the many scholars whose career he has nurtured.

Notes

1. Richard Gunther, ed., *Politics, Society, and Democracy: The Case of Spain* (Boulder: Westview, 1993); H. E. Chehabi and Alfred Stepan, eds., *Politics, Society, and Democracy: Comparative Studies* (Boulder: Westview, 1995). For Linz's own reflections on his career, see his "Between Nations and Disciplines: Personal Experience and Intellectual Understanding of Societies and Political Regimes," in Hans Daalder, ed., *The Intellectual Autobiography of Comparative Politics* (Casell/Pinter, forthcoming).

2. "An Authoritarian Regime: Spain," in Erik Allaradt and Yrjo Littunen, eds., *Cleavages, Ideologies, and Party Systems* (Helsinki: Westermarck Society, 1964), p. 291. This essay was reprinted in the more readily available Erik Allardt and Stein Rokkan, eds., *Mass Politics: Studies in Political Sociology* (New York: Free Press, 1970), pp. 251-83 and 374-81. For further elaboration, see Linz's "From Falange to Movimiento-Organización: The Spanish Single Party and the Franco Regime, 1936-1968," in Samuel Huntington and Clement Moore, eds., *Authoritarian Politics in Modern Society: The Dynamics of Established One Party Systems* (New York: Basic Books, 1970), pp. 128-201; and "Opposition in and under an Authoritarian Regime: The Case of Spain," in Robert A. Dahl, ed., *Regimes and Oppositions* (New Haven : Yale University Press, 1973), pp. 171-259.

3. For a critical analysis of this point, see Bolivar Lamounier, "Ideologia em Regimes Autoritários: Uma Crítica a Juan J. Linz," *Estudos CEBRAP* No. 7 (1974): 69-92.

4. "Totalitarian and Authoritarian Regimes," in Nelson Polsby and Fred Greenstein, eds., *Handbook of Political Science* (Reading, MA: Addison and Wesley, 1975), pp. 175–411.

5. In Juan J. Linz and Alfred Stepan, *Problems of Democratic Transition and Consolidation* (Baltimore: Johns Hopkins University Press, 1996).

6. Among others, see James M. Malloy, ed., *Authoritarianism and Corporatism in Latin America* (Pittsburgh: University of Pittsburgh Press, 1977); Susan Kaufman Purcell, *The Mexican Profit-Sharing Decision* (Berkeley: University of California Press, 1975); Guillermo O'Donnell, *Modernization and Bureaucratic-Authoritarianism* (Berkeley: Institute of International Studies, 1973); Philippe C. Schmitter, *Interest Conflict and Political Change in Brazil* (Stanford: Stanford University Press, 1971), especially pp. 377–86.

7. "The Future of an Authoritarian Situation or the Institutionalization of an Authoritarian Regime: The Case of Brazil" (New Haven: Yale University Press, 1973), pp. 233–54. Bolivar Lamounier builds on this analysis in his "O Discurso e o Processo: Da Distensão às Opções do Regime Brasileiro," in Henrique Rattner, ed., *Brasil 1990: Caminhos Alternativos do Desenvolvimento* (São Paulo: Brasiliense, 1979), pp. 88–120.

8. Golbery conveyed his reaction to Linz's article in an interview with Alfred Stepan. See Stepan's *Rethinking Military Politics: Brazil and the Southern Cone* (Princeton: Princeton University Press, 1988), p. 33.

9. "*Authoritarian Brazil* Revisited: The Impact of Elections on the *Abertura*," in Alfred Stepan, ed., *Democratizing Brazil: Problems of Transition and Consolidation* (New York and Oxford: Oxford University Press, 1989), especially pp. 44–45.

10. O'Donnell, *Modernization and Bureaucratic-Authoritarianism*; Stepan, *The Military in Politics: Changing Patterns in Brazil* (Princeton: Princeton University Press, 1971). Noteworthy contributions after the publication of *The Breakdown of Democratic Regimes* include David Collier, ed., *The New Authoritarianism in Latin America*, and Wanderley Guilherme dos Santos, *Sessenta e Quatro: Anatomia da Crise* (São Paulo: Vértice, 1986).

11. *The Breakdown of Democratic Regimes: Crisis, Breakdown, and Reequilibration*, pp. 4–5. For excellent analyses that in broad terms follow a Linzian approach to democratic breakdown, see Alfred Stepan, "Political Leadership and Regime Breakdown: Brazil," in Linz and Stepan, eds., *The Breakdown of Democratic Regimes: Latin America*, pp. 110–37; and Arturo Valenzuela, *The Breakdown of Democratic Regimes: Chile*.

12. Ibid., pp. 16–17. Linz also authored the chapter on the breakdown of democracy in Spain. See "From Great Hopes to Civil War: The Breakdown of Democracy in Spain," in Linz and Stepan, eds., *The Breakdown of Democratic Regimes: Europe*, pp. 142–215. For further analysis of legitimacy, see Linz's "Legitimacy of Democracy and the Socioeconomic System," in Mattei Dogan, ed., *Comparing Pluralist Democracies: Strains on Legitimacy* (Boulder: Westview, 1988), pp. 65–113. For a critique of approaches that understand the erosion of authoritarian regimes in terms of legitimacy, see Adam Przeworski, "Some

Problems in the Study of the Transition to Democracy," in Guillermo O'Donnell, Philippe Schmitter, and Laurence Whitehead, eds., *Transitions from Authoritarian Rule: Prospects for Democracy* (Baltimore: Johns Hopkins University Press, 1986), Part 3, especially pp. 50–53.

13. Linz, *The Breakdown of Democratic Regimes: Crisis, Breakdown, and Re-equilibration,* p. 5. On the advantages of Linz's procedural definition of democracy, see Yossi Shain, "Minimum Claims, Maximum Gains: The Advantages of Juan Linz's Definition of Democracy," in Chehabi and Stepan, eds., *Politics, Society, and Democracy: Comparative Studies,* pp. 45–56.

14. Dietrich Rueschemeyer, Evelyne Huber Stephens, and John D. Stephens, *Capitalist Development and Democracy* (Chicago: University of Chicago Press, 1992), p. 34.

15. "Change and Continuity in the Nature of Contemporary Democracies," in Garry Marks and Larry Diamond, eds., *Reexamining Democracy: Essays in Honor of Seymour Martin Lipset* (Newbury Park, CA: Sage, 1992), p. 201.

16. On changes in how Latin American scholars have perceived democracy, see Robert Barros, "The Left and Democracy: Recent Debates in Latin America," *Telos* 68 (Summer 1986), pp. 49–70; Jorge Castañeda, *Utopia Unarmed: The Latin American Left after the Cold War* (New York: Knopf, 1993); Bolivar Lamounier, "Representação Política: A Importância de Certos Formalismos," in Bolivar Lamounier, Francisco C. Weffort, and Maria Victória Benevides, eds., *Direito, Cidadania e Participação* (São Paulo: T. A. Queiroz, 1981), pp. 230–57; Robert A. Packenham, "The Changing Political Discourse in Brazil," in Wayne A. Selcher, ed., *Political Liberalization in Brazil: Dynamics, Dilemmas, and Future Prospects* (Boulder: Westview, 1986), pp. 135–73; Francisco Weffort, *Por Que Democracia* (São Paulo: Brasiliense, 1985).

17. "Some Comparative Thoughts on the Transition to Democracy in Portugal and Spain," in Jorge Braga de Macedo and Simon Serfaty, eds., *Portugal Since the Revolution: Economic and Political Perspectives* (Boulder: Westview, 1981), pp. 25–45. O'Donnell and Schmitter, *Tentative Conclusions about Uncertain Democracies,* O'Donnell, Schmitter, and Whitehead, eds., *Transitions from Authoritarian Rule: Prospects for Democracy,* Part 4, distinguish between transitions in which the authoritarian regime is in a relatively strong position and those in which it is weaker. Scott Mainwaring and Eduardo Viola, "Transitions to Democracy: Brazil and Argentina in the 1980s," *Journal of International Affairs* 38 (Winter 1985), pp. 193–219, expanded the typology into a threefold one: transitions from above (like the Spanish), transitions through extrication, and transitions after regime breakdown (like the Portuguese). Alfred Stepan, "Paths toward Redemocratization: Theoretical and Comparative Considerations," in O'Donnell, Schmitter, and Whitehead, eds., *Transitions from Authoritarian Rule: Prospects for Democracy,* Part 3, pp. 64–84, develops a tenfold typology, but the basic Linzian inspiration is still visible. See also J. Samuel Valenzuela, "Democratic Consolidation in Post-Transitional Settings: Notion, Process, and Facilitating Conditions," in Scott Mainwaring, Guillermo O'Donnell, and J. Samuel Valenzuela, eds., *Issues in Democratic Consolidation:*

The New South American Democracies in Comparative Perspective (Notre Dame: University of Notre Dame Press, 1992), especially pp. 73–78.

18. "Political Crafting of Democratic Consolidation or Destruction: European and South American Comparisons," in Robert A. Pastor, ed., *Democracy in the Americas: Stopping the Pendulum* (New York: Holmes & Meier, 1989), pp. 41, 46.

19. For example, see Howard J. Wiarda, "Can Democracy Be Exported? The Quest for Democracy in U.S.-Latin American Policy," in Kevin Middlebrook and Carlos Rico, eds., *The United States and Latin America in the 1980s: Contending Perspectives on a Decade of Crisis* (Pittsburgh: University of Pittsburgh Press, 1986), pp. 325–51.

20. For a work that epitomizes many Linzian themes, see Giuseppe Di Palma, *To Craft Democracies: An Essay on Democratic Transitions* (Berkeley: University of California Press, 1990).

21. See his "Innovative Leadership in the Transition to Democracy and a New Democracy: The Case of Spain," in Gabriel Sheffer, ed., *Innovative Leaders in International Politics* (Albany: State University of New York Press, 1993), pp. 141–86.

22. Juan J. Linz and Alfred Stepan, "Political Identities and Electoral Sequences: Spain, the Soviet Union, and Yugoslavia," *Daedalus* 121, 2 (Spring 1992), p. 125.

23. Larry Diamond and Juan J. Linz, "Introduction: Politics, Society, and Democracy in Latin America," in Larry Diamond, Juan J. Linz, and Seymour Martin Lipset, eds., *Democracy in Developing Countries: Latin America* (Boulder: Lynne Rienner, 1989), pp. 1–58.

24. Guillermo O'Donnell, Philippe Schmitter, and Laurence Whitehead, eds., *Transitions from Authoritarian Rule: Prospects for Democracy* (Baltimore: Johns Hopkins University Press, 1978). Nancy Bermeo, "Rethinking Regime Change," *Comparative Politics* 23, 3 (April 1990), pp. 359–77. Bermeo remarks that "Schmitter and O'Donnell's earlier work is unambiguously and unabashedly 'structuralist' in its approach" (p. 360) and argues that they had moved in a direction more akin to Linz and Stepan.

25. "The Perils of Presidentialism," *The Journal of Democracy* 1 (1990): 51–69; "Presidential or Parliamentary Democracy: Does It Make a Difference?" in Juan J. Linz and Arturo Valenzuela, eds., *The Failure of Presidential Democracy* (Baltimore: Johns Hopkins University Press, 1994), pp. 3–87.

26. Linz, "Presidential or Parliamentary Democracy," p. 7.

27. Ibid., p. 18.

28. In Argentina it was published by the Consejo de Consolidación Democrática in *Presidencialismo vs. parlamentarismo* (Buenos Aires: EUDEBA, 1988). In Chile it appeared in Oscar Godoy Arcaya, ed., *Hacia una democracia moderna: La opción parlamentaria* (Santiago: Ed. Universidad Católica de Chile, 1990). In Brazil, it was published in Bolivar Lamounier, ed., *A Opção Parlamentarista* (São Paulo: Sumaré/IDESP, 1991), pp. 61–120.

29. Most of the contributors to Linz and Valenzuela, eds., *The Failure of Presidential Democracy* agreed with Linz. The chapters by Catharine Conaghan, Jonathan Hartlyn, Cynthia McClintock, and especially Giovanni Sartori diverge somewhat from Linz's analysis. Linz directed the dissertation of Luis Eduardo González, which was later published as *Political Structures and Democracy in Uruguay* (Notre Dame: University of Notre Dame Press, 1992). This fine book bears many of Linz's marks, including the analysis of presidentialism. For analyses critical of presidentialism, see also Carlos Santiago Nino, et al., *El presidencialismo puesto a prueba* (Madrid: *Centro de Estudios Constitucionales*, 1992); Scott Mainwaring, "Presidentialism, Multipartism, and Democracy: The Difficult Combination," *Comparative Political Studies* 26, 2 (July 1993): 198–228; Fred Riggs, "The Survival of Presidentialism in America: Para-Constitutional Practices," *International Political Science Review* 9 (October 1988): 247–78; Bolivar Lamounier, ed., *Presidencialismo ou Parlamentarismo: Perpsectives sobre a Reorganização Institucional Brasileira* (São Paulo: Loyola/IDESP, 1993). For analyses that diverge more from Linz's line, see Matthew S. Shugart and John Carey, *Presidents and Assemblies* (New York and Cambridge: Cambridge University Press, 1992); Donald Horowitz, "Comparing Democratic Systems," *Journal of Democracy* 1, 4 (Fall 1990): 73–79; Seymour Martin Lipset, "The Centrality of Political Culture," *Journal of Democracy* 1, 4 (Fall 1990): 80–83; Scott Mainwaring and Matthew S. Shugart, eds., *Presidentialism and Democracy in Latin America* (New York and Cambridge: Cambridge University Press, 1997). See also Linz's response to Lipset and Horowitz, "The Virtues of Parliamentarism," *Journal of Democracy* 1, 4 (Fall 1990): 138–45.

30. See Consejo para la Consolidación de la Democracia, *Reforma constitucional: Dictamen preliminar del Consejo para la Consolidación Democrática* (Buenos Aires: EUDEBA, 1986).

31. The article, coauthored with Seymour Martin Lipset, Paul F. Lazarsfeld, and Allen H. Barton, is "The Psychology of Voting: An Analysis of Political Behavior," in Gardner Lindzey, ed., *Handbook of Social Psychology*, vol. 2 (Reading, MA: Addison-Wesley, 1954), pp. 1124–75. His Ph.D. dissertation, "The Social Bases of West German Politics" (Columbia University, 1959) unfortunately was never published as a book. Part of it appeared as "Cleavages and Consensus in West German Politics in the Early Fifties," in Seymour Martin Lipset and Stein Rokkan, eds., *Party Systems and Voter Alignments* (New York: Free Press, 1967), pp. 283–321. On Linz's dissertation, see the personal account by his advisor and later collaborator, Seymour Martin Lipset, "Juan Linz: Student—Colleague—Friend," in Chehabi and Stepan, eds., *Politics, Society, and Democracy*, pp. 3–12. Also see the appraisal and update by Elisabeth Nolle-Neumann, "Juan Linz's Dissertation on West Germany: An Empirical Follow-up, Thirty Years Later," in Chehabi and Stepan, eds., *Politics, Society, and Democracy*, pp. 13–41.

32. For example, see Juan J. Linz, Francisco Andrés Orizo, Manuel Gómez-Reino, and Darío Vila, *Informe sociológico sobre el cambio político en España 1975–1981* (Madrid: Fundación FOESSA, Euramérica, 1982).

33. Some results of the earlier comparative work in Brazil and the southern cone countries are published in Judith Muszynski and Antonio Manuel Teixeira Mendes, "Democratização e Opinião Pública no Brasil," in Bolívar Lamounier, ed., *De Geisel a Collor: O Balanço da Transição* (São Paulo: Sumaré, 1990), pp. 61–80. Linz and Stepan publish some results of the Latinobarometro study in *Problems of Democratic Transition and Consolidation.*

34. His list of publications on this subject is too extensive to reproduce here. For a sample, see Juan J. Linz, "The Party System of Spain: Past and Future," in Lipset and Rokkan, eds., *Party Systems and Voter Alignments,* pp. 197–282; Juan J. Linz, "The New Spanish Party System," in Richard Rose, ed., *Electoral Participation: A Comparative Analysis* (London and Beverly Hills: Sage, 1980), pp. 101–89; Juan J. Linz and José Ramón Montero, eds., *Crisis y cambio: Electores y partidos en la España de los años ochenta* (Madrid: Centro de Estudios Constitucionales, 1986).

35. Juan J. Linz and Amando de Miguel, "Within-Nation Differences and Comparisons: The Eight Spains," in Richard L. Merritt and Stein Rokkan, eds., *Comparing Nations: The Use of Quantitative Data in Cross-National Research* (New Haven: Yale University Press, 1966), pp. 267–319.

36. Personal communication, August 22, 1996.

37. *The Capitalist State and the Politics of Class* (Cambridge, MA: Winthrop, 1978). Szymanski states in the preface (p. xiii) that "I owe more to Juan Linz than to any other teacher I have ever had. He not only excited my interest in the field, taught me the methods of doing political sociology, opened up a vast literature to me and was the source of innumerable ideas, but he served as the model of scholarship and seriousness which the subject deserves."

[37] Linz, "Between Nations and Disciplines."

2

The Failure of Presidential Authoritarianism: Transition in Mexico

Miguel Angel Centeno

The work of Juan Linz has covered an immense variety of political experiences including cases as disparate as Brazil, Germany, and of course, Spain.[1] He has analyzed the conditions that lead to the breakdown of democracy as well as those that foster its reappearance.[2] He has written on electoral systems and voting distributions and provided the classic definition of authoritarianism.[3] In recent years he has been especially concerned with the costs and benefits associated with presidentialist vs. parliamentary systems and how each of these contributes to the development or downfall of democratic practices.[4]

Despite the truly outstanding breadth and scope of his work, there are clear common strands in all of Linz's works. First, the often expressed debt to his beloved Max Weber. Second, a commitment to the defense of the most basic attributes of a democracy: regular elections which can lead to the replacement of office holders. Third, and most important, a political perspective that may be called pragmatic idealism. By the latter I mean his analytical emphasis on the importance of symbols, laws, and cultural norms in helping to shape political destinies. No student who ever presented Professor Linz with a thesis proposal that overprivileged economics or simplistic conflict models can ever forget his responses and his concern with apparently empty emblems. Linz's idealism also encompassed a deep faith in democratic practices and scorn for those who asked, "*Votos, para que?*" Yet this same idealism is tempered by a pragmatic awareness that democracy is not perfect, that it could not—and, if it wanted to survive, should not—

attempt to resolve injustices outside of the limited realm of politics. His pragmatism sought answers for political questions in the daily compromises, debates, adjustments, and alliances of concrete actors. Always distrustful of grand theorizing, he is friendliest to historical accounts that seek first to establish who did what to whom, when, where, how, and why.

This pragmatic attachment to the specifics of the case has often frustrated those of us who were his students or who used his work. There are common links and familiar, recognizable perspectives, but as yet there is no complete theory of the state or of democracy that encompassed all his interests. A collection of papers such as this Festschrift using his theoretical insights to analyze a wide variety of regimes might represent the beginning of such a synthesis.

Given the central role of authoritarianism in Linz's work, it is interesting that he never addressed the case of postrevolutionary Mexico.[5] This is especially surprising given the importance of Linz's contributions in Mexican academic circles. At least in such leading institutions as the Colegio de México, the model of authoritarianism used to describe the Mexican regime is explicitly borrowed from Linz. This essay is an attempt to fit Linz's thoughts onto a country that in many ways exemplifies the concerns that have guided his career. It focuses on two distinct strands of his work: the categorization of regime types and the analysis of presidentialism. How does the ultimate *sui generis* case fit into Linz's categories? How does more recent work on the failure of presidential democracy inform the structure of Mexican *presidencialismo*, perhaps the most extreme form of such concentration of power? I hope that this effort will both improve our understanding of the dynamics and particular characteristics of the Mexican regime and further illuminate aspects of Linz's thoughts.

Categorizing the Mexican Regime

Let us begin with Linz's definition of democracy: "legal freedom to formulate and advocate political alternatives with concomitant rights... free and nonviolent opposition among leaders with periodic validation of their claim to rule; inclusion of all effective political offices in the democratic process; and provision for the participation of all members of the political community, whatever their political preferences."[6] Linz emphasizes that such a definition "does not require a turnover of parties in power, but the possibility of such a takeover" and that "deviation from the democratic ideal does not necessarily constitute its denial."[7]

Using this definition, arguments could be made for considering Mexico a democracy. A short review of the criteria is important since such formal guarantees have always helped define the regime, no matter what its practices. Certainly since 1934, there have been few *institutional or legal* restrictions on the advocacy of political alternatives. Exceptions include the decades-long prohibition on the Communist party and special cases such as the Federación de Partidos del Pueblo in 1954 and the Frente Electoral del Pueblo in 1963. The government, however, never attempted to *systematically and officially* exclude or limit the activities of the major opposition party, the National Action Party (Partido Acción Nacional, PAN).[8] The Party of the Democratic Revolution (Partido de la Revolución Democratica, PRD) experienced much more violent repression, but even in this case the government did not move to suppress it legally. The fact that Cárdenas could hold rallies in the *zocalo* questioning the legitimacy of the regime does suggest a certain liberality.

With regard to concomitant democratic rights, there exist constitutional guarantees for a free press, and the regime never institutionalized censorship offices. All major federal offices, with the exception of Mayor of the Federal District, are filled by regularly held direct elections. (This office will be elective after 1996). Since 1952 there have been no systemic exclusions of any part of the adult population by race, gender, or creed.[9] This is not to deny that Indians in the South, to name one obvious example, often had their votes stolen through fraud or intimidation and that this often worked as a form of electoral apartheid. Yet the regime steadfastly maintained at least the legal fiction of universal suffrage, even if it was not always very effective.

Nevertheless, it would be difficult to find a single authority on Mexican politics who would be comfortable with labeling Mexico a democracy, at least before 1994.[10] There have always been stringent limits on the roles of political alternatives to the ruling Institutional Revolutionary Party (Partido Institucional Revolucionario, PRI). The litany of PRI victories is well known: The party has won every presidential election since its inception as the National Revolutionary Party (Partido Nacional Revolucionario, PNR) in 1929. Until 1988, the PRI had won every senatorial race and until 1989, every gubernatorial campaign. While the opposition did win some seats in the House of Representatives and was allotted some representational slots, the PRI (again until 1988) always possessed a commanding majority in the lower house. Even after the 1988 elections the PRI was the majority party in that chamber and its candidates won 60 of the 64 senatorial races. The election of 1991 brought back practically absolute control over the legislature. Despite the watershed 1994 election, the PRI still occupies 61 percent of the lower house and 74 percent of the Senate while retaining control over 26 of 31 governorships.

Some prominent politicians have argued that the PRI should not be penalized for its successes; that the regime should not be labeled undemocratic simply because it is popular or because its party enjoys hegemonic control. Unfortunately, many of the votes "earned" by the PRI reflect more its well-developed capacity for fraud than real electoral support. In those elections where the opposition has managed to organize resources adequate for policing the electoral process, a consistent pattern of fraud has been uncovered. The "green vote" from the rural South is well known to reflect the power of local *caciques* in small communities throughout Mexico's most impoverished states. The central labor organization and major unions such as the oil workers were well known for providing workers with premarked ballots in exchange for their blank sheets. The massive use of fraudulent credentials and multiple voting techniques have also been regularly reported. Last-minute changes in voting sites, polling booth intimidation, and simple destruction of boxes containing the votes of well-known opposition strongholds have also been amply documented.

The evidence of electoral fraud in Mexico is more anecdotal than systematic. We know it is there, but we lack a conclusive measure of how much it matters. On the national level practically all sources agree that massive fraud occurred in the 1940 and 1952 presidential elections when PRI dissidents decided to support a nonofficial candidate. The results of the 1988 elections also remain disputed.[11] We know, thanks to revelations by internal players, that the infamous computer crash was caused more by political malfeasance than electronic failure. The subsequent destruction of the paper trail of ballots and district counting sheets also raises suspicions. Yet Jorge Alcocer, an opposition congressman elected in 1988, estimated that while fraud had elevated the PRI totals by 6–8 percent, Carlos Salinas would still have won by a small margin without the fraud.[12]

It would be an error to completely dismiss the PRI's electoral appeal. Until 1968 the party and the regime enjoyed wide popular legitimacy, and even after the Tlatelolco Massacre, the PRI's "revolutionary mantle" and apparent success in providing economic growth attracted the support of large segments of the peasant and working classes. Despite the prevalence of fraud, PRI presidential candidates (with the possible exception of Salinas in 1988) would probably have won all the presidential elections since 1946 even if these had been administered fairly. The margins of victory would have been smaller, but the outcome would have remained the same. The 1994 election was certainly not fair (see below), but almost all sources agree that it was free of decisive fraud.[13] The case of local and congressional elections is less clear since fraud is more prevalent below the national level. But even with these one could argue that the PRI would have won a large number (though certainly not all) of these elections. While it progressively lost support from the 1970s onwards, the PRI arguably was the majority party in Mexico well into the 1980s.[14]

The perpetual victories of the PRI not only served to monopolize power but also effectively weakened the formulation and voicing of political alternatives by demonstrating the futility of such efforts. This demonstration effect curtailed opposition in two ways: encouraging voter apathy and discouraging the organization of opposition forces. The first is indicated by the consistently high levels of absenteeism. After an increase in participation in the 1960s and 1970s, 48 percent of the population did not bother to vote in 1988.[15] This was reversed with the dramatic turnout of 1994 (78 percent). Nevertheless, a significant part of the Mexican population consistently fails to participate politically, and the PRI probably has often depended on such passivity for control. While nonparticipation arguably represented a vote against the PRI and thereby weakened the legitimacy of the regime, such practices had little, if any, practical consequences: nonvotes do not count. Moreover, such abstention also made the job of the PRI easier since the number of votes that it had to mobilize in order to ensure victory was smaller. Combined with its control of resources, this allowed the PRI to consistently win elections even in the absence of explicit and blatant fraud and intimidation.

Perhaps more importantly, the almost certain guarantee of defeat also discouraged even the pretense of opposition, at least until 1988. Given the low probability of winning and the likelihood of reprisal, it is surprising that opposition parties such as the PAN continued to exist. Even such dedicated opposition institutions tended to admit defeat as, for example, in 1976 when José López Portillo ran unopposed. The grassroots "explosion" following the earthquake of 1985, the rise of a left opposition in 1988, the consolidation of the left opposition after the government recognized its victories, and the increasing competitiveness of local elections appear to have changed this dynamic.[16] Nevertheless, given the significant lag in developing what may be called an "opposition culture," Mexican politics still suffers from the learned powerlessness of the previous decades.

Those rights associated with the practice of democracy—a free press and the opportunity to associate and organize—have also been restricted through nonofficial means. The Mexican government has never had to formally prohibit publication of a newspaper or magazine. (One possible exception would be Echeverría's assault on *Excelsior* in

1976). Instead, through its former monopoly on newsprint and advertising revenue, it allowed the intimidation of the market to exercise censoring authority.[17] Sticks have also been accompanied by carrots such as the practice of bribing journalists. The alliance of the government with Televisa is based on a simple exchange: the private network has a monopoly on advertising, and the government has a monopoly on the voicing of political analysis. The support of the television monopoly is critical, since over 90 percent of Mexicans receive their news from this medium. Studies of television coverage even in 1994 demonstrated that the government candidate enjoyed an overwhelming advantage.[18]

Partly because of these practices, the Mexican regime has generally not used systematic violence in order to maintain its power, at least not at the levels seen in the Southern Cone in the 1970s.[19] This is not to deny the very real use of violence and the threat thereof but to distinguish the Mexican variant of such activities. There have been moments of violent suppression, including that during the disputed election of 1940, during the railroad strike of 1958, and the student massacre of 1968. The shock caused by the latter, however, in many ways serves to indicate how rare violence had been in the political lexicon of postrevolutionary Mexico. In the 1970s government-sponsored and -directed violence against the opposition increased, the most famous example being the *halcones* incident of 1971. In the state of Guererro the battle against the guerrilla movement also brought about an increase in violent actions. During the last two decades the activities of the government in controlling labor and peasant organizations has involved explicit repression, including the murder of dissidents and the creation of mafias and private armies. More recently dozens of journalists (especially in the provinces) have been killed, and prominent opposition intellectuals have been harassed and threatened by thugs with obvious links to the Ministry of Government. Since 1 January 1994 the army has occupied large parts of Chiapas and has expanded its presence in similar regions such as Guererro and Oaxaca. The Mexican army's policy in Chiapas, however, has been remarkably restrained by the standards of its continental counterparts. One can only imagine what the Peruvian, Chilean, or Guatemalan armed forces would have done under similar circumstances. The Mexican system *was* a "perfect dictatorship" whose infrequent recourse to public repression masked the efficiency of its control.

Mexico, therefore, represents a special case of Linz's category of authoritarian regimes. This definition emphasized the existence of "limited, not responsible, political pluralism."[20] The "deviation" from democratic ideals is great enough to minimize the effectiveness of electoral mechanisms for popular participation. At least until 1994 no one would have thought of the PRI as a government *pro tempore*. As in many of the cases identified by Linz, the PRI is an official or single party, created from above rather than in the grassroots, the product of an alliance among elites already in power rather than an instrument for obtaining power. Such a party can institutionalize political participation by opposition groups without risking a defeat. The regime has been dominated by a bureaucratic-technocratic elite that has increasingly discouraged participation and mobilization. Other than reliance on nationalistic appeals and an increasingly vague revolutionary legacy, the regime has never formulated an explicit ideology with which it sought to control the daily life of its citizens. It therefore lacks the "totalist" qualities associated with totalitarian regimes.

Using Linz's subtypes, we could speak of Mexico as spanning the boundary between mobilizational-authoritarian and bureaucratic-military.[21] Unlike the classic cases of mobilizational-authoritarian regimes, the PRI does not represent an alternative power to the central bureaucracy but rather is part of it. The PRI has never been a "disciplined, ideological mass movement" but was always "a flexible machine that maintained solidarity among its members by appealing to their self-interest while allowing for the play of factions...relying characteristically on the attraction of material rewards rather than enthusiasm for political principles."[22] But neither is Mexico an example of bureaucratic-militarism. For one thing, civilians have been in charge since the 1930s. Moreover, at least for the first forty years, the party was not a simple facade behind which the bureaucratic-military elite conducted "real politics" but served as both an organizational arena for elite settlements and a means to organize the population into corporatist sectors and mobilize support for and legitimize the government. While it never represented an independent power base, it did serve as a vital channel of communication and patronage between state and society and as a cohesive force inside the elite.[23] In the words of Cosio Villegas, "El PRI se respira en todas partes" [one breathes the PRI everywhere].

Was the PRI representative? It was arguably so through the 1960s. The last two decades, however, have seen a tightening of the relevant elite to those associated with a small group within the ruling circle.[24] One prominent sign of this greater exclusivity was the break within the PRI beginning with Cuauhtémoc Cárdenas in 1987. The circulatory mechanism has broken down and the regime has become arguably much less representative of the country's population. Linz's concept of an authoritarian mentality (as opposed to ideology) is clearly relevant here. The technocratic elite that ruled(s?) Mexico rejected even the limited voicing of interests embodied in the traditional system and in its place asserted the existence of optimal solutions to social problems. This elite shared a frustration with representational politics (even as practiced in Mexico). According to them, pressure from interest groups made it impossible for the government to pursue long-term solutions to the country's problems. The answer was to empower a group with no such prior commitments who could and would choose what was best for the country *as a whole*. In many ways the new elite embodied the assumptions or mentalities associated with the Organic Statism of Brazil and the Southern Cone of the 1960s and 1970s. But it went further than these since it rejected even corporatist mechanisms. In their place the technocrats proposed a national commitment to "modernization"; to a greater common good that would follow the logic of the international market place.

How to categorize Mexico in the 1990s? Borrowing from both Linz and Guillermo O'Donnell,[25] we could label Mexico a "delegative authoritarian" regime in which the president increasingly came to embody the entire nation and served as the main custodian and definer of its interests. Elections served to confirm the regular circulation of new elites into the first circle of the bureaucracy. This system had gradually replaced a more inclusive corporatism or "representative authoritarianism." The current political crisis in Mexico does not stem from the death of the PRI, as traditionally understood. The party has been in decline for at least two decades. It is the office of the president and the particular form of technocratic authoritarianism that has been practiced in Mexico since the late 1970s that is in crisis. The reasons for this and possible consequences lead us to the analysis of a second major theme of Linz's work.

Presidentialism

As defined by Linz, presidentialism is characterized by "an executive with considerable powers...and generally full control over the composition of his cabinet and the administration is elected...for a fixed period of time and is not dependent on a formal vote of confidence."[26] The most important attributes of presidentialism are: concentration of power and constitutional rigidity. While Linz's analysis largely concerns presidential democracies, his discussion also helps us to better understand the Mexican system.

The advantages of presidentialism, as identified by Linz, parallel arguments made for such a system in the Mexican case beginning in the nineteenth century. A strong chief executive was thought necessary for the creation of a unified state following the chaos of the postindependence period. Similarly, following the violence of the Revolution and the instability of the 1920s, a strong presidential system appeared to provide an institutional brake on the incipient *caudillismo* or warlordism. Moreover, the concentrated power of the presidency also allowed Cárdenas to successfully challenge Calles's attempts to remain the *líder máximo* through the 1930s. The no-reelection clause theoretically balanced the power of the office with limitations on tenure, thereby preventing the consolidation of power such as had occurred during the Porfiriato. Both the PRI and the strong presidency did provide the institutional stability that allowed Mexico to recuperate from the Revolution. The concentration of power in the incumbent, combined with the no-reelection clause, also prevented the consolidation of one-man rule.

As Linz takes great pain to point out, however, some of the supposed benefits of presidentialism lose a great part of their appeal on closer inspection. A perfect example is the claim that in presidential systems the voters know what they are voting for, as opposed to the more general vote for a parliamentary party. Certainly in Mexico the opposite has been the case. Neither government nor opposition candidates are known commodities. In the case of the latter, this partly reflects the media's effective blackout of opposition voices. But the mystery surrounding the PRI candidate is often equally great. The reason is that government candidates have never originated in public careers involving constituency building. From the very beginning candidates were drawn from within the "Revolutionary Family." Anyone thought likely to move outside it was automatically disqualified.

In the past twenty-five years this trend has become even more pronounced. The limited exposure to the six "precandidates" of the PRI in 1987 revealed how little was actually known about the men being considered. Even in 1993 Colosio's positions on a wide variety of issues were unknown and his most minimal utterances were probed for signs on where he stood. In Zedillo's case (or de la Madrid's before him) the candidate was practically an unknown even to many in the political class.

The dynamics of succession make the mystery even more profound, since the type of behavior rewarded is precisely that designed to disguise true intentions and honest feelings. Even those doing the "real" choosing (the ruling president) have found that they knew little about their successors. To great extent, the future president remains a cipher until his inauguration. The population barely knows him or her (and in any case has had little to say about the choice). His superiors and colleagues can only attest to his abilities as a courtier or perhaps as a technical expert. No one can have the slightest idea how he will perform as the temporary monarch of a nation of 90 million.

Such an enigma is particularly dangerous given how much rides on a single individual. In the absence of countervailing institutions, the legitimacy of the regime at any point in time has come increasingly to rely on the actions of the office of the presidency and by extension, the incumbent. Legitimacy crises are particularly problematic when combined with the rigidity that is a basic institutional characteristic of presidentialism. This rigidity is particularly pronounced in a system with no reelections, since the president is completely unaccountable. There is no possible electoral "give-and-take" with the population. Whatever the president's actions, the populace will never have another opportunity to express its opinion. Under a parliamentary regime, failure, if catastrophic enough, can lead to a change in government. Under a presidential system, an early departure from office, even if voluntary, can produce an even greater crisis.

The identification of a regime with a single person can have benefits. It could be argued that the largely discredited PRI rode Salinas's coattails in the 1991 elections. Zedillo's rags-to-riches biography and his well-known honesty helped cleanse the party of some of the dirt accumulated through sweetheart deals and support by the Mexican billionaires' club. But since the 1950s the regime has also had to weather the costs associated with the "divorce" of the president from power. Whenever the president was seen as betraying the legacy of the Revolution (Gustavo Díaz Ordaz), or expanding such a legacy beyond its accepted bounds (Luis Echeverría), or when the president could not control corruption or participated in it (Miguel Alemán and José López Portillo), or when his administration could no longer deliver economic growth (de la Madrid), the very legitimacy of the regime was called into question. Salinas's departure was particularly disastrous. But more than the immediate damage seen in 1994, the historical link between the president and the regime had deleterious long-term results. First, it forced the next incumbent to break with the legacy of his predecessor and disrupted interadministration continuity. Second, and more importantly, it required the suppression of any assaults on the president, since these could be so destabilizing. The first helped prevent the construction of a stable civil service which could act as an institutional brake on personalistic rule; the second encouraged authoritarian control.

This single-focus legitimization is also associated with the polarization of public opinion. Certainly in the case of Mexico the central political dividing line is between those who support the regime and those who oppose it. All ideological and even partisan considerations pale next to this choice.[27] This makes it very difficult to publicly articulate, much less implement, compromise policies. The NAFTA decision is a perfect example. Mexico did not possess an institutional space in which the agreement could both be supported *and* amended. Similarly, the collapse of the peso might have been avoided if there had existed the possibility of creating an alternative to neoliberal triumphalism within policy-making circles or even civil society. Mexico did not have the institutional equivalents of Chile's CIEPLAN or the Concertación.[28] The concentration of resources and legitimation in the office of the president was partly responsible for this, since no other channel existed for communication. The absence of dissident voices not only made the Mexican system not only unresponsive and authoritarian but also reduced its policy-making efficiency as it was increasingly susceptible to all the problems of groupthink and denial.

The extent of power also makes presidential contests "winner-take-all" struggles, thereby raising the stakes of the game and exacerbating political tensions. Such situations are particularly problematic for societies in which there is no solid social consensus regarding public policy goals. Since the president's claim to legitimacy is partly based on the fact that his is the only office that seeks to represent the entire population (as opposed to a regional or corporatist section), any opposition to positions taken by the president may be seen as a form of betrayal or political irresponsibility. This was certainly a feature of the presidentialist discourse since the advent of the technocrats. Even previously, however, challenging the word of the president bordered on treason. Combined with sycophancy, which is endemic in such institutions, this often leads the incumbent president to begin associating his fate and interests with those of the nation.

In some ways, the president is trapped by the totality of his mandate. Presidentialist systems, and particularly those with no-reelection clauses, force a time limit on the office holders, thereby increasing the pressure to reject compromises and complete the presidential agenda as soon as possible. The combination of this almost absolute power (at least until 1994) and the limit on incumbency creates a particularly disastrous dynamic. The temptation of power makes office holders believe that they can accomplish the impossible. The awareness that they will have no power after six years gives their mission a special sense of urgency. Moreover, since the judgment of history (always a consideration for such persons) will be based on those relatively short six years, the temptation to "damn the torpedoes" is particularly strong. On the positive side, this can produce decisive leadership. On the other side, it causes presidents to commit to policies that would benefit from longer-term assessment. Worse still, presidents grow terrified of failure in their sixth year. They use all resources at their disposal to postpone bad news even if it is inevitable. The catastrophic postponement of currency devaluation is only the most recent and prominent example.

The concentration of power in the Mexican presidency has also contributed to the absence of a real opposition. Because only one office counted and this office had all resources at its disposal, the "zero-sum" aspect of presidentialist systems has been particularly manifest in Mexico. Whoever controlled the presidency could literally dictate the direction of the government. There was no possibility of limiting or conditioning the imposition of a political perspective through other political institutions such as Congress. Those committed to a particular development model could not afford to lose their monopoly on this one office as it would necessarily involve a radical social, political, and economic reorientation of the regime. This tended to discourage political efforts at the grassroots level and even in legislative races. The PRD clearly suffered from this syndrome, as its obsession with Cárdenas's claims to the presidency obscured the more realistic and vital need to develop an institutional base and to perhaps even bargain for a share of power on the provincial level. As much as national level agreements may have helped the PAN's resurgence since 1988, it could capture governorships and congressional seats only because it possessed a well-organized party apparatus in these regions.

The central role of the presidency and the cycle of six year "monarchies" also encouraged the personalization of politics. Since the president controlled all posts and government resources, only those associated with him could hope to succeed professionally or have their policies implemented. Combined with the absence of a civil service tradition that would have ensured the autonomy of the bureaucracy, this fostered the development of patronage networks within the regime. In order to accomplish all his goals within the allotted period, the president had to depend on his *camarilla* or personal clique.[29] Every six years an incumbent's *camarilla* would replace that of his predecessor. Only those whom the president could trust would be allowed to play a role in the formulation or implementation of public policy. Such dependence on a personal relationship with one man reduced the possibility of dissent within the regime which lead to a homogeneity of perspectives and the exclusion of alternative voices.

The circulation of elite subgroups could have led to the development of a Japanese-type model in which the various factions within the PRI would serve as partylike institutions clustered around an ideological center, each representing varying social groups and interests. But beginning with the *sexenio* of Luis Echeverría, the office of the presidency and the *camarillas* that orbited it established an even more pronounced control over the bureaucracy. Simultaneously, partly because of Echeverría's attempts to relegitimize the regime through welfare populism and partly thanks to the massive increase in revenues following the oil boom, the resources available to this inner circle also increased. This combination of immense concentration of power within a set of institutions and the personalization of rule through the *camarillas* increasingly characterized the current Mexican system and played an important role in the development of the current crisis.

The no-reelection clause, the one feature of the Mexican system that could be seen as contributing to a democratic regime, is also partly responsible for the failure to develop more democratic mechanisms.[30] The no-reelection clause was meant to prevent a repetition of the Porfiriato through which one man was able to impose his control over the government for three decades. Recently, similar restrictions have become popular in the United States as a means to limit the power accruing to incumbents and the resulting low turnover rate. In his analysis of authoritarian regimes and presidentialist systems Linz also discusses this institution, but without making an explicit judgment on its desirability.[31] The Mexican case indicates that in their attempt to force limits on incumbents' power, such constitutional provisions may also discourage the development of alternative voices.

The principle of no-reelection supports the stability of ruling parties by providing incentives for loyalty and discouraging the development of internal opposition. Since each elite group or faction has, at least theoretically, the possibility of achieving power within a prescribed period of time, there is no need to go outside institutional channels in order to make a claim to rule. Thus, despite the immense resources that accrued to whatever faction or *camarilla* controlled the presidency at any one point in time, other elite groups could expect that their turn would come eventually. No-reelection, and the circulation of elites that accompanied it, provided adequate spaces for all those with political aspirations within the PRI. Only when significant groups within the PRI perceived a dramatic decline in such probabilities (as in 1940, 1952, and most significantly, 1988) did the party provide the oppositional voices necessary to make its monopoly on rule more representational.

More importantly, the prohibition on re-election prevented the development of political bases outside of the presidentially controlled bureaucracy. Even under the best circumstances a politician's career would be extremely short. Only if he or she could progress up the electoral ladder (Congress, Senate, Governor) could a politician expect to remain in power for any extended period. Even those few who could manage such a progression would see their career limited to fifteen years. The division between the public and private spheres that existed in Mexico until the 1980s would also limit the professional future awaiting even the most successful of candidates. The fruits of corruption provided some comfort (and helped grease the wheels of elite circulation), but ambitious politicians would see their professional lives cut short at very young ages. Thus, the only professional alternative was entry into a bureaucracy that, despite the cyclical changes, could provide a relative assurance of employment. This helps explain the passivity of the Mexican Congress which, despite its broad constitutional powers, has traditionally served as a rubber stamp for the president.[32] No politician could afford to anger his or her future employer or get a reputation for disloyal behavior. Those whose principles might push them to challenge the authority of the president would be excluded from the system. Assuming that access to power is central to a politician's agenda, no-reelection deprived elite members of a means to power independent of central control. If they could not expect to be ever reelected, there was no incentive for them to cultivate a popular constituency. Why provide services to voters who could not return such favors with electoral support?

The failure to develop individual constituencies, in turn, deprived politicians of access to resources not controlled by the central bureaucracy and by extension, the president. Not only were they dependent on his favors for employment, they also possessed no bargaining chips with which to exert pressure in negotiations. The corporatist sectors could perhaps have developed into such independent bases. But these owed their very existence to the presidential office. More importantly, in order to ensure their monopoly over their relevant social groups, they became increasingly linked to and dominated by the central authorities as well.

It is these mechanisms that help distinguish Mexico from similar hegemonic or dominant party regimes with more democratic characteristics, such as Japan, Congress Party India, or Christian Democracy in Italy. In these cases politicians and their factions did develop both electoral and financial constituencies. These ensured a more competitive arena in which the various cliques could fight over the spoils of the system. In Mexico only one voice counted, and the person with that one voice also held all the purse strings. What mattered was establishing personal relationships with one of the *camarillas* that could claim some access to the presidential office. Since these were based on trust and obedience, no opposition voices could develop internally. Thus, even with greater respect for electoral norms, the development of the Mexican system might not have been much different. When a subgroup within the regime was able to establish its monopoly over the presidential office and impose its particular model on public policy, opponents within the regime had to rely on the very same electoral mechanisms they had previously helped to circumvent in order to voice alternatives.

If, as I have argued elsewhere,[33] presidential authoritarianism was partly responsible for the success of the Salinas project of restructuring the Mexican economy, it also may be blamed for much of the resulting disaster. Aside from whatever costs or benefits *salinastroika* might have had, presidentialism allowed the technocratic elite to become increasingly insulated, not only from the population but also from the very real dangers of their policies and the many warning signs that appeared beginning in 1992. Alternative sources of power or even channels of communication might not have prevented the explosions of January and December 1994. Yet an earlier discussion of armed discontent in Chiapas and of the peso overvaluation might have softened the blows. It could even be argued that a wider diffusion of institutional powers and greater openness might have prevented the kinds of pressures that exploded with the killings of Colosio and Ruiz Massieu.

Después del desmadre:
Effective Suffrage and Reelection

Is Mexico moving towards a more competitive democracy? Clearly 1994, perhaps even more than 1988, was a significant milestone. Several aspects of the election deserve attention.

First, the huge turnout indicated that the government could not continue to rely on the passivity of the population. If nothing else, this makes the management of fraud much more complicated and may tax the organizational capacities of the PRI. By expressing their faith in the democratic system the population may be helping to guarantee its honesty.

Second, despite the fact that many bemoaned the PRI's attempts to gain millions from leading businessmen, this effort indicated that the party no longer felt so safe in using government resources. One may wish for better representatives of "civil society" than Emilio Azcarraga or Carlos Slim, but the PRI's need for money made it much more susceptible to external voices and influence. The results may be corruption and sweetheart deals, but the wall between the PRI and society erected over the past twenty years is being dismantled.

Third, the opposition lost and accepted it. One may respect Cárdenas's lonely campaign against the legitimacy of the Salinas election, but his efforts tended to obscure the importance of a loyal opposition. In order for democracy to work in Mexico, basic parameters of the regime must be accepted by all the players. An argument about the rules should not feature in every round of electoral competition.

Fourth, these rules are increasingly leveling the playing field. The creation of an independent electoral bureau and cleaner and fairer voter registration and identifications has drastically reduced the possibilities for significant fraud, at least at the national level. This is not to deny that the election was unfair and that the distribution of resources will still benefit the incumbent, but these problems are in many ways closer to the conditions of democratic competition in the United States than the electoral shams of 1970s Mexico.

Fifth, whatever one's ideological preferences, the PAN will serve as a much more effective opposition in a transition environment than the PRD. There are several reasons for this: The PAN is much more of a political party than the PRD which was really a coalition of grassroots groups linked through the candidacy of Cárdenas. A victory by the latter would have resulted in a political mutant, a PRD head on a PRI body. The PAN's greater organizational capacity ensures that once a PAN president is elected, he (a she is almost out of the question) can rely on some support both in the legislature and in the provinces. Perhaps more important, precisely because the ideological space between the PRI and the PAN has shrunk so dramatically over the past decade, a technocratic government is much more likely to accept defeat from the reft than from the left. (The record of state level elections over the past eight years confirms this). Relatedly, a victory by the PAN will not be associated with fears of capital flight or economic disaster. For Mexican democracy to consolidate, it is vital that election results be somewhat divorced from immediate economic expectations. Finally, the United States (which has developed an effective veto through the emergency loans) is much more likely to see the victory of the PAN as a legitimate expression of democracy and to reward such behavior with the kind of policies that are desperately needed if the Mexican economy is to recover (for example, debt relief).

These same conditions also indicate the continuing Achilles heel of any Mexican democracy. The fact that in a country with the horrific poverty and rampant inequality of Mexico,[34] the left is still not a viable political alternative highlights the limits of the kind of formal democracy that Juan Linz has always emphasized. As much as one may rejoice in the ultimate collapse of the "perfect dictatorship" of the PRI, it is unclear how much a PAN victory will mean for those citizens on the bottom of the social and economic ladder. Linz has always detested confusing democratic liberty with socioeconomic equality (as hundreds of students who have dared to broach this topic can attest). Yet a case such as Mexico's may require that we look farther than the guarantees of competition and circulation and look to the range of options being offered.

This is of particular concern given the likely scenario for a PRI defeat. There exists the possibility of an PAN victory in the 1997 legislative elections as well as in the presidential elections of the year 2000. Yet the PAN, despite all its strength, is not prepared to compete in large parts of the country (for example, the rural South). It is likely that a PAN president would have to rely on a coalition of PAN and rightist PRIistas. This would effectively check the influence of the PRD and of voices calling for more redistributive social and economic policies. It might also lead to a worsening of regional tensions, as it could evolve into a new version of the Northern dynasty.

Can democracy make a difference? It will not surprise anyone to hear a student of Linz answering yes. Obviously a more accountable government is more likely to prosecute those who violate laws and who betray public trust. A democratic government will be more sensitive to public perceptions of conflict of interests and perhaps less likely to insist on having the majority pay for the luxuries and the mistakes of the few. Democracy may even do more. It could offer an opportunity to expand the choices of polices available and make the government truly representative of Mexican social reality. This will require perhaps a paradoxical radical shift in the Mexican constitution: the elimination of the prohibition on reelection.

The Mexican constitution is not particularly presidentialist.[35] Following its formal laws could create a strong president balanced by an equally strong legislature. Federalism would also potentially create a third balance on central executive power. These countervailing forces, however, cannot develop as long as the principle of no-reelection prevents the creation of stable electoral careers. Reelection gives the population the opportunity to reward politicians who have confronted and challenged the presidency. It also offers an opportunity for local and regional party machines to establish their autonomy from the capital.[36] Reelection would support a democratic transition no matter which party dominates in the next century. If the PRI maintains its position, the possibility of reelection would strengthen forces dependent on elections and allow them to challenge the presidency. A PAN government would have to seek support in new areas and sectors of the population and develop a platform for creating a more equitable society. The PRD could use this opportunity to begin to create a truly integrated national apparatus with which to implement its preferred policies.

A repeal of the no-reelection clause (with perhaps a change in the presidential term to four years) would provide Mexico with a mechanism with which to build a more democratic regime *from below*. Such a mechanism might be slower and more frustrating than the presidential imposition some have suggested to Zedillo, but presidential dominance, even for a good cause, would only strengthen an institution that desperately needs to be weakened.

While he has never written on this subject, I suspect that Linz would be pleased with such a solution. It would avoid the kind of totalist and radical change he has always argued against and that he sees as representing a grave threat to young democracies. It would accept the reality that politicians need to make a living and will adjust their behavior accordingly. Most important, it places voting and the possibility of both removal from or retention in office at the very center of political life.

Notes

1. On Brazil, see his "The Future of an Authoritarian Situation" in Alfred Stepan, ed., *Authoritarian Brazil* (New Haven: Yale University Press, 1973). On Germany, see his dissertation, "The Social Bases of West German Politics," University of Ann Arbor, 1963. The work on Spain is obviously too long and well known to list.

2. *The Breakdown of Democratic Regimes*, edited with Alfred Stepan (Baltimore: Johns Hopkins Press, 1978); *Democracy in Developing Countries*, edited with Larry Diamond and Seymour M. Lipset (Boulder, CO: Lynne Rienner, 1989).

3. His contributions to the analysis of voting behavior began almost forty years ago with an article (coauthored with Seymour M. Lipset, P. F. Lazarfeld and A. H. Barton) in Gardner Lindzey, ed., *Handbook of Social Psychology*, vol. 2 (Reading, MA: Addison-Wesley, 1954). The first conceptualization of authoritarianism came in "An Authoritarian Regime: The Case of Spain," in E. Allardt and Y. Littunen, eds., *Cleavages, Ideologies, and Party Systems* (Helsinki: The Academic Bookstore, 1964).

4. See Juan Linz and Arturo Valenzuela, eds., *The Failure of Presidential Democracy*, vols. 1 and 2 (Baltimore: Johns Hopkins University Press, 1994).

5. This is not to deny the many allusions to Mexico in Linz's work, but I have not been able to locate an explicit analysis of this regime.

6. Juan Linz, *Crisis, Breakdown, and Reequilibration*, vol. 1 of Linz and Stepan, *The Breakdown of Democratic Regimes*. A similar set of criteria may be found in "Totalitarian and Authoritarian Regimes," in Fred Greenstein and Nelson Polsby, eds., *Handbook of Political Science*, vol. 3 (Reading, MA: Addison-Wesley, 1975), p. 184.

7. *Crisis*, p. 6.

8. Not all agree on this point. Juan Molinar Horcasitas, for example, believes that the PRI made it *almost* impossible for PRI dissenters to participate in federal elections. See his *El tiempo de la legitimidad* (Mexico, D.F.: Cal y Arena, 1991). Much of the debate on this issue comes down to the definition of the "almost" emphasized above.

9. The one exception was the prohibition on clerics from participating in the political process which was removed with the constitutional amendments of 1991.

10. The most optimistic appraisals are found in W. P. Tucker, *The Mexican Government Today* (Minneapolis: University of Minnesota Press, 1957), and R. E. Scott, *Mexican Government in Transition* (Urbana: University of Illinois Press, 1964). See also Pablo Gonzalez Casanova, *La democracia en México* (Mexico: Editorial Era, 1965). Certainly all academic analyses since 1968 have accepted the essentially authoritarian nature of the regime.

11. Not surprisingly, the most extensive analysis has been done by the opposition. See J. Barberan, et al., *Radiografía del fraude* (Mexico: Colección Los Grandes Problemas Nacionales, 1988), and Partido Acción Nacional, *Mitos y verdades de las elecciones presidenciales de 1988* (Mexico: PAN, 1988). Unfortunately, we still do not have a good scholarly account of fraud in Mexico, but see E. Butler and J. Bustamante, eds., *Sucesión Presidencial* (Boulder: Westview, 1991).

12. Cited in Jorge Castañeda, *The Mexican Shock* (New York: New Press, 1995), p. 129.

13. Sergio Aguayo Quezada, "A Mexican Milestone," *Journal of Democracy* 6, 2 (April 1995).

14. The polls cited by Jorge Dominguez and James A. McCann in their *Democratizing Mexico* (Baltimore: Johns Hopkins University Press, 1996) indicate that the PRI has often accurately articulated majority views.

15. Miguel Basañez, *El pulso de los sexenios* (Mexico: Siglo XXI, 1990), and Jaime Gonzalez Graf, ed., *Las elecciones de 1988* (Mexico: IMEP, 1989).

16. According to one estimate, nearly ninety percent of electoral districts are now competitive. Joseph Klesner, "The 1994 Mexican Elections," *Mexican Studies* (Winter 1995).

17. For an illuminating account of the relationship between the government and the press, see Julio Scherer Garcia, *Los presidentes* (Mexico: Editorial Grijalbo, 1986).

18. See Andreas Oppenheimer, *Bordering on Chaos* (New York: Little, Brown, 1996), pp. 131–35.

19. On this issue, see Judith Adler Hellman, *Mexico in Crisis* (New York: Holmes and Meier, 1983), chapter 5.

20. "An Authoritarian Regime: The Case of Spain," in Erik Allardt and Stein Rokkan, eds., *Mass Politics: Studies in Political Sociology* (New York: Free Press, 1970), p. 235. See also José Luis Reyna and R. Weinert, *Authoritarianism in*

Mexico (Philadelphia: ISHI, 1977), and Kevin J. Middlebrook, *Political Liberalization in an Authoritarian Regime* (San Diego, CA: Center for U.S.-Mexican Studies, 1985).

21. On the application of the bureaucratic-authoritarian model, see Guillermo O'Donnell, *Modernization and Bureaucratic-Authoritarianism* (Berkeley: Institute for international Studies, 1979), p. 91.

22. "Totalitarian and Authoritarian Regimes," p. 324.

23. In the 1960s there was considerable debate regarding the extent to which the party did serve to represent the disparate interests within it. Martin C. Needler, Leon Vincent Padgett, and Robert E. Scott contended that it did represent them while Frank Brandenburg and Roger D. Hansen saw it more as a controlling, as opposed to representative, institution. After 1968, most analysts agreed with the latter perspective.

24. See Miguel Angel Centeno, *Democracy within Reason: Technocratic Revolution in Mexico* (University Park: Penn State University Press, 1994).

25. Guillermo O'Donnell, "Delegative Democracy," *Journal of Democracy* 5, 1 (January 1994).

26. "Presidential or Parliamentary Democracy" in Linz and Valenzuela, *Failure of Presidential Democracy*, p. 6. For a summary of other views on presidentialism, see the essays in the same volume and Scott Mainwaring, "Presidentialism in Latin America," *Latin American Research Review* 25, 1 (1990).

27. Much of Dominguez and McCann, *Democratizing Mexico*, emphasizes this characteristic.

28. Recent success with political reform legislation indicates that Congress could develop into an institution capable of managing compromises.

29. On this institution, see Rogelio Hernández Rodriguez, "Los Hombres de Miguel de la Madrid," *Foro Internacional* XXVIII, 2 (July–September 1987): 25–32, and Roderic Camp, "*Camarillas* in Mexican Politics," *Estudios Mexicanos* 6, 1 (1990): 1.

30. The following discussion owes much to Jeffrey Weldon who is currently writing a book on the origins of this clause and the process through which it was accepted by Congress. See his contribution to Scott Mainwaring and Matthew Shugart, eds., *Presidentialism and Democracy in Latin America* (Cambridge University Press, forthcoming).

31. "Presidential or Parliamentary Democracy," pp. 16–18.

32. Legislators can be reelected, but not consecutively.

33. Centeno, *Democracy within Reason*.

34. One survey estimated that 66 percent of Mexicans live below the poverty line. Another estimated that inequality has actually grown since 1983 and is almost at the level of Brazil. See Wayne Cornelius, *Mexican Politics in Transition* (La Jolla, UCSD U.S.-Mexican Studies Center, 1996), pp. 99–106.

35. Jeff Weldon and Juan Molinar Horcasitas have been emphasizing this point for several years.

36. Obviously this does not always promote more democratic procedures, as the case of Tabasco illustrates.

3

Communist States as Ideocracies? Lessons from Cuba

Susan Eckstein

Juan Linz's work distinguishing authoritarian, totalitarian, and democratic regime types was pathbreaking.[1] His understanding of authoritarian regimes has influenced Latin American scholarship ever since.

Our understanding of totalitarian states, particularly their communist variant, remains weak, however. Anticommunist sentiment in the Western world, combined with the difficulties of doing research in communist countries, has stood in the way. In Latin America they have thwarted our understanding of Cuba under Fidel Castro's rule. The present chapter attempts to address this lacuna.

Totalitarian states, in Linz's view, have, in their ideal-typical form, the following combination of characteristics: (l) power concentrated in an individual who is not accountable to any large constituency and who cannot be dislodged from power by institutionalized, peaceful means; (2) a single mass party, together with other mobilization organizations; (3) an exclusive, autonomous, and more or less intellectually elaborate ideology with which the ruling leadership and the party serving the leader identify, an ideology that guides policy or is manipulated to legitimate policy; and (4) active citizen participation that is encouraged, demanded, and rewarded by the party through which it is channeled.

Totalitarian states are presumed to be strong in relation to civil society. While other writers have suggested that such regimes tend to obliterate the distinction between state and society as society is totally politicized, Linz has noted that the tension between the two never disappears (p. 188). Even so, Linz does not portray society as a constraining force. To the extent that he addresses constraints on the leadership's and party's ability to do what they want, he focuses on organizational dynamics internal to the ruling party and on dynamics grounded in the routinization of charisma. That is, he focuses on informal dynamics operating within formal political institutions, not on the society in which those institutions are embedded.

Ideology is said to be of such consequence to totalitarian regimes that some scholars, as Linz notes, have considered these states to be ideocracies, with ideology operating as a powerful "independent variable" (p. 196). Ideology purportedly limits the range of policy options (p. 196) while serving as a source of legitimacy and providing a sense of mission. Linz adds that while ideology imposes some constraints on rulers and their actions under totalitarian systems, the relationship is not one-sided. Much effort in such systems goes into the manipulation, adaptation, and selective interpretation of the ideological heritage. The simultaneous weakening and ossification of the ideology tend to isolate the ruling group and contribute to a power vacuum that tends to be filled by more coercive bureaucratic control, including greater reliance on praetorian police (p. 198). A replacement of ideology by pragmatic bases of policy formulation and the acceptance of heteronomous sources for ideas and central policies, he says, will lead to changes away from the totalitarian model. In essence, ideology is not inherently static, and dynamics at the ideological level may be of systemic consequence.

As the Cold War partially thawed it became less fashionable to call communist states "totalitarian." Political analysts began to highlight differences between and among fascist and communist regimes, both categorized previously as totalitarian. Yet the prevailing conception of communist states changed little: Communist states were still assumed to be strong, hegemonic, and ideologically driven, with power highly centralized and concentrated in the hand of the ruler and the ruling party. Society, in turn, continued to be portrayed as weak.[2] The main modification of the totalitarian conception of communism centered on the formal political apparatus. It was argued that bureaucracies, though state-affiliated, might develop institutional interests of their own which they defended and promoted.[3]

The speed and ease with which so much of the communist world collapsed between 1989 and 1991 suggest not merely that the regimes were unpopular politically and ineffective economically but that they were also misunderstood abroad. Society proved to be stronger and the governments weaker than had been assumed. Official Marxism-Leninism and "vanguard" party rule mystified the outer world more than folk who experienced them directly.

A new approach is needed to understand communist states, one that is political-economic rather than exclusively political and society- rather than merely state-centric. Even when the "means of production" are (in the main) nationalized and political control is formally concentrated in a "vanguard" party, global political-economic forces, on one hand, and informal domestic sociopolitical dynamics, on the other, may affect what communist regimes do. They therefore must be taken into account analytically.[4]

All states necessarily concern themselves with institutional economic, administrative, and political matters. However, they have differed in how they attempt to address such concerns and how effective they have been. Communist states with similar political structures have varied in their economic capacities, in their resources, and in the extent to which their resources have been externally or domestically generated. They also have varied in their dependence on trade, foreign technology, and capital. The more economically dependent, the more vulnerable the state to external economic conditions. Communist regimes not only relied on intra-Soviet bloc trade and aid, they also sought, when possible, Western goods and financing to attain items unavailable—at a comparable price or quality— from fellow Marxist-Leninist states. The communist bloc was not a self-contained economic entity. Ideological antipathy to capitalism did not keep the governments from seeking the products of capitalism or capitalist financing to attain them. Western economic ties, in turn, subjected communist states to Western market, political, and geopolitical forces.

Societal constraints may emanate, as Linz noted and bureaucratic interest group analyses elaborated, from within the interstices of the state apparatus itself. Organizational analyses, meanwhile, have highlighted how the desire of persons in positions of authority to advance their own interests may result in the diversion of resources for private ends. Robert Michels argued that all organizations, including socialist organizations with egalitarian goals, had such tendencies.[5] Accordingly, bureaucracies can be expected to operate in a less unified and hierarchical fashion than formal organizational blueprints specify. Although communist states have claimed to rule in the name of Marxist-Leninist moral principles and, specifically, in the interests of the proletariat, there are structurally rooted reasons why their ruling elites may put their own individual and institutional interests first.

Forces constraining what communist states do may emanate from people in subordinate as well as authoritative positions. Potentially conflicting viewpoints and interests are rooted in positions of domination and subordination. Even if elites try to obscure disparities of interests at the ideological level, subordinates do not necessarily internalize the official point of view. If dissatisfied with the regime in general or with specific policies, and if grievance articulation is illegal or personally risky, they are apt either to privatize their grievances or to turn to informal, seemingly uncoordinated covert ways to defy conditions they dislike. The weaker the autonomous, formally sanctioned organizational fabric of society, that is, the weaker the civil society,[6] the more likely people are to rely on covert means—such as foot-dragging, arson, sabotage, hoarding, tax evasion, absenteeism, desertion, pilferage, black marketeering, and sideline activity—to oppose conditions they dislike and to press for change.[7] Under communism such forms of disobedience can undermine official control over production and distribution, state revenue appropriation, and regime authority. Studies of communism that focused merely on formal institutional activity left unanalyzed the multitude of quiet ways that ordinary folk, as well as members of the bureaucratic elite, could and did "sabotage" state plans and state authority. Society, therefore, needs to be brought into the analysis of state socialism, even when formal structures suggest that society is tightly controlled by a single leader and political party and a centralized administrative apparatus.

The role of ideology and state/society relations under communism are examined below with reference to Cuba in the latter 1980s, one of the two periods under Fidel Castro's (and the Cuban Communist Party's) rule when policy appeared to be especially ideologically driven. (The other period was the late 1960s, when the government officially pushed for speeding up the transition to communism). Linz recognized that the utility of his ideal-type constructs was grounded in historically concrete textured analyses. If communist regimes are ideologically propelled and if their control over society is pervasive, such characteristics should be apparent in the period under study.

Not only was the ideological emphasis in the late 1980s strong but so too was the emphasis on state ownership and control. Castro and the Cuban Communist Party then called for a "rectification of errors and negative tendencies." The so-called Rectification Process (RP) called for collective forms of organizing production and labor and the primacy of Marxist-Leninist and Guevarist principles.

The RP appeared to outside observers as economically and politically irrational and out of sync with world trends.[8] I will show, though, that the ideologically legitimated policy shift reflected an effort by the state to address emergent pragmatic institutional concerns, especially mounting fiscal problems. The state's fiscal health deteriorated even when macrostatistics gave reason for optimism earlier in the decade. According to official estimates the economy had grown, on average, about 7 percent a year between 1981 and 1985.[9] Islanders at the time had become more efficient, but not in ways that allowed the government to address effectively its economic exigencies. People pursued their own interests at the state's expense. I will also show that while the "rectification campaign" appeared to revitalize Marxism-Leninism in theory and practice, it was designed in no small part to improve, paradoxical as it seems, the island's external hard currency relations. As further evidence that the reforms were advanced for institutional reasons and that they were not primarily ideologically driven, some projects initiated during this period will be shown to be antithetical to Marxist-Leninist moral precepts. Pragmatic and ideological emphasis will be shown to be intertwined, not polar opposites.

Below, moral themes and policies associated with the "rectification process" are described.[10] Then reasons for the seemingly irrational ideologically driven campaign are examined. The chapter ends with a discussion of the impact of the RP and the theoretical implications of the case study. Castro launched the RP when communism still appeared a viable—even if disdained in the West—alternative to authoritarian and democratic regimes.

The Campaign to Rectify Errors and Negative Tendencies

The RP, Castro asserted, was a "battle of ideas." It involved political and ideological work to correct "negative tendencies." There was a trend toward mercantilism and economism, a reactionary, counter-revolutionary, and petty bourgeois spirit that had to be corrected, so he claimed.[11]

In one of Castro's first speeches on the struggle against negative tendencies, he specified that "socialism must be built with awareness and with moral incentives."[12] On another occasion he noted that the country was going downhill in moral terms with inevitable economic and political consequences. Workers were corrupted by attempting to solve all problems with money: "[T]echnocrats and bureaucrats were suffering from and transmitting a sort of ideological AIDS...that was destroying the revolution's defenses."[13] And "two-bit capitalists" were criticized for profiteering at the public's expense.

Ernesto "Che" Guevara symbolized the values guiding the RP. In a speech marking the twentieth year since Che's death, Castro commented that the country was rectifying "all that was a negation of Che's ideas, Che's style and Che's spirit."[14] Castro mentioned that islanders were to rectify those things—and there were many—that strayed from revolutionary spirit, revolutionary work, revolutionary virtue, revolutionary effort, and revolutionary responsibility.

The RP thus appears to have been ideologically driven. Yet reasons both for the ideological surge and for the implementation of policies that were inconsistent with the new ideological thrust need be explained.

Policies Associated with "Rectification"

The drive for ideological purity was associated with a range of policy changes. The RP included a clampdown on certain market features and profiteering that had been tolerated in the early 1980s, a new emphasis on collective forms of organizing labor, and an expansion of the state's role in the economy, consistent with an ideal-typical socialist system. But the RP also included policies antithetical to the interest of labor, the class in whose name the government claimed to rule, and antithetical to the revolution's initial nationalist, anticapitalist thrust.

The market clampdown affected the housing, agricultural, commercial, and service sectors. An early 1980s toleration of private housing construction and sales was declared a mistake. To "rectify" the error the state became a compulsory partner in the construction as well as buying and selling of homes. The RP also included the closing of the private Farmer Markets permitted since 1980. The markets were said to have generated inequities and "too many millionaires." Merchants had been able to charge what the market would bear. And although the government had permitted private service work since 1976, with "rectification" it prohibited private manufacturing and street vending and it derided self-employment. The antimarket measures strengthened the state's direct role in the economy.

Concomitantly, the government and party promoted collective forms of labor. For one, in housing they promoted minibrigades, comprised of enterprise volunteers who committed themselves for two years to do construction work. Minibrigades built housing as well as health care units, schools, day care centers, and hotels. Second, Cubans were called upon to do volunteer work. In 1987 more than 400,000 people contributed 20 million hours of voluntary labor, and two years later there was a "Red Sunday" mobilization in which over two million workers reportedly contributed a day's voluntary labor. Minibrigade and other volunteer work was said to involve the "communist work spirit," a "recovery of the work spirit" advocated by Che.[15] Third, private independent farming was discouraged. The government encouraged remaining independent farmers to join cooperatives, a "higher" form, in Marxist thinking, of private economic activity. By 1989 cooperatives came to absorb 86 percent of all land not held by the state, and the portion of total land operated by independent farmers dropped to 2 percent.[16] Agriculture was the one sector in which private ownership had been tolerated since the nationalization of most of the economy in the 1960s. Fourth, construction contingents were promoted, involving workers hired in teams. By early 1990 some 33,000 Cubans were involved in such contingents.[17]

The government and Party at the same time called for a "rectification of errors" in more conventional forms of employment. The "errors" involved policies that had generated inequities in earnings, excessive emphasis on material reward, and inefficiencies in the use of labor. Workers were castigated for having absented themselves from their state sector jobs in the early 1980s to engage in private economic activity and for collecting their official wage when so doing. Meanwhile, work "norms," the job obligations required for receipt of basic wages, were said to have become so slack that almost all workers fulfilled them four to five times over. Workers were paid for their extra work. Work shifts had, in addition, often been shortened, with millions of overtime hours reported. Deliberate footdragging or creeping inefficiency in the normal work day allowed workers to increase their earnings through overtime work. Labor, in essence, manipulated work rules to their own advantage, at enterprises' and the state's expense.[18] Workers were not as powerless as state control of the formal union movement suggested.

To address these problems the government tried to increase job performance requirements for receipt of basic wages. It also attacked bureaucratic tendencies. Castro and the Party newspaper criticized functionaries who acted selfishly, technocratically, and passively, who ruled and managed "from above" without contact with the masses, and who violated rules and regulations or tolerated infractions by others.

The values stressed with "rectification" would suggest a state committed to the furthering of worker interests. Yet the RP was associated with the introduction of some labor policies more characteristic of the ideal-typical capitalist than the ideal-typical socialist economy—and of the nonunionized "informal" sector of capitalist economies at that. In the latter 1980s the state came out against employment security, wage guarantees, and unemployment and seniority rights.[19] The government praised enterprises that reduced their payrolls and it castigated others that did not.

Indicative of the turn on labor, professional construction sector workers were to be paid according to their performance and the amount of time they worked.[20] Since production in the sector often was halted because of supply shortages (associated with austerity policies, described below), workers had to shoulder costs of conditions not of their making. And state enterprises were granted permission to hire on a piecework basis, further undermining worker security and rights to a minimum wage.

Though not apparent at the ideological level, brigades, contingents, and minibrigades provided the state with a means to undermine union authority and historically won union rights. Workers who headed brigades were named by enterprise management (subject to approval by brigade members), and unions were to be reorganized along brigade lines. Meanwhile, in exchange for material benefits brigade and contingent workers conceded their right to an eight-hour work day, a right that organized labor had won prior to the 1959 revolution. Mini-brigade members also worked more than an eight-hour day. The government turned on labor precisely when official discourse would suggest labor-friendly policies, in line with Marxist-Leninist and Guevarist priorities.

Other labor policies of the late 1980s attacked institutional rigidities without either undermining worker employment rights or subjecting workers to market-type vagaries. A newly sanctioned *multioficio* (multiple-job, or "broader job profile") principle permitted managers to call on employees for diverse economic tasks, to combine a number of work norms (job descriptions). Management at many work places had, previous to the reform, experienced difficulty assigning laborers to tasks for which they had not officially been hired, owing to labor resistance.[21] The *multioficio* system was to allow for more efficient use of labor by weakening worker control over the labor process.

The government at the same time attempted to reduce the number of job classifications. The number of job classifications had jumped from 10,000 in 1975 to 14,000 in 1983, after the 1980 wage reform increased earnings for workers in skilled categories.[22] The rise in job classifications reflected yet another way that labor had manipulated the system to its own advantage: to increase the number of higher paying positions. Like the "broader job profile" principle, fewer job classifications allowed for greater state flexibility in the use of labor and weakened labor's power.

The renewed ideological concern with revolutionary and socialist virtue also fails to explain certain consumer policies implemented in the latter 1980s. The government reduced supplies of milk, petroleum, kerosene, and textiles and raised the price of consumer goods, transport, and electricity. Urban transport fares doubled and electricity tariffs increased about 30 percent. Prices of some rationed goods had never before been raised. The price hikes occurred, moreover, at a time when the average wage fell slightly (from 188 pesos in 1986 to 184 pesos in 1987). According to U.S. estimates, workers experienced cuts from 7 to 15 percent in their purchasing power as a result of the measures.[23] Simultaneously, the government cut food subsidies to state agencies. It stopped providing snacks at work centers and replaced the afternoon meal offered at child care institutions with a snack.

The ideology of "rectification" cannot, in addition, account for the government's aggressive pursuit of Western economic ties and its initiation of new forms of economic ownership of a capitalist sort in the latter 1980s. The government looked for Western management expertise, Western assistance in export markets, and Western investment. Joint venture agreements were reached in electronics, mechanical engineering, petrochemicals, pharmaceuticals, textiles, and tourism. Various plants available for joint ventures were publicized.[24]

Even government ministries and state agencies directly sponsored joint production and distribution deals with foreign public and private entities. The Cuban Public Health Ministry, for example, signed an agreement for cooperation in quality control in medicine production, joint production and distribution of medicines, and a bilateral consultancy in 1990.[25] The state agency Cubatabaco went so far as to try to take over private foreign cigar companies (with only one success, the British Knight Brothers Company).

Sociedades Anónimas (SAs), for-profit enterprises that operate in hard currency with considerable autonomy from day-to-day budgetary constraints of ministers of state, moreover, grew in number and significance. Among the best known during this period was Cubanacán. It quickly moved beyond its initial tourism mission. By the end of the 1980s it had negotiated contracts worth tens of millions of dollars with Brazil to export meningitis B vaccine and melagenina for treatment of vitiligo.[26] Cubanacán in addition established clinics abroad to treat vitiligo with the exported medicine.

Cimex became the largest SA Registered in Panama, Cimex by the end of the 1980s included forty-eight subsidiaries and twelve associated companies that operated in seventeen countries. Cimex ran tourist shops and a car rental enterprise, arranged flights and accommodations, and organized tours. Havanatur, a Cimex subsidiary with tourist offices abroad, brought half a million tourists to Cuba between 1979 and 1989. Cimex's involvement in tourism spurred ventures in trade, manufacturing, finance, and consulting. It exported seafood, meat products, sugar, cigars, rum, sugar industry software, and biotechnology products, and it imported for island hard currency stores and for any entity with money to pay. Cimex, in addition, had a small merchant fleet in Panama which delivered goods in the Caribbean. Through its activity Cimex developed expertise in international law which it subsequently marketed through Consultoría Jurídica Internacional. It also became one of the main depositors in Cuba's Banco Financiero (BF), a bank that operated in international stock and commodity markets. Cimex's subsidiary Caribsugar, which refined, imported, and exported sugar, also operated in overseas financial markets, and its subsidiary Afinco executed and supervised investments in tourism.

Such aggressive, officially sanctioned Western-oriented activity gained force at the same time that Castro criticized individuals and enterprises for "teaming up with capitalist hucksters...playing at capitalism, [and] beginning to think and act like capitalists.[27] Moreover, the government granted businesses initiated by SAs, such as a Spanish-Cuban joint venture hotel at Varadero beach, flexibility in hiring and firing workers. Toleration and encouragement of archetypical pro-capitalist, antisocialist practices while advocating a "rectification of errors and negative tendencies" are explicable, but at the institutional, not ideological, level.

In sum, islanders in the early 1980s had covertly defied official rules and regulations in ways that advanced their interests at the state's expense. In the name of moral rectitude the government sought to counter such tendencies. Yet policies associated with "rectification" contradicted the rhetoric of the campaign in a number of respects. The government and Party tolerated and, at times, actively encouraged market features; they undermined revolutionary and prerevolutionary labor gains; they implemented policies that caused people's living standards to drop; and they encouraged foreign investment and SAs that operated like capitalist ventures, all while claiming to give new life to Marxism-Leninist and Guevarist ideological orthodoxy. State pursuit of its own institutional economic and political concerns, described below, underlay the apparent contradiction between ideology and practice.

The State's Fiscal Crisis and Efforts to Address It through Rectification

Although Cuba experienced — according to official sources — an impressive growth rate during the period of "market opening" in the early 1980s when many other Latin American countries did poorly, it concomitantly experienced a mounting fiscal crisis. Both the island's hard currency current account balance and its domestic budget deficit increased at the time.[28]

The early 1980s' economic expansion had been tied very much to imports, including from Western bloc countries, and not merely to domestic market reforms. But the government's capacity to finance hard currency imports deteriorated in the mid-1980s. In 1986, the year the RP was launched, the government had both to suspend debt payments and to slash imports.[29] It was unable to reschedule Western debt payments that were due, and it attained no new money to finance imports. Meanwhile, its export earnings were adversely affected by a drop both in world sugar and world oil prices. (In the 1980s Moscow had allowed Havana to reexport some of its oil for hard currency, to the point that oil became the island's principal hard currency earner.) The 1985 world market sugar price was the lowest in nominal terms since 1970 and in real terms since the Depression of the 1930s.[30] The world price affected the portion of island production not purchased by Soviet bloc countries. Compounding government problems, the island's hard currency situation was hurt indirectly by the fall in the value of the dollar.[31]

Western commentators viewed the drop in Western trade, as a percentage of total trade, as an indication of the RP's anticapitalist bent, consistent with the ideology of the campaign. The increased communist bloc trade dependence, which peaked at about 87 percent in 1988, was not, however, of Cuba's own choosing. With limited hard currency export earnings and access to no new Western loans, Cuba could trade little with market economies. To imply that the island's Western trade marginalization resulted from new ideological orthodoxy conceals the heart of the matter.

Several policies initiated in the latter 1980s that were antithetical to socialist principles and the ideology of "rectification" reflect state efforts to address the mounting hard currency crisis. For one, the SAs which the government promoted were intended to generate hard currency. Second, austerity policies that caused islander living standards to plunge were partly a response to the hard currency squeeze. The government, for example, increased the amount of textiles earmarked for export while decreasing textile rations, and it slashed sugar and motor vehicle gas allocations to increase the amount of each item available for export. The government also raised the electricity tariff to encourage more rational electricity use so as to free petroleum for sale abroad. Third, tourism and foreign investment, initially condemned on moral grounds, were tolerated during "rectification" because they generated hard currency. Nearly all tourist revenue was in hard currency.

The RP may have been a response to a growing trade deficit with the Soviet Union as well as with the West. The trade deficit with the then still superpower had doubled between 1983 and 1984, and it continued to mount during the next two years.[32] However, since Moscow tolerated the island's Soviet trade imbalance and foreign debt, and since Gorbachev expanded trade and aid dealings in the latter 1980s, this seems not to have been a major force behind "rectification." Soviet economic aid for 1986 to 1990 increased 50 percent over the 1981 to 1985 period.[33]

The underlying fiscal crisis that induced the RP had roots in the domestic as well as the external sector, though. After a slight budgetary deficit in 1984, state expenditures exceeded state revenue substantially the following year.[34] In conjunction with the RP, the government sought to reduce expenditures and increase revenue (with mixed results, as discussed below).

The market reforms that had gradually been initiated since the latter 1970s had benefited individuals and enterprises partly at the state's expense, in ways that macroeconomic data conceal. By restricting private commerce the government could, in principle, better control what agriculturalists produced, minimize diversion of goods from the export to the domestic market, and profit more from domestic sales. The government could profit by buying foods from farmers at one price and selling them to the public at state outlets for more. Government efforts to benefit fiscally from private commerce through taxation had met with resistance.[35] The government indeed took advantage of the closing of the Farmer Markets to raise some state-run parallel market retail prices, and revenue in turn.

Production in the state sector, moreover, had suffered—in both the city and the countryside—as labor and supplies were diverted to private activity. People stole resources from their state jobs for sideline activity; they absented themselves from work to profit from private initiatives while drawing their official wage; and they sought early retirement, collecting state pensions while pursuing private endeavors. That is, enterprises and individuals manipulated the situation to their own advantage. They pursued the best of both worlds, compounding the state's fiscal burdens: the wage, unemployment, and retirement guarantees associated with state employment, and the opportunities for additional income that market activity allowed. Restrictions on private sideline activity and the Farmer Markets were to enhance state revenue and accumulation. The government announced that in 1988 alone the clampdown on private production and service activity would allow production to expand ten–fold; it would add 250 to 300 million pesos to its coffer and make about 300 items cheaper for consumers.[36]

Market reforms in the state sector had also created problems that the RP was to address. Under the so-called New Management System state enterprises had been able to retain a portion of the profits they generated. Intended to stimulate productivity, the entitlement contri-buted to enterprise hoarding of material and labor inputs.[37] Payrolls had become inflated as enterprises competed for scarce labor.

The market reforms also led to enterprise concentration on the most profitable economic activity, not necessarily the full range of activity needed for the smooth functioning of the economy and the fulfillment of state plans. Here, too, enterprises manipulated the system to their own advantage, with the state (and ultimately the consumer) having to bear the costs. What was profitable to a government-owned enterprise and its labor force was not necessarily equally profitable and beneficial to the state. As a result, the "right" things were not always produced and projects, for example, in construction, were left unfinished because the value of the final stages of building are lower than the initial stages.[38] Indeed, at the time of the launching of the RP, the number of unfinished projects had allegedly gotten out of hand. Minibrigades and contingents were to complete such projects and in so doing recoup state investments.

The restructuring of work norms and the attack on "unwarranted" bonuses described above were, similarly, in principle cost-saving measures. They were designed both to minimize idle and inefficient labor (by linking wage payments to efficiency) and to reduce the wage bill.

The ideological work associated with Rectification was itself to improve work productivity along with revolutionary purity. Said Castro, rectification involved a "[b]attle of ideas...that can be transferred into material wealth" and save hundreds of millions of pesos.[39] He warned that "we have to be careful not to fall into...errors of excessive idealism...we must be careful...not [to] do anything which could hamper production."[40]

As the fiscally strapped government had to slash imports, and as domestic production suffered in turn, the government had added reason to stress work as a revolutionary duty, not an opportunity for personal gain. Castro acknowledged the matter: "[R]ight now," he said, "the revolution is not able to provide a counterpart to that effort in money because there is no counterpart in goods."[41] The RP, in essence, made virtue out of necessity.

Even a wage increase granted to the poorest paid workers addressed state economic concerns. This socially just measure involved an added expenditure at a time of budgetary belt-tightening. Though seemingly inconsistent with the fiscal austerity emphasis of the time, it was designed, in no small part, to attract labor to such poorly paid sectors as agriculture and to reduce labor turnover in low-paid industries. Unable to strike for higher wages, workers in those sectors had been voting with their feet. Laborers had opted, when possible, for better paying, less backbreaking work. Farm hands had come to be in short supply and farm labor turnover had not been high. A wage raise for cane cutters in the latter 1980s is said to have helped attract 8,000 laborers.[42]

The collective forms of economic organization promoted in the latter 1980s — worker brigades and contingents, agricultural cooperatives, and construction minibrigades — were consistent as well with government economic concerns at the time. That is, the state had economic and not merely political and ideological reasons for promoting the collective forms of labor organization. The worker brigades were designed to increase labor productivity, including sectors where labor turnover and absenteeism had been high because the work was hard and dirty.[43] Brigade workers were deployed as shock troops to resolve problems or complete priority projects quickly.[44] Minibrigades, in turn, allowed for employment flexibility. They could be expanded and contracted with the availability of building supplies. Even though they were less efficient than professional construction workers, in relying on them the government avoided the fiscal and political costs involved in laying off professional builders during "bad times"; unemployed workers received 70 percent of their former salary while not contributing to the economy. It was more expedient to halt minibrigade mobilizations than to release professional construction workers when bottlenecks arose.

Agricultural cooperatives, moreover, in principle permitted economies of scale, not merely a "higher" form of social organization consonant with Marxist principles. As the rural population became more educated and resistant to farm work, a more capital intensive organization of agriculture made sense (in sectors not requiring labor-intensive work). And large farm units could make better use of farm equipment than small land holdings, thereby expanding the market for domestic farm manufactures. The manufacturing of tractors and other farm equipment had expanded in the 1980s.

If there was an "underlying" political-economic rationale for the domestically oriented reforms that the state justified ideologically, the same was true of the reforms for which the state had no such justification. The labor policies that eroded worker employment security and earnings, in violation of socialist principles, addressed state economizing concerns. Tolerance of part-time hiring and payment on a piecework basis, elimination of seniority rights, and encouragement of employment cutbacks encourage labor efficiency and minimize nonproductivity linked labor expenditures.

The austerity policies that caused islander living standards to plunge similarly addressed the state's fiscal deficit — and in a manner that minimized regime opposition. Price hikes and consumer cutbacks were designed to reduce state fiscal outlays as well as increase the stock of goods available for export. Islanders were told to tolerate the deprivations for moral reasons.

Impact of the Rectification Process

By the end of the 1980s the RP resolved neither the state's economic nor its political problems. But problems persisted largely because of unforeseen changes abroad and domestic resistance to the morally justified campaign, not because ideology drove the leadership to implement economically irrational policies.

Performance of certain sectors specifically targeted with the "rectification campaign" improved. Construction grew 16 percent and agriculture, including sugar, about 10 percent in 1988 (versus, on average, 4.5 percent yearly between 1981 and 1985).[45]

Yet, the island's convertible currency debt rose to 6,700 million pesos in 1988, dropping only slightly the next year. While the RP failed to keep the hard currency debt from mounting, the amount owed foreign creditors undoubtedly would have been greater had Western imports not been slashed and hard currency earning exports and tourism not been encouraged in conjunction with the RP. Moreover, the debt increased mainly because of conditions beyond the government's control. Seventy-two percent of the increase in the debt has been attributed to the depreciation of the dollar.[46] Meanwhile, the government had to turn increasingly to expensive suppliers' credit to finance imports, as less costly government and bank loans ceased to be forthcoming.[47]

Partly because the government's fiscal strength remained so tied to the external sector, the RP did not resolve domestic budgetary problems either. The balance between revenue and expenditures improved between 1985 and 1986, but it deteriorated dramatically thereafter. Revenue remained relatively constant while expenditures climbed. The deficit, like the foreign debt, might have been worse in the absence of RP reforms. The RP included cost-cutting initiatives.

The government's ability to remake society was undermined not merely, however, by unfavorable global economic conditions (and unfavorable climatic conditions) but also by the indifference and disobedience of manual workers, the proletariat in whose name the leadership claimed to rule. Despite "rectification" emphasis on productivity and socialist morality, absenteeism, at least in certain sectors, remained high (for example, 20 percent in a part of the clothing industry). And people, according to the Minister of Health, still frequently feigned illness. Moreover, the entire national committee of the sugar workers' union was replaced in March 1989, apparently because it failed to secure worker conformity with new labor policies.

Meanwhile, bureaucratic inadequacies remained. A Cuban survey found most respondents critical of mistreatment and poor and slow service.[48] And illegal activity not only persisted but took on new dimensions, despite the efforts to promote socialist morality. A black market immediately emerged with the closing of the Farmer Markets, and persons illegally started to sell places at the front of queues for goods that came to be in short supply.[49] In 1988 nearly half of 125,000 retail establishments scrutinized violated price and other regulations, and audits uncovered 12 million pesos of undeclared earnings by wholesale outlets and 19 million pesos of undeclared earnings by state ministries.[50] Government employees continued to "sabotage" state efforts to maintain "law and order" and collect revenue. People, individually and on an enterprise basis, took advantage of their positions for their own ends, the RP moral campaign notwithstanding.

Public revelations of serious criminal involvements by high level ministerial and military officers in 1989 illustrate how ineffective the moral campaign for "rectification" was even among the ruling stratum. Four of Castro's most trusted comrades were executed while many more were imprisoned and fired from their jobs. The high-ranking officials were purportedly guilty of illegal drug and hard currency dealings, among other crimes. The state's hard currency preoccupation became an instrument of high-level private abuse of office, an unintended consequence of island dealings with the capitalist world. Functionaries took advantage of their privileged access to foreign exchange, both to enrich themselves and to build up informal followings in the Latin American patron-client tradition.

The 1989 trials implied that the criminal activity was rooted in the misbehavior of selective individuals, a common strategy for treating leadership opponents in totalitarian regimes, as Linz notes. However, extraordinary numbers of ordinary folk collaborated with the accused, through acquisitions of illegally attained goods. And because "rectification" did not tame people's material wants, the trials did not put an end to petty and organized crime. Reported crimes increased the following year.[51]

Conclusion

Official discourse conveyed the impression that the RP was ideologically driven by a renewed state commitment to Marxism-Leninism and

Guevarism. However, the state had institutional and not merely ideological reasons for launching the campaign. In the name of revolutionary and socialist morality the government set about to address fiscal and political concerns. Policies associated with the RP were designed, above all, to increase state earnings and reduce state expenditures, and to deal with their political ramifications.

While the RP resolved neither state economic nor state political problems, the reason was not rooted in "ideocracy." Forces rooted in the external economy and domestically, within the state apparatus itself as well as in society, limited what the state was able to accomplish. The institutional perspective advanced here helps explain state implementation of policies that contradict the very ideology Castro and the Party espoused. "Rectification" moral themes were of some consequence, but more to legitimate policies that otherwise might have stirred disquietude than to induce structural reform. At the time, price hikes in other Latin American countries sparked protests[52] and dissatisfaction with economic and political conditions led the people of Eastern Europe to bring their regimes down.

Although there was an economic logic to the launching of the RP, the "offensive" was not economistically determined. The Soviet Union, Eastern Europe, and China, not to mention Third World Western bloc countries, responded differently, in certain respects, to similar fiscal concerns. Within the context of economic constraints, ideology and political considerations shaped the strategy the state chose.

While the "rectification" campaign may have helped Castro weather the international anticommunist tide that swept Eastern Europe, the Soviet Union, and China between 1989 and 1991, neither ordinary citizens nor high-level bureaucrats completely internalized the values stressed. Cubans continued to resort to footdragging, absenteeism, abuse of office, and other illicit activity. The 1989 leadership shake-up revealed a crisis within the state, and not merely in the society in which state institutions were embedded.

The Cuban experience accordingly suggests the need for revisionist thinking about totalitarian societies. Linz's democratic and authoritarian regime types have been better elaborated. The portrayal of totalitarian systems as ideologically driven and as premised on strong states/weak societies obscures important dynamics of such regimes. For one, the role of ideology needs to be reinterpreted. Linz correctly recognized that ideology may be manipulated as well as manipulating. But, concretely, ideology and pragmatism are not necessarily alternative bases of policymaking, and ideology may serve economic as well as political functions, points not well elaborated in the ideal-typical schema. If state policy was not ideologically driven during a period of stepped up ideological emphasis, it is even less likely to have such an effect in periods when it is downplayed. Second, under "totalitarianism" the distinction between state and society does not necessarily disappear, with the latter subordinated to and subsumed by the former. Linz suggested that distinctions between the two remain, but the reason is not merely, as he emphasized, because of informal dynamics operating within formal political institutions. When formal channels of "interest articulation" are blocked, a populace is likely to turn to informal, covert channels to pursue self-defined concerns. Informal involvements typically are patterned, and they may be of substantial consequence, whether or not so intended. If society asserts itself in Castro's Cuba, in one of the communist regimes where autonomous and quasi-autonomous involvements have been most contained, its influence in other totalitarian regimes is likely to be (or to have been) even greater. The informal and unofficial ways that individuals and institutions address their own concerns when formal institutional channels are wanting must become part of any full understanding of totalitarian regimes. Third, totalitarian state initiatives must be understood in a global context, including in relation to the capitalist world. Ideological differences among states do not preclude economic relations, relations that may have domestic consequences. There is no predetermined causal relationship between regime type, as ideal-typically defined, and economic dynamics.

In the 1990s, with the collapse of the communist bloc and the Soviet Union, the role of ideology as a guiding force and the subordination of society to the state withered away. Cuba continued, formally, to retain attributes of an ideal-typical totalitarian state—namely power concentrated in a single individual and a single party to which state-linked organizations were subordinated. And officially the ruling ideology remained unchanged. However, the "new world order" compelled the government to once more open to market forces and to downplay Marxism-Leninism. Islanders did not press for a democratic-capitalist transition as did their former Soviet bloc comrades, but their informal covert involvements contributed to a political-economic restructuring beneath the veneer of communist political continuity. An analysis of these changes is, though, beyond the scope of this chapter.[53]

Notes

1. Juan Linz, "Totalitarian and Authoritarian Regimes," in Fred Greenstein and Nelson Polsby, eds., *Handbook of Political Science, Volume 3: Macropolitical*

Theory (Reading, MA: Addison–Wesley, 1975), pp. 175–411. The page references I cite are to this version of his writing on the three ideal-typical regime types.

2. On the characterization of communist regimes as premised on strong states/weak societies within the context of the Third World, see Joel Migdal, *Strong Societies and Weak States* (Princeton: Princeton University Press, 1988).

3. On the interest group approach to the study of communist regimes, see H. Gordon Skilling and Franklyn Griffiths, eds., *Interest Groups in Soviet Politics* (Princeton: Princeton University Press, 1964). With reference to Cuba, see William LeoGrande, "A Bureaucratic Approach to Civil-Military Relations in Communist Political Systems: The Case of Cuba," in Dale Herspring and Ivan Volgyes, eds., *Civil-Military Relations in Communist Systems* (Boulder, CO: Westview Press, 1978), pp. 201–18.

4. I discuss reasons why these factors are of consequence at greater length in Eckstein, *Back from the Future: Cuba under Castro* (Princeton: Princeton University Press, 1994), chapter 1.

5. Robert Michels, *Political Parties: A Sociological Study of the Oligarchical Tendencies of Modern Democracy* (New York: The Free Press, 1962).

6. Civil society refers here to the social fabric formed by the array of formal organizations that exist independent of the state. Society, by contrast, refers to the people collectively comprising a community who are informally but not formally organized. The state, civil society, and society are analytically but not necessarily empirically distinguishable.

7. On the forms and effects of such "everyday forms of resistance," see James Scott, *Weapons of the Weak: Everyday Forms of Peasant Resistance* (New Haven, CT: Yale University Press, 1986).

8. For an early statement of the purported irrationality of "rectification," see Carmelo Mesa-Lago, "Cuba's Economic Counter Reform (Rectification): Causes, Policies and Effects," in Richard Gillespie, ed., *Cuba after Thirty Years: Rectification and the Revolution* (London: Frank Cass, 1990).

9. *Granma Weekly Review (GWR)* 27 August 1989: 12.

10. I discuss the rectification process in greater detail in "The Rectification of Errors or the Errors of the Rectification Process in Cuba," *Cuban Studies/Estudios Cubanos* 20 (1990). See also the published exchange between Mesa-Lago and myself in this and the succeeding volume of the journal.

11. *GWR* 22 January 1989: 4 (supplement).

12. *GWR* 15 June 1986: 3.

13. *GWR* 13 December 1987: 19.

14. *GWR* 18 October 1987: 4.

15. *GWR* 7 February 1988: 9; Economist Intelligence Unit (EIU), *Cuba: Country Report* no. 1 (1990): 4.

16. Cuba, Comité Estatal de Estadísticas (CEE), *Aunario Estadístico de Cuba 1989* (Havana: CEE, 1991): 195.

17. *GWR* 10 December 1989: 4.

18. Labor strategies to increase earnings independently of productivity undermined enterprise interests when enterprises were responsible for their cost accounting and expenditures reduced retainable profits; when enterprises were not allotted a profit fund, the state bore the labor costs. Labor, in defense of their own interests, argued for continued material incentives. See the May 1987 issue of *Trabajadores*. By contrast, the Union of Young Communists in their publication, *Juventud Rebelde*, argued at the time in favor of moral incentives.

19. *GWR* 3 August 1986: 5.

20. EIU no. 3 (1988): 11.

21. *GWR* 12 February 1989: 3.

22. *GWR* 21 February 1989: 3.

23. Mesa-Lago, "Cuba's Economic Counter-Reform."

24. *Cuba Business* (*CB*) August 1989: 16.

25. *CB* February 1990: 14.

26. *CB* February 1990: 16.

27. *GWR* 18 October 1987: 6.

28. Eckstein, *Back from the Future*, p. 223.

29. EIU no. 3 (1989): 14.

30. *GWR* 16 September 1990: 3.

31. Hard currency commodity trade is negotiated in dollars, while Castro's Cuba's western loans were necessarily contracted in other hard currencies owing to Washington's continued enforcement of the embargo.

32. Mesa-Lago and Fernando Gil, "Soviet Economic Relations with Cuba," in Eusebio Mujal-Leon, ed., *The USSR and Latin America: A Developing Relationship* (Boston: Unwin and Hyman, 1989), p. 195.

33. Mesa-Lago and Gil, "Soviet Economic Relations," p. 218.

34. Eckstein, *Back from the Future*, p. 223.

35. Medea Benjamin, Joseph Collins, and Michael Scott, *No Free Lunch* (San Francisco: Institute for Food and Development Policy, 1985), pp. 84–86.

36. Cited in Mesa-Lago, "Cuba's Counter Economic Reform," p. 108.

37. Such tendencies are characteristic of scarcity economies. See J. Kornai, "Resource-Constrained versus Demand-Constrained Systems," *Econometrica* (July 1979): 801–19; "'Hard' and 'Soft' Budget Constraint," *Acta Oeconomica* 25 (1980): 231–46; "The Soft Budget Constraint," *Kylos* 39 (1986): 3–30.

38. *GWR* 18 October 1987: 6.

39. *GWR* 13 December 1987: 9; *GWR* 15 February 1987: 4–5.

40. *GWR* 1 February 1987: 2.

41. *GWR* 12 October 1986: 4.

42. *CB* August 1988: EIU no. 1 (1988): 12.

43. *CB* October 1989: 8.

44. Ibid.

45. *CB* December 1988: 12.

46. Ibid., 11.

47. *CB* April 1990: 3. In 1980 suppliers accounted for 0.9 percent of Cuba's hard currency debt; 9 years later they accounted for 22.8 percent of that debt. Elena Alvarez, *The External Sector of the Cuban Economy in the 80's* (Havana: Instituto de Investigaciones Económicas, JUCEPLAN, n.d.), p. 13.

48. *GWR* 1 October 1989: 4.

49. EIU no. 4 (1988): 9.

50. EIU no. 3 (1988): 10.

51. *GWR* 22 July 1990: 9.

52. John Walton, "Debt, Protest and the State in Latin America," in Susan Eckstein, ed., *Power and Popular Protest: Latin American Social Movements* (Berkeley: University of California Press, 1989), pp. 299–328.

53. Changes in the early 1990s are documented in my book *Back from the Future,* chapter 4.

4

The Pinochet Regime:
A Comparative Analysis with the
Franco Regime

*Carlos Huneeus**

Two themes are dominant in the academic work of Juan Linz: the study of authoritarian regimes, and the analysis of democratic crises and breakdowns. His endeavors in these two areas of research have proven enormously useful for understanding the political developments that have taken place in Latin America during the last quarter of a century. Linz's model of authoritarian regimes[1] and his conceptual framework for the study of the causes and dynamics of democratic crises and breakdowns[2] have contributed significantly to the effort to fathom the remarkable political changes that transpired in the region. Actors and analysts alike wondered how democracy could possibly have collapsed in countries that for decades had succeeded in following a trajectory of consolidation. They also sought an explanation for the brutal coercive measures deployed against broad sections of the political elite and the citizenry when the dictatorships were installed. Unlike their historical antecedents, these violent regimes did not function as "mere interregnums" between democratic regimes, but pursued programs of profound economic and political innovation. After a wave of military regimes swept across the continent starting with the Brazilian coup d'état in 1964, such concerns became a major preoccupation for politicians and for social scientists.

*I would like to thank the Federal Republic of Germany's Volkswagen Foundation for support to undertake this research. I am entirely responsible for its contents.

When the first coups occurred, political scientists did not immediately study the military regimes that were established but focused instead on explaining the causes of the military's "intervention in politics." As a consequence, for a considerable time almost nothing was known about the power structures in these regimes, the composition of their ruling elite, or the political projects they aimed to implement. Nor were the factors which explained the regimes' stability, or their lack of it, identified. Instead, contemporary analyses dwelt exclusively on the range of causes that had provoked members of the military to perpetrate coups d'état.

At the time of the Latin American coups, Linz had already presented a model of sufficient breadth, flexibility, and clarity that it could be used to comprehend both the failure of democracy *and* the attributes of the political systems established after democratic break-down. Nevertheless, the study of authoritarian and military regimes remained exceedingly limited. No sooner had analysis of the military regimes commenced in earnest with some commentators, convinced of the invincible strength of such regimes, predicting their inevitable proliferation throughout the region, military regimes in Latin America promptly began to collapse, giving way to astounding processes of democratic transition. The attention of analysts then shifted to the dynamics of political regime change; overlooked were the authoritarian influences on the transition process, the economic and political pre-conditions of democracy, and, in particular, the enormous difficulties faced by the democracies, obstacles that have subsequently impeded the process of democratic consolidation. Accordingly, much remains to be learned about both the structure of those authoritarian regimes or military dictatorships which for several years dominated "south of the Rio Grande," and their policies, which are still having an impact upon the new democracies. So far, the problems of the new democracies have been traced only to the behavior of democrats, and not to the conditions left by authoritarianism. From the hyper-historicism of the 1960s there has been a swing to the opposite extreme: a dismissal of the legacy of the recent past.

A return to Linz's classic theme of the authoritarian regime is germane for the pursuit of two objectives: (1) a more complete comprehension of a form of government widespread throughout Latin America during the 1960s and 1970s (and in Paraguay and Chile, until the 1980s), and (2) an adequate grasp of several characteristics of the politics of democratic transition. Linz's abiding analytical-ethical interest was the empirical study of democracy, demonstrated by the fact that the concept of "limited pluralism" — so central to his model of the authoritarian regime — was developed through a process of comparison with democratic regimes. It was not by chance that as soon as Franco's dictatorship ended, Linz shifted his analytical focus to the transition and was never again concerned to further develop his model of the authoritarian regime.

A comparative perspective is very useful for analyzing the Chilean experience given that Chile represents the quite rare case of a long-lived and highly stable authoritarian regime that profoundly transformed the state, the economy, and society. Chile's postauthoritarian politics cannot be explained without reference to the seventeen years of General Augusto Pinochet's regime. Pinochet was the only dictator among those of the "new authoritarianism" who remained chief-of-state from beginning to end. Even now, he retains his post as commander-in-chief of the army.

Further analysis of authoritarianism is also warranted by the fact that the bibliography on Latin America and Spain is still rather slim. Writing in 1977, Guy Hermet concluded that "Franco's Spain constitutes a territory which is three-quarters virgin to political investigation,"[3] and in the case of Pinochet's Chile, analysis may be even more limited.[4] Considering the recent boom in studies on transition and the consolidation of democracy, it is likely that research on nondemocratic forms of government will continue without awakening any special interest among political scientists. In the analysis of Latin American authoritarian regimes, attention must be paid to the Franco experience, not only because Franco was Linz's touchstone, but because his regime was admired from afar by the extreme right wing groups which supported military regimes in Latin America.

The authoritarian regimes in Spain (1939–1975) and Chile (1973–1990) attracted a great deal of attention in the international community for the dramatic conditions in which they arose—a bloody civil war in the first case, during the prelude to World War II; a failed experiment of "transition to socialism by legal means" in a country having a long and respected democratic tradition in the second—and for the form in which they exercised power. Forceful coercive measures, especially pronounced in the initial phases of each of these authoritarian experiments, exacted very high human costs and provoked strong emotional reactions among the populations of the respective countries and in international public opinion. Franco and Pinochet, each in their own time and manner, felt the weight of international isolation.

Comparative analysis of two authoritarian regimes such as those of Franco and Pinochet is important to comprehend the nature of the transition to democracy in Spain and Chile. In fact, these countries' respective transitions to democracy can be characterized as having followed a path of reform using the legal framework established by the authoritarian regime to ensure its continuity[5] with a high level of consensus among the elite groups. The contextual differences between these two countries, stemming from dissimilar processes of state formation,[6] are well understood and do not constitute an obstacle to this analysis since the comparative method stems from the assumption that no countries have truly identical contexts.

Certain fundamental directions taken during the transformation of the Chilean regime, such as the accord between the Socialists and the Christian Democrats which later enabled the construction of a political alternative capable of defeating Pinochet in the plebiscite of October 5, 1988, may only be understood by examining politics under authoritarianism. The accord between the Socialists and the Christian Democrats came to form the basis of a party coalition that has subsequently supported two democratic governments. Leaders of political groups antagonistic to one another during the final phase of the democratic crisis came together under the dictatorship in the struggle to defend human rights. The foundation for a strategic alliance was created which, in turn, led to the Democratic Alliance (Alianza Democrática) in 1983 and to the Parties' Agreement (Concertación de Partidos) at the beginning of 1988. The latter would become the basis of the current governing coalition. Some of the singularities of the new Chilean democracy, such as the fact that the former dictator remains commander-in-chief of the army, may only be understood by examining the features of authoritarianism. Such a perspective also helps to explain the peculiarities of the Chilean right wing, which has recently split into two parties, thereby effecting a return to the pattern that had existed up until the mid-1960s.

The analysis of an authoritarian regime becomes less difficult once the regime has ceased to exist, not only because more information is available but also because a defunct regime loses its demonic aura. Consequently, its various elements and the dynamics of its development may be viewed with the requisite composure, and other of its relevant features–its general characteristics and less visible contours–may be identified.

This essay concentrates on an analysis of the Pinochet regime, comparing it with the Franco regime. The analysis is organized around an examination of three central aspects of Linz's model. First, the relative positions of dictators and military organizations in the Chilean and Spanish political systems are discussed, along with the associated issues of personalization and institutionalization under authoritarian rule. Second, and directly linked to the first, is an analysis of the uses of coercion and a reassessment of the definition of authoritarianism both as "limited pluralism" and as "limited synchronization" (that is, partial cancellation of previously existing democratic structures). Third, mechanisms for the cooptation and political integration of civilian groups through economic incentives, developed by the regimes in the absence of other structures of political participation, are examined; in this context, the promotion of economic transformation by both regimes was a decisive factor. Analysis of each of these elements furthers both our understanding of the Pinochet regime and our comprehension of several characteristics of politics under the democratic regime inaugurated in Chile in 1990.[7]

The Personalization and Institutionalization of Power: Political Roles Played by Franco and Pinochet

The authoritarian regimes of Spain and Chile were strongly identified with their respective heads of state, both army generals, which demonstrates the high degree of personalization of their power. "Franco's" regime and "Pinochet's" regime revolved to a considerable extent around the persona of the Generalísimo and the Captain General, with a stronger institutional framework supporting the former than the latter. It is not by chance that in both cases these leaders controlled the central power of the state from the beginning to the end of their respective regimes. General Pinochet was the only military chief of the "new militarisms" who was able to remain in power during the entire authoritarian experience.[8] In addition, he retained his position as commander-in-chief of the army after President Patricio Aylwin had taken office and in spite of the fact that he had been defeated through the plebiscite of October 5, 1988 in his aim to be "reelected" as president for eight more years.[9]

"The Franco regime" was not viable after its leader's death; nor was Pinochet's regime imaginable without his presence. Despite the high degree of institutionalization of the former regime, which distinguishes it from the latter and from other military dictatorships, it is quite evident that following Franco's death his regime lost all viability.[10] Above all, Franco and Pinochet were members of the military in the strict sense of the word; they viewed politics as the continuation of war by different means. Their principal advisors were military officers. When the stability of his regime was threatened, neither leader hesitated to implement highly coercive measures. Despite international protests and pleas for mercy from several chiefs of state, including Pope Paul VI, Franco proceeded to ratify the death sentences of five Basque terrorists only weeks before he died.

Franco grounded his authority and power in a one-party system, the Falange-Organización, and in structures of corporatist representation, the Courts (las Cortes). Together these allowed the diverse groups of his governing coalition to participate in the decision-making process.

If it is true, as Tusell has stated, that Franco's rule was never a dictatorship of the army as an organization nor tended toward praetorianism,[11] the same cannot be said of the Pinochet regime. In fact, Pinochet had members of the military and specifically, army officers, as his principal collaborators. Army officers occupied ministerial posts. As governors and local officials, they supervised the regions and provinces. They were appointed as university rectors and even controlled the national television broadcasting organization.[12] Retired army officers were made ambassadors and mayors, and so forth. A broad but cohesive ruling elite, subordinated to Pinochet in his triple role as head of the army, commander-in-chief, and president of the republic, was thereby created.[13] The governing junta, composed of the chiefs of the three branches of the armed forces and the police director, exercised legislative power with the support of civilian advisors integrated into the so-called "legislative commissions." These "legislative commissions" assisted in the drafting of legislation but enjoyed no decision-making autonomy.

Under Pinochet, there was practically no area of government in which the military presence was not visible. In each field of public service, members of the military were assigned to high positions as part of the annual personnel assignment plan. In the economic sector as well (in which a monolithic presence of civil technocrats might have been expected, as was the case in Spain), there was also a strong military component. By 1983, the military headed the ministries of finance and economics along with the corresponding undersecretaries, as well as the presidency of the Central Bank. Even during the period from 1976 to 1982, when the "Chicago boys" were in full control of the economic sector, military personnel held the undersecretary positions in finance and in economics.

The presence of a homogeneous network of high-ranking officers from the armed forces not only lent cohesion to the governing elite but also brought unity of leadership to the political system and effectiveness in the formulation and implementation of policies. The role of military officers was not limited to the sphere of the army; they acted as arbiters and performed an integrative function in their respective governing coalitions. In both regimes the heads of government were required to play the role of arbiter since the governing elite was formed by broad and heterogeneous coalitions of individuals and groups with differing interests, giving rise to tensions and conflicts that had to be resolved.

The analyst must not see them as passive subjects forced to resolve differences only, however, but also as agents of integration and mediation. At critical moments, both Franco and Pinochet made decisions that signified sweeping changes in policy. Comparing the two, Franco's role was more highly concentrated on leadership of the state, rather than the government. Responsibility for the latter was delegated to Carrero Blanco, a distribution of leadership made possible by a complex institutional network and the existence of the Falange-Organización as a force for the cooptation and mobilization of politicians.

General Pinochet carried all functions–head of state, head of government, and commander-in-chief of the army–with equal energy since he was aware that his source of authority and power was based upon the exercise of all three. There was not a second- or third-in-command, such as Franco had. Instead, Pinochet maintained direct control of the government,[14] assisted by an effective governing body composed of civil servants and ranking army officers, the General Secretariat of the Presidency, authorized to collect information from each ministry, thereby establishing a direct channel of information and of government control. Thus, the personalization of power in General Pinochet was more intense than that of Franco.

In Chile, both the delay in the implementation of the regime's planned development of the 1980 constitution, and the urgency with which numerous laws were promulgated following Pinochet's loss in the 1988 plebiscite, may be attributed to the regime's low degree of institutionalization. It was feared that in the absence of guiding legal norms, democrats would enjoy wider margins within which to pursue political action. In the period from the plebiscite of 5 October 1988 to the inauguration of democracy on 11 March 1990, the military regime enacted 226 new laws regulating a wide variety of areas. Among these were changes to five basic statutes including the charter of the Central Bank, an entity which, according to the constitution, enjoyed autonomy from the government.[15] Most of these laws were promulgated between October 1989 and 11 March 1990, regardless of the fact that on 14 December 1990 a new president would assume office. The notion of "everything tied and well tied" that had defined the format of succession for the Franco regime, was even more extensively applied in Chile. Law 18.919, promulgated in January 1990, prohibited the national Congress from indicting persons for actions taken prior to 11 March 1990. Under this law, administrative abuses perpetrated during the privatization process could not be prosecuted.[16] On 11 March 1990, the army was even granted certain economic privileges by an amendment to its charter statute. Unlike Franco, who effectively ceased ruling years before his death on 20 November 1975, Pinochet ruled until his very last day in office.

As Tusell has noted,[17] the military component of the Franco regime must be seen in light of the Civil War, during which Franco consolidated his military and political power and from which the new political order emerged victorious. Franco established the authoritarian order in 1939 without having to consolidate his authority and power politically since this had already been achieved in 1936 during the first few weeks of the war. General Pinochet faced a different situation in 1973, not only because he was the newest of the commanders-in-chief of the armed forces–having been named two weeks before the coup d'état after the dramatic resignation of his predecessor, General Carlos Prats, under pressure from his subordinates[18]–but also because a collegial government of the armed forces was initially planned, as was present in Uruguay and to some extent in Argentina.[19] General Pinochet, therefore, had to consolidate his power first within the armed forces and then on a national level. In the end, the greater military component of Pinochet's power and authority must be understood in the context of a political order in which there was no party organization to serve as a political support base through which the middle- and upper-class elite could be recruited, as Franco possessed with the Falange. The absence of a party increased Pinochet's flexibility in the recruitment of his collaborators, but at the same time it required him to rely upon another kind of basic structure to ensure the continuity and coherence of his government and his policies, and this he found in the Army.[20]

The strong military component of the Pinochet regime is also the key to explaining the speed with which he consolidated his institutional and personal power. The coercion exercised by the DINA (National Intelligence Agency), composed of members of the three branches of the armed forces under the direction of Colonel Manuel Contreras, was of enormous importance for the suppression of the opposition, carried out not only in Chile but also abroad, as evidenced by the assassination of Orlando Letelier in Washington D.C. in September 1976.[21] Military force was used against opposition demonstrations on numerous occasions including the Chilean winter of 1983 and during the opposition's "mobilization" activities of subsequent years. Between 1983 and 1985, 134 persons were killed, most of them as a result of military operations.

It is important to take into account the fact that the military components in the leadership of Franco and Pinochet differed in their intensity as well. Franco's Armed Forces were institutionally weak, a result of the high priority placed on economic development. This led to a decline in military expenditures which, at the end, was so severe that in Western Europe only Luxembourg spent less on defense.[22] This produced a deterioration in the level of arms supplies and especially in the standard of living of members of the armed forces, who received such low salaries that a high percentage of officers were forced to bolster their income with extra-military activities–making use of the secondary job market, just like civilians.[23] Despite its weak participation in the Franco regime, the military was seen by the Spanish citizenry as a major powerholder. In fact, FOESSA Study III, carried out in September and October 1973, showed that people perceived the military as the group holding the greatest degree of power in Spain, much higher than the banks, Opus dei, or the unions.[24]

In General Pinochet's Chile, the armed forces maintained and even increased their level of defense expenditures, so much so that by the end of the regime they were extremely strong institutionally. This fact must be considered in the analysis of the role of the armed forces in the transition to and consolidation of democracy.

In sum, the military presence in the Pinochet regime was stronger and more permanent than that of Franco's Spain. This distinction can be explained not only by considering the different conditions under which each regime arose, but also by taking into account the disparate institutional styles adopted in each case, determined, among other factors, by the unequal duration of each political system. In Franco's Spain, the political center of gravity was formed by "the institutions," that is to say, the civilian personnel assigned to the varied and differentiated network of institutional and political channels; in Pinochet's Chile, the system revolved around the army as an institution, and as a recruitment source for key leaders.

Limited Synchronization and the Uses of Coercion

A central element in Linz's conceptualization of the authoritarian regime is "limited pluralism."[25] With this term he seeks to express, in the first place, a clear differentiation from totalitarianism, in which pluralism is almost nonexistent,[26] and from democracy, in which it "is in principle almost unlimited."[27] This concept is very useful in analyzing the extent of the freedom of political action available to those who oppose the regime. Along with this element, Linz added that apathy predominates in an authoritarian society, the result of the depoliticization sought by the regime.

The concept of "limited pluralism"[28] is fruitful in comprehending the nature of an authoritarian regime that has already consolidated its power. It lacks the same heuristic utility, however, in the analysis of the preceding phase of authoritarianism, that is to say, the instauration of military rule, a phase that is decisive to its subsequent consolidation. In practice, during this phase pluralism disappears or is radically suspended as the new governing coalition is preoccupied with establishing power over the population and a new structure of authority that will ensure the effective consolidation of authoritarianism. To achieve this goal, strong coercive measures are exercised over broad strata of society and over political and social leaders. These measures are aimed not only at weakening the parties and unions but also at provoking a strong shock reaction among the population and the elite groups that will linger as a latent threat that at any moment the coercive action may be repeated, thereby inhibiting political action. Once the authoritarian system has been consolidated, it then permits and encourages certain limited freedoms which make up the limited pluralism analyzed so perceptively by Juan Linz. It is not sufficient to explain the establishment of authoritarianism by reducing it to the exercise of coercion, but neither should such analysis be avoided, consigning it to a "black hole" in the history of authoritarian regimes.[29]

To better comprehend all of this, it seems appropriate to analyze "limited pluralism" together with another concept mentioned by Linz in the later version of his model published in the *Handbook of Political Science*.[30] The concept referred to is "limited synchronization," derived in part from the German term *Gleichschaltung*, used to describe the seizure of power by the Nazis through the destruction of political institutions and the neutralization of interest groups. Linz notes that an authoritarian regime must achieve a "limited synchronization" in order to establish a new political system in the wake of a democratic political order.

The totalitarian version of synchronization eliminates pluralism while politicizing society with its ideology, articulated through a single party; the limited synchronization of authoritarianism cedes some latitude to liberty, in which the citizens and parties who have survived the phase of authoritarian instauration may operate. Both of these concepts can be placed on a continuum: greater synchronization, less pluralistic freedom; less synchronization, more latitude for liberty and political action for the groups and parties of the opposition. The scope and significance of limited synchronization are defined not only by the number and significance of eliminated or controlled institutions, but also by the political style employed, and especially by the use of coercion. Thus, authoritarian regimes could well be classified according to the synchronization strategy used to establish themselves in power.

The Franco and Pinochet regimes differ according to the scope of limited pluralism, as evidenced by the divergent manner in which their levels of semisynchronization were achieved. The authoritarian consolidation of power in Spain took place in a politically, economically, and morally fragmented country, a result of the long and bloody civil war that had caused thousands of deaths and enormous material damages and economic reversals and during which the political institutions (the polity) either disappeared or were sharply restricted in their usual functions. The weakened condition of Spanish political development up to the outbreak of the civil war—including the brief and unsuccessful Second Republic (1931–1936), the first democratic experience in the context of mass politics[31]—did not permit the rise of a party system at the national level; organized parties existed only on the periphery, in the Basque and Catalan country, nor did an influential associative network arise which could have survived the war and which would have been necessary to synchronize in 1939.[32] As a consequence, Franco in 1939 did not need to confront the problem of synchronizing strong political and social institutions, as did Pinochet in Chile, since these had been shattered by the effects of the war. Even so, the first years of the Franco regime were characterized by strict political control and the broad use of coercion.[33]

Certain interest groups such as the Catholic Church, having seen their organizing capacity severely diminished, had reoriented their political or social line in reaction to political conflicts during the Second Republic, and, as a result, had lost their apostolic and social influence in broad sectors of society. The anticlerical policies of the *bienio negro*[34] translated into profound legal changes and excesses by minority groups–including the burning of churches and the assassination of priests and nuns–and provided precedents under which the Church adopted a negative attitude toward the Republic. Later, the Church assisted Franco's "crusade" during the civil war and subsequently supported his political regime. This situation continued until the late 1960s when Pope Paul VI openly rejected the Franco regime.

During the 1950s and 1960s, when the system had been consolidated and Spanish society was modernizing, the regime was compelled, under its own initiative or as a response to opposition pressure, to establish certain liberties. These came to constitute a limited pluralism in which social or political groups were able to express themselves, albeit within narrow limitations and with extreme prudence. Freedoms were granted especially within the regime itself–for example, in political associations and in elections for deputies of the Cortes. In municipal elections the "semi-opposition" (but not the opposition), were given space to participate.[35] Thus, at the time of Franco's death, with the exception of the Communist Party[36] and the nationalist parties of the Basque and Catalan country, there were no organized political parties. These arose and developed in the heat of the transition to democracy. The principal party of the transition, the Union of the Democratic Center (Unión de Centro Democrático, UCD), was founded just a few weeks prior to the first general elections of 15 June 1977 and disappeared in 1982.[37] This is also the reason that the decisive actors of the transition had their origin in the "semi-opposition" and not in the opposition.

In Chile, the semisynchronization enforced by General Pinochet took place under different conditions. The country possessed a broad and differentiated political and social structure, a result of its long and continuous democratic evolution,[38] out of which arose a party system that permeated society, extending to the union and student movements and including interest groups with a high level of organization and affiliation.[39] There was a parliament which enjoyed a tradition of almost a century-and-a-half of activity, along with an autonomous judicial branch. The Catholic Church possessed a high level of organization and social influence,[40] not only by virtue of its presence in the educational system, including three universities,[41] but also because the opinions and activities of its hierarchy were taken seriously by the political class as contributions to the political and social development of the country.[42]

The democratic crisis that occurred in the late 1960s, particularly during the Popular Unity government (Unidad Popular), did not break or destroy this institutional network,[43] although it seriously fragmented it. In addition, during these years a "hypermobilization" took place that produced, among its various effects, a strong politicization of society and an intense ideologicizing of debate and political conflict.[44] As a result, in order to establish and consolidate his authority, Pinochet carried out an energetic "semisynchronization" program that rapidly and severely restricted the scope of pluralism in Chilean society. Moreover, the use of coercion was a factor of fundamental importance in this strategy. The seizure of power was dramatic, symbolized by the bombing of the seat of the presidency, the Palacio de la Moneda, by Air Force planes, with the consequent suicide of President Salvador Allende; by the proposal to "eradicate the Marxist cancer";[45] by the application of a state of "internal war"; by the detention of thousands of people in various centers, principally the National Stadium; and by the summary executions of scores of detainees immediately following the coup d'état.[46] Together these established a climate of fear in broad strata of the population and among the politicians of the center and left. People's feeling of terror lingered in latent form in Chile and remained a significant factor impeding political action.

The limited synchronization encompassed political institutions and interest groups.[47] Congress was closed and the judicial branch saw its legal independence severely curtailed through the new government's declaration of a state of siege and later through the states of emergency, during which the right of habeas corpus was suspended. Political parties were prohibited and progressively persecuted beginning with the parties of the left, followed later by the Christian Democrats.[48] The Worker's Central (Central Unica de Trabajadores, CUT) was suppressed and many leaders and members of worker's groups or unions were persecuted. Thousands of Chileans were forced to seek asylum in embassies and petition for exile.

Pinochet's limited synchronization was not able to eliminate the roots of institutional development in the country—nor was this its aim. The historical parties that had been active during democratic times managed to maintain a minimal organizational base, permitting them to reconstitute themselves substantially when more freedom was granted;[49] unions and student and professional organizations were not suppressed but merely controlled;[50] and radio stations remained on the air which gave broad opportunities to the opposition to an extent that never existed in Franco's Spain.[51] The Catholic Church established opportunities for freedom that were of enormous importance for the survival of individuals and groups during the most difficult years of the regime.[52] Thus, for example, the Cardinal Archbishop of Santiago, Raúl Silva Henriquez, created the Vicarage of Solidarity—crucial to the effort to protect human rights—and the Academy for Christian Humanism, founded so that academics expelled from the universities who wished to remain in Chile would have a place to continue their work.[53]

In analyzing limited pluralism in Pinochet's Chile, one must consider the changes produced by the economic crisis of 1982–1983 which triggered an intense social mobilization against the regime, encompassing workers, students, and segments of the middle classes.[54] The opposition was able to exploit the greater latitude of liberty rapidly and effectively thanks to the latent organization maintained since the beginning of the regime. This allowed for the resurgence of political parties and interest groups. Thus, strong pressure was placed upon the regime which reacted with a policy of liberalization *and* a high level of coercion. The regime's initial repressive reaction in August and September 1983 resulted in 37 dead, 113 injured, and 1,951 detained.[55] At the end of the authoritarian period, Chile manifested a higher level of politicization than did Spain at the end of the Franco regime. In fact, while the Spanish population two years before Franco's death was clearly depoliticized—3 percent were "very interested" and 12 percent "somewhat interested" in politics[56]—Chileans in April 1989 gave percentages of 11 and 25 percent respectively.[57] A 1985 study in Santiago showed that 34 percent had a strong interest and 32 percent little interest in politics.[58]

This greater development of civil society shows why in Chile, in contrast to Spain, the fundamental factor for explaining the transition from authoritarianism to democracy was the role of the opposition rather than the "semi-opposition." The latter did not exist in Chile, due more to the presence and important clandestine activities of a real opposition than to the fact that the regime itself did not permit such quasi-opposition groups to function. As a result, the democratic insfrastructure–parties and interest groups–arose with great vigor *before* the authoritarian regime had ended. Starting with protests during the apertura or "opening" in mid-1983, parties derived from the pre-authoritarian period honed their political activity in struggle against the regime, winning the plebiscite of 5 October 1988, and participating successfully in the presidential and parliamentary elections of 14 December 1989. Hence, with the inauguration of democracy on 11 March 1990, Chile already possessed political parties with a significant level of organization.

The crucial test of democracy was the indictment of Manuel Contreras for his involvement in the 1976 assassination of Orlando Letelier in Washington, D.C. As chief of the DINA (later transformed into the CNI), Contreras was at the apex of a harsh, centralized system of coercion during the years of authoritarian rule. The Supreme Court finally sentenced him to eight years imprisonment. After initially threatening to ignore the sentence of the court, Contreras was incarcerated in Punto Peuco in the winter of 1995. The military demanded a special prison facility for officers found guilty of human rights violations. Nevertheless, they could not prevent the democratic government from implementing the laws—the so-called *leyes Cumplido*—under which human rights violators were tried and sentenced.[59]

In conclusion, differences in the manner in which semisynchronization was implemented and the scope of the limited pluralism that resulted, explain important distinctions between the power structures of authoritarian Spain and Chile. Furthermore, they also serve to explain the different political conditions under which the transition from authoritarian rule to democracy took place.

The Recruitment of the Civilian Elite and the Political Uses of Economic Transformation

The strategy of taking power through a process of limited or partial synchronization, the use of coercion, and the presence of a broad and differentiated military elite, were not the only factors that explain the stability of the Pinochet regime. A broad civilian elite, highly trained and loyal to the military, occupied many middlerange positions within the regime, including ministerial posts, regional ministerial director-ships, and at the local level, municipal leadership positions.

How can the collaboration of hundreds of people, especially young people, be explained? Where are these people now, and what do they do? Naturally, they were not motivated by the idea of collaborating in the politics of semisynchronization, nor did they identify with the project of establishing an authoritarian regime of indefinite longevity. Accepting positions at various levels of responsibility, they were moved to collaborate with the regime by other interests and incentives. In order to understand the enormous capacity that the authoritarian regime apparently exercised in incorporating hundreds of civilians into political positions, it is not sufficient to consider only the political factors associated with the trauma of the democratic breakdown or the conflicts that arose during the tenure of the Popular Unity government. The role played by economic policy must also be taken into account. In other words, it is not sufficient to consider the role of "passions" in politics; the role of "interests" must also be factored in.[60] "Interests" more than "passions" explain the civilian elite's unqualified defense and support of the military regime, including their silence in the face of human rights violations.

Authoritarian regimes establish institutional mechanisms for political participation in order to create a political arena where intra-elite groups may express their views, and, more importantly, to recruit new members, thereby renewing the ruling elite. When authoritarian regimes do not rely on such mechanisms–as in the case of the Pinochet regime–recruitment of elite civilian staff must be conducted through other means. The Pinochet regime utilized appointments to government ministries (the ODEPLAN, in particular) and "legislative commissions."

In the case of Spain, the existence of an institutional network of cooptation and political participation in which the various organizations of the Movement (the vertical unions, the youth organizations, the local authorities, etc.) played an important but not exclusive role, provided very effective opportunities for social mobility to large numbers of village and city youth who had been unable to better their social positions within the framework of traditional society. The existence of a broad and complex state apparatus constituted an important "clientelistic" power, not only for the jobs it could offer but also for its vast economic resources earmarked for investment in infrastructure and development, for example in tourism. An analysis of the party officials who led the transition, beginning with Adolfo Suárez, the leader of the UCD, shows the recruitment of leaders from the middle and lower-middle classes of the villages and medium-sized cities. Party membership and the belief in an ideology (or mentality, using Linz's term), and not only or uniquely one's social class as it had been before, were the keys to social advancement and consequently to a better economic situation. In sum, the policy of cooptation broadened the social base of the Spanish political elite.

The Pinochet regime differed from Franco's in this respect. Given that the goal was to build a "new Chile," civilian recruitment efforts were not aimed at right wing politicians (notably, the National Party, which won 20 percent of the vote in the 1973 parliamentary elections), but rather, were targeted at professionals and leaders of interest groups. One of the main elements of the project for a "new Chile" was the proposed transformation of the private sector into the linchpin both of the economy and politics, irrespective of who was to control the government. Thus, the regime's economic policies and its program of appointments within the public sector economy responded not only to technical imperatives but also to the exigencies of the regime's long-term political goals. Indeed, it was essentially here, "from within," that a "new Chile" was being forged.

This was a necessary step as a consequence of the regime's rejection of the democracy that collapsed on 11 September 1973 which the military saw as the inevitable result of "decadent" political developments since the 1930s. Various instances of cooptation were seen at the level of the central government, centered on the national secretariats for youth, women, and labor unions. At the same time, the regime utilized institutional channels for political cooptation which had been established during the 1960s, such as mothers' centers, neighborhood committees, and youth organizations. Emphasis was also placed on the recruitment of new leaders and on political influence at the local government level through municipal reforms that granted municipalities significant responsibility for social policy, especially in the areas of education and health, and made investment capital available through the Municipal Development Fund, administered by the central government. Under this system, Chile's mayors gained important resources for cooptation and local political influence.

At the central government level, recruitment was effected through ODEPLAN, headed during the first years of the regime by a retired naval officer, Roberto Kelly. Kelly acted as a link between the navy and a group of civilians who, during the tenure of the Allende government, had designed an economic program known as "the Brick." This group of civilians became the authoritarian regime's chief economic team, and many of the proposals it generated were implemented during the seventeen years of military rule; Chile's private pension system is a prime example.[61] Kelly's successor, the economist Miguel Kast, systematically invited young people from Santiago's universities, and especially those at the Catholic University, to "collaborate" with the government. Kast offered these young people inducements that appealed to both their passions and their interests. Foreign study opportunities were made available through "President of the Republic" scholarships, accompanied by the promise of a government appointment on repatriation. In view of the government's plans to transform the entrepreneurial state through a process of privatization, these scholarship programs were extremely attractive. Those who preferred to join the private sector could pursue corporate careers as stockholding executives in a range of newly privatized enterprises.

In the period from 1981 until the demise of the Pinochet regime, under the auspices of the ODEPLAN scholarship program, more than 800 students went to study abroad, principally to the United States. The hope was that a highly trained elite could be relied upon to collaborate in the development of the regime from public sector positions and from the universities. Two hundred seventy one students who attended U.S. universities were surveyed following the collapse of the military regime. The study showed that the predominant major was economics (40 percent), followed by engineering (14 percent), natural sciences (12 percent), social sciences (11 percent), basic science (7 percent), and education (4 percent). Of the 271 students surveyed, 108 (40 percent) undertook Ph.D. programs, 139 (51 percent) obtained Master's level degrees, and 24 (9 percent) pursued other specialized programs.[62]

In addition to these academic training inducements, elite recruitment efforts were sustained by emerging economic interests. These interests sprang from the economic transformation, at the center of which was a drastic program of privatization accompanied by deregulation of domestic markets and the reduction of barriers to international trade.[63] Unlike privatization programs in democratic countries where a clear separation between private and public interests assures the transparency of the decision-making process and thereby excludes those who decide what and how to privatize from afterwards purchasing privatized enterprises, the separation between private and public interests under authoritarian regimes is less than clearcut. Consequently, any analysis of the Chilean regime's manipulation of the privatization process cannot adequately proceed from the notion of "corruption." Nevertheless it must be recognized that the idiosyncrasies of the regime's privatization program established a set of political and ethical standards that have profoundly affected the ethical contours of the new democratic marketplace. Those who supervised the sale of public enterprises and the creation of economic institutions (such as the AFP and the ISAPRES),[64] later purchased the enterprises and managed the institutions. This practice has adversely affected both the institutionalization of the modern market and the formation of an appropriate articulation of economic and political institutions under democratic rule.

Close ties between the Pinochet regime's elite public sector managers and the executives and major stockholders of leading corporations have persisted. Most of the former civilian ministers in the Pinochet regime are now to be found in the private sector, either as presidents of the country's largest companies, or as members of their boards. That private sector leaders share a common political background is illustrated by the fact that in 1996, years after the fall of the military regime, most of the company directors elected to the AFP were former collaborators or partisans of the military regime; of thirty-one persons occupying thirty-four directorships elected by the shareholders' boards of companies with stocks in the AFP, only three were not former partisans of the military regime, while only one had previously been a minister under the first democratic government.[65]

Pinochet's former collaborators did not participate in the transition to democracy directly, that is, through political parties. Instead, they utilized the press and entrepreneurial interest groups. They succeeded in reintroducing the rightist politics of the 1950s, a form of politics centered around personalities and opposed to partisan politics which, it was believed, would lead inevitably to partyarchy.[66] Very few, with the notable exception of Jaime Guzmán, principal ideologist of the military regime, participated through party structures. Guzmán established a party, the Independent Democratic Union (the Unión Demócrata Independiente, UDI), and was elected senator for Santiago in 1989. A former subsecretary, Jovino Novoa, was elected president of the UDI. Only two former Pinochet ministers were elected to the Senate: National Renewal's Sergio Onofre Jarpa, who did not run for reelection in 1993 when his term expired, and General Bruno Siebert (ret.), elected in 1989 for an eight year term. Sergio Fernández, former minister of the interior, joined the Senate as an "appointed senator" (that is, he was appointed by General Pinochet). This was also the fortune of Santiago Sinclair, who had previously held the position of secretary of the presidency. In Chile, the rightist political elite has been formed by independent professionals and business proprietors. They have occupied middle-range positions such as governorships and municipality-level leadership positions: some were formerly members of the "legislative commissions." Others, such as the president of National Renewal, Andrés Allamand, and his collaborator, Deputy Alberto Espina, have kept themselves apart, forming a diffuse "semi-opposition." Only one former subsecretary, Alberto Cardemil of National Renewal, is currently a member of the Chamber of Deputies.

On this score, a significant difference exists between democratic Spain and democratic Chile. Outstanding former ministers from the Franco regime—Laureano López Rodó, Federico Silva, and Fernando Suárez, among others—participated in the transition through a party structure, the Popular Alliance (Alianza Popular), then headed by Manuel Fraga Iribarne. Although they have not acted as direct participants in political parties, Pinochet's former collaborators have successfully sought to influence decisions made within the UDI and National Renewal. Their influence explains both parties' continued public defense of the military regime. This circumstance represents another difference between the Spanish and Chilean right wings. Support for Franco rapidly subsided in Spain. The pro-Franco orientation of the "New Force" (Fuerza Nueva) was not shared by the Popular Alliance (Alianza Popular). The Popular Party (Partido Popular), headed by José María Aznar, which assumed office in 1996, has signaled both its detachment from Franquism and its commitment to democracy by highlighting the role of the UCD in democratization. The Popular Party has established relations with the Chilean PDC (Christian Democrat Party), rather than with National Renewal. It has also publicly condemned the Pinochet regime.

The influence of the members of Chile's former military regime has not waned with the passing of the years; their hold over the right wing has been steadily maintained. They have demonstrated a capacity to influence National Renewal, which earlier on had attempted to differentiate itself from the UDI along these lines. National Renewal's leader, Andrés Allamand, has been forced to acknowledge the existence of a dependency relation. On 11 September 1996, Allamand for the first time attended a mass, organized each year by the military academy; in previous years, Allamand could afford not to attend this annual commemoration of the military "intervention."

The dependence of the right wing on former members of the military regime is firmly reflected in the expressed opinions of both rightist parties' supporters; UDI and National Renewal voters have few differences of opinion regarding the military regime.[67] In a survey voters were asked whether they thought there would have been more, the same, or less development if Chile had always been a democracy instead of a military regime. The answers of UDI voters were similar to those of National Renewal voters. It should be recalled that Chileans' evaluations of the military regime are generally very charitable. In 1996, only 35 percent of those interviewed thought that there would have been more development if Chile had remained a democracy, a percentage slightly lower than the 1995 result of 39 percent. Among voters on the left the percentage is higher than average; 50 percent of socialists said they thought that there would have been more development if Chile had remained a democracy; 41 percent of Christian Democrat (PDC) and Democracy Party (PPD) voters expressed the same opinion (Table 4.1).

UDI and National Renewal voters' evaluations of the Pinochet regime are also similar although the former are more "Pinochetist" than the latter. Whereas 62 percent of UDI voters think that the military regime was good, only 48 percent of National Renewal voters express the same opinion. However, their differences with Concertación voters on this point are evident; a very low percentage of Concertación voters think that the military regime was good, while a high percentage declare that it was either bad, or "partly good and partly bad" (Table 4.2).

These opinions have remained relatively constant throughout the period of democratic rule though some fluctuations have arisen in response to Pinochet's direct political interventions, for example the *ejercicio de enlace* (linking exercise) in December 1990 and the *boinazo* in May 1993.

Chileans' evaluations of the Pinochet regime do not differ greatly from those expressed between 1984 and 1989 by Spaniards about Franco, nor from those offered in 1985 by Portuguese, Greeks, and Italians about their respective nondemocratic regimes. With the exception of Portugal, in all of these cases slightly less than half of the population thought that their respective regimes displayed both good and bad characteristics; one in five thought their regime was bad, and one in eight expressed the view that their regime was "generally good" (Table 4.3).

The prospects for Chilean right wing parties under democracy cannot be ascertained without taking into account the legacy of the Pinochet regime, including the former dictator's current role as commander-in-chief of the armed forces. This ongoing influence has deep economic, political, and symbolic roots. In consequence, it will not subside after Pinochet leaves his position as head of the army in 1998. He could continue to exercise influence as an appointed senator, or simply as former president. Even were the position of "appointed senator" to be eliminated by constitutional amendment—as some sections of the right wing and members of Concertación now propose— the influence of Pinochet (in view of his age, health permitting) and the members of the former authoritarian regime would not fade automatically. Instead, it would merely shift to another arena.

Table 4.1 Voter Evaluations of the Military Regime and Development

QUESTION: "If Chile had always been a democracy, and General Pinochet's military regime had not been established, do you think there would have been more development, the same, or less?"

	PDC %	PPD %	PS %	RN %	UDI %	Others %	None %	N/A %	1996 Total %	1995 Total %
More	41	41	50	14	10	28	24	26	33	39
Same	31	29	25	30	22	25	28	34	29	33
Less	22	29	19	53	68	43	37	25	31	20
Did not know/no answer	6	1	7	4	-	4	11	15	7	7
N	305	127	95	109	52	72	228	173	1200	1240

Source: National Survey CERC, July 1996.

Table 4.2 Voter Evaluations of the Pinochet Regime

QUESTION: "Do you think that General Augusto Pinochet's regime was good, bad, or partly good, partly bad?"

	PDC %	PPD %	PS %	RN %	UDI %	Others %	None %	N/A %	Total %
Partly good, partly bad	56	52	42	41	34	52	56	51	50
Bad	34	42	51	8	4	20	22	24	29
Good	7	4	5	48	62	26	18	15	17
Did not know/no answer	3	2	1	3	-	3	4	11	4
N	305	127	95	109	52	72	228	173	1200

Source: National Survey CERC, July 1996.

Table 4.3 Public Evaluations of the Franco Regime (1984–1989), and of the Dictatorships in Portugal, Greece, and Italy (1985).

| | Spain | | | Portugal 1985 % | Greece 1985 % | Italy 1985 % |
	1984 %	1985 %	1989 %			
Partly good, partly bad	46	44	45	44	31	43
Bad	27	29	26	29	59	37
Generally Good	18	17	13	13	6	6
Did not know/no answer	9	10	16	14	4	13
N	2490	2488	3371	2000	1998	2074

Source: José Ramón Montero and Mariano Torcal, "La cultura política de los españoles: pautas de continuidad y cambio," *Sistema* 99 (November, 1990): 57.

Conclusion

"Franco's" and "Pinochet's" authoritarian regimes were not mere interregnums between two democratic regimes; rather, they represent stages of each country's political development which left strong imprints upon the politics, society, culture, and economy of their respective nations, Spain and Chile. Although both belong to the same type of political system, they manifested significant differences that can be explained by considering the unique political development in each state and the different strategies used to achieve and consolidate power. Comparative analysis, highlighting the differences in specific areas, allows us once again to verify that the model of authoritarian regimes formulated by Linz is a useful analytical instrument for comprehending one of the crucial stages of contemporary political development.

Notes

1. Juan Linz, "An Authoritarian Regime: Spain," in E. Allardt and Y. Littunen, eds., *Cleavages, Ideologies and Party Systems* (Helsinski: Transactions of the Westermarck Society, 1964), pp. 297-301.

2. Juan Linz, *Crisis, Breakdown, and Reequilibration* (Baltimore: Johns Hopkins University Press, 1978).

3. Guy Hermet, "La España de Franco: formas cambiantes de una situación autoritaria," in M. Tuñon de Lara, et al., *Ideología y sociedad en la España contemporánea. Por un análisis del franquismo, Pau Colloquium VII* (Madrid: EDICUSA, 1977), pp. 103-30, especially p. 120. The various studies by Linz will be cited throughout the present essay. See also Klaus von Beyme, *Vom Faschismus zur Entwicklunqsdiktatur-Machtelite und Opposition in Spanien* (Munich: R. Piper and Co. Verlag, 1971); Amando de Miguel, *Sociología del franquismo* (Barcelona: Editorial Euros, 1975); Paul Preston, ed., *Spain in Crisis* (London: The Harvester Press, 1976); Stanley G. Payne, *The Franco Regime 1936-1975* (Madison: The University of Wisconsin Press, 1987).

4. For a historical treatment, see Ascanio Cavallo, Manuel Salazar, and Oscar Sepúlveda, *La historia oculta del régimen militar* (Santiago: Antártica, 1989).

5. Carlos Huneeus, "La inauguración de la democracia en Chile. Reforma en el procedimiento y ruptura en el contenido democrático?" *Revista de Ciencia Política* 8, 1-2 (1986): 22-87.

6. Consider in the case of Spain, for example, the uniqueness of its imperial tradition, its peripheral national groups, its greater degree of industrialization and urbanization, the bloody civil war (1936-1939), and its location in Europe, all of which represent enormous differences from Chile.

7. Linz reserves the term "authoritarian regime" for those particular cases in which a high degree of institutionalization is achieved. In this article, the terms "authoritarian regime," "military regime," and "dictatorship" are used interchangeably to characterize Pinochet's regime.

8. Neither General Velasco Alvarado in Peru nor General Videla in Argentina were able to achieve this. In Brazil the military government decreed that the president would be elected by an electoral college every four years, without possibility for reelection, in order to avoid the personalization of power.

9. The first "election" took place in the form of the plebiscite of 11 September 1980 which ratified the constitution of that year. Carlos Huneeus, "Elecciones no-competitivas en las dictaduras burocrático-autoritarias en América Latina," *Revista Española de Investigaciones Sociológicas* 13 (1981).

10. With respect to his work on Brazil, dating from the early 1970s, Linz may be criticized postfactum for overemphasizing the extent to which institutionalization constitutes the basis of authoritarianism. The Spanish experience demonstrated the regime's vulnerability as soon as Franco ceased ruling directly and began to rule through Arias Navarro. Moreover, in the case of Chile, weak institutionalization was associated with the protraction of authoritarian rule. See Juan Linz, "The Future of an Authoritarian Situation or the Institutionalization of an Authoritarian Regime: The Case of Brazil," in Alfred Stepan, ed., *Authoritarian Brazil* (New Haven: Yale University Press, 1973).

11. Javier Tusell, *La dictadura de Franco* (Madrid: Alianza Editorial, 1988), p. 162.

12. Carlos Huneeus, "El Ejército y la política en el Chile de Pinochet. Su magnitud y alcances," *Opciones* 14 (1988): 89-136.

13. Carlos Huneeus and Jorge Olave, "La participación de los militares en los nuevos autoritarismos. Chile en una perspectiva comparada," *Opciones* 11 (1987): 119-62.

14. The well-known phrase of General Pinochet to describe his power, "not so much as a leaf moves without permission," was not mere rhetoric but reflected the extreme concentration of power in his person.

15. During the tenure of the first democratic government (1990-1994), 473 laws were promulgated, twice as many as had been promulgated by Pinochet during the final period of his rule.

16. One such irregularity was the purchase of state enterprises by members of the civilian authorities who had both designed the new regulatory environments of key economic sectors (for example, energy) and managed the related state enterprises immediately prior to privatization.

17. Tusell, *La dictadura de Franco*, p. 162.

18. Carlos Prats, *Memorias* (Santiago: Pehuén, 1985).

19. Daniel García Delgado and Marcelo Stiletano, "La participación de los militares en los nuevos autoritarismos: la Argentina del 'proceso' (1976-1983)," *Opciones* (1988): 55-88.

20. Until the plebiscite of 1980, the military elite consisted of the three branches of the armed forces and the *Carabineros* (Chile's uniformed national police force). Afterward, it became more of an elite of the army. Huneeus, "El Ejército en el Chile de Pinochet."

21. See *Informe Comisión de Verdad y Reconciliación*, vol. 1 (Santiago: 1991).

22. Tusell, *La dictadura de Franco*.

23. Julio Busquets, *El militar de carrera en España* (Barcelona: Editorial Ariel, 1966).

24. On a scale from one to ten, the average for the military was 5.7; the banks, 4.94; the influential Opus Dei, 3.5; the unions, 3.84; business owners, 3.78. *Estudios sociológicos sobre la situación social de España 1975* (Madrid: Fundación FOESSA, Euramérica, 1976), Table 1.68, p. 1212. The field work for this study was carried out between 15 September and 15 October 1973 and encompassed 4,397 cases.

25. Linz, "An Authoritarian Regime: Spain."

26. Ibid., p. 299.

27. Ibid., p. 300.

28. There has been extensive discussion of this element of Linz's model. The reader is referred to the summary of this debate provided by Tusell, *La dictadura de Franco*, chapter 2.

29. If the literature on authoritarian regimes is still limited, this can be said with even more justification about analysis of the functions of coercion. For example, this theme is not examined by Amos Perlmutter, *Modern Authoritarianism* (New Haven: Yale University Press, 1981).

30. Juan Linz, "Totalitarian and Authoritarian Regimes," in F. Greenstein and N. Polsby, eds., *Handbook of Political Science*, vol. 3 (Reading, MA: Addison-Wesley, 1975).

31. Juan Linz, "From Great Hopes to Civil War: The Breakdown of Democracy in Spain," in Juan Linz and Alfred Stepan, eds., *The Breakdown of Democratic Regimes* (Baltimore: Johns Hopkins University Press, 1978).

32. Juan Linz, "The Party System in Spain: Past and Future," in Seymour M. Lipset and Stein Rokkan, eds., *Party Systems and Voter Alignments: Cross National Perspectives* (New York: The Free Press, 1967); Juan Linz, "A Century of Politics and Interests in Spain," in Suzanne D. Berger, ed., *Organizing Interests in Western Europe* (Cambridge: Cambridge University Press, 1981).

33. It is estimated that 23,000 summary executions took place after the civil war, eighty percent of them between 1939 and 1941. At the end of the war there were approximately 250,000 prisoners, a number that did not decrease to 200,000 until 1941. In 1945 there were still 43,000, and in 1950, 30,000. Tusell, *La Dictadura de Franco*, pp. 226-27.

34. Translation: "black biennium."

35. Here Linz's concept is used, from "Opposition to and under an Authoritarian Regime: The Case of Spain," in Robert Dahl, ed., *Regimes and Oppositions* (New Haven: Yale University Press, 1973).

36. Maravall notes that in 1974 the Spanish Socialist Workers' Party had scarcely 4,000 militants, *La Política de la Transición* (Madrid: Taurus, 1982). Regarding the PCE, see Eusebio Mujal-León, *Communism and Political Change in Spain* (Bloomington: Indiana University Press, 1983).

37. Carlos Huneeus, *La Unión de Centro Democrático y la transición a la democracia en España* (Madrid: Centro de Investigaciones Sociológicas, Siglo XXI Editores, 1985).

38. Federico Gil, *El sistema político de Chile* (Santiago: Editorial Andrés Bello, 1969).

39. Alan Angell, *Partidos políticos y movimiento obrero en Chile* (Mexico: ERA, 1974).

40. Brian H. Smith, *The Church and Politics in Chile* (Princeton: Princeton University Press, 1982).

41. The three universities are Catholic University in Chile, Catholic University of Valparaíso, and the Catholic University of the North.

42. See the three volumes by Cardinal Silva Henríquez, *Memorias* (Santiago: Copygraph, 1981).

43. On the crisis and fall of democracy, see Carlos Huneeus, *Der Zusammenbruch der Demokratie in Chile* (Heidelberg: Esprint Verlag, 1981); Arturo Valenzuela, *The Breakdown of Democratic Regimes: Chile* (Baltimore: Johns Hopkins University Press, 1978).

44. Henry Landsberger and Tim McDaniel, "Hypermobilization in Chile, 1970-1973," *World Politics* 23 (1976).

45. Words of the Air Force chief and member of the governing junta, General Gustavo Leigh.

46. See Patricia Verdugo, *Los zarpazos de Puma* (Santiago: CESOC, 1989).

47. The Commission on Truth and Reconciliation appointed by President Aylwin confirmed 2,115 cases of human rights violations and 164 victims of political violence. See *Informe de la Comisión Nacional de Verdad y Reconciliación* (Santiago, 1991).

48. An inquiry made by the author among the National Executive Committee (*Junta Nacional*) of the PDC in July 1985 showed that 37 percent had been detained, tortured, relocated or exiled; 20 percent had been expelled from their place of employment or study, and 16 percent were subject to various other forms of intimidation.

49. Carlos Huneeus, "Sistema de partidos políticos en Chile: Cambio y Continuidad," *Opciones* 13 (1988): 163-98.

50. Guillermo A. Campero and José A. Valenzuela, *El movimiento sindical en el régimen militar chileno 1973-1981* (Santiago: Estudios ILET, 1984).

51. Radio Cooperativa should be mentioned. The station conducted extremely important work throughout the military regime, securing the largest audience nationwide.

52. It was naturally affected by the authoritarian system. The universities, for example, suffered interference and came to be controlled by the regime.

53. The Church possessed a radio station with national range (Radio Chilena) and others with regional range, depending upon the diocese. These were free to broadcast some news although prudence was required to avoid being censored. Furthermore, various dioceses supported social development activities and projects that helped advance the formation of the social fabric of democracy, thus broadening the scope of limited pluralism.

54. Analyzed by the author in "From Diarchy to Polyarchy: Prospects for Democracy in Chile," in Enrique Baloyra, ed., *Comparing Democracies* (Boulder: Westview Press, 1987).

55. Huneeus, "La política de la apertura y sus implicancias para la inauguración de la democracia en Chile," *Revista de Ciencia Política* 7, 1 (1995): 25–84.

56. In Spain in 1971, five percent had a strong interest in politics and 51 percent no interest; in 1976, when the transition to democracy had been achieved, the percentages were 11 percent and 35 percent respectively. Rafael López Pintor, *La opción pública española: Del franquismo a la democracia* (Madrid: Centro de Investigaciones Sociológicas, 1982), p. 93.

57. The Spanish data come from *Estudios sociológicos de la situación social de España 1975* (Madrid: Fundación FOESSA, Euramérica, 1976), pp. 1176ff.. The field work was completed between 15 September and 15 October 1973 and comprised 4,397 cases. The Chilean study was done by CERC with 2,500 cases representative of the population eighteen years old and older. *Informe CERC* (April 1989).

58. CED-FLACSO study carried out during November and December 1985.

59. The *leyes Cumplido* are named after Francisco Cumplido, minister of justice in the first democratic government. See also, Carlos Huneeus, "En defensa de la transición: el primer gobierno de la democracia en Chile," in Dieter Nohlen, comp., *Democracia y neocrítica en América Latina* (Frankfurt am Main: Vervuert-Iberoamericana, 1995), pp. 192-224. Also reproduced by *Ibero-Amerikanisches Archiv* 21, 1-2 (1995): 21-55.

60. For an elaboration of the distinction between "passions" and "interests," see Albert Hirschman's *The Passions and the Interests* (Princeton: Princeton University Press, 1997).

61. See Arturo Fontaine, *Los economistas y el Presidente Pinochet* (Santiago: Zig-Zag, 1988).

62. Programa Especial de Becas D.F.L. 22/81 a U.S.A. 1981-1990, draft.

63. Dominique Hachette and Rolf Lüders, *La privatización en Chile* (Santiago: CINDE, 1992).

64. The AFP is the Pension Funds Administration (Administradora de Fondos de Pensiones); it manages the private sector's pension plan system. The ISAPRE (Institución de Salud Previsional) administers the private health insurance and services system.

65. A list of directors elected to the AFP in 1996 is found in Superintendencia Administradora de Fondos de Pensiones, *Boletín Estadístico*

133 (1996): 300-340; information about those elected in 1995, and the presidents and directors of the AFP, appears in the *Boletín* 128 (1995): 331-48.

66. The writings by Gonzalo Fernández de la Mora were well-known and much admired by the members of the right wing grouped around former president Jorge Alessandri (1958-1964). Alessandri symbolized the politics of "independents."

67. This is evident from the results of a series of surveys conducted by CERC between 1990 and 1996.

5

Political Continuities, Missed Opportunities, and Institutional Rigidities: Another Look at Democratic Transitions in Latin America

Jonathan Hartlyn*

Numerous publications have addressed democratic transitions, focusing especially on the recent processes of democratization in Latin America and Southern and Eastern Europe. This literature has produced useful insights regarding different kinds of transition processes as well as arguments linking transition types to the emergence of different types of political democracy and to the possibilities of their consolidation. However, following the initial focus on democratic transitions and as increasing awareness of the difficulties of consolidation have re-emerged, questions remain regarding the importance of the kind of transition to the subsequent likelihood of democratic consolidation.

Many of the initial, invaluable writings on democratic transitions (and even some subsequent articles) emphasized the importance that should be placed on the mode of transition in explaining subsequent democratic evolution. Stepan, for example, argued "the actual route taken toward...redemocratization has an independent weight," and then goes on to note that one central challenge is to isolate and assess its particular contribution.[1] In a review essay, Kitschelt noted that a

---

* I appreciate the thoughtful comments of Scott Mainwaring and of the two anonymous readers of the volume.

"guiding hypothesis of revisionist thinking is that the process of transition is a better predictor of eventual regime outcomes than structural preconditions that precede the advent of liberalization."[2] Then, as events unfolded in the countries that had experienced democratic transitions, several scholars argued that greater emphasis should be placed on other factors, both socioeconomic and political in nature, in explaining consolidation. For Cavarozzi, the problem with the transition framework was that it tended "to neglect long-term historic processes...[which] have a more decisive influence on the politics of democratic consolidation."[3] In developing his concept of "delegative democracy," O'Donnell emphasized that historical processes and the extent and nature of contemporary socioeconomic crises experienced in various countries were more critical factors in explaining the different types of democratic regimes that were emerging and could be consolidated than the mode of transition.[4] A third group of scholars, more structuralist in their orientation, have largely avoided the debate on transitions to focus more on socioeconomic factors critical for democratic consolidation that tend to change only slowly over time, in the tradition of Barrington Moore.[5]

Without completely eschewing the importance of structural factors, Juan Linz's work has tended to fall more into the first and second camps.[6] This short piece does as well. Its goal is to articulate a broader framework within which to place the insights from the transitions literature alongside consideration of other key factors relevant to the evolution of democracy following a transition. It does so by presenting an expanded three part framework of modalities of transition that can be employed to help structure explanations for why predictions based solely on transition modes, narrowly construed, have not always been borne out and to identify features that may help to explain disparate outcomes in seemingly similar transition processes. In the context of this framework, Latin American examples are employed to demonstrate that differing transition modes do not always have opposing consequences nor do similar transition modes necessarily produce the same outcome.

The first section below reviews some of the arguments proffered as to how and why transition modes matter. It then presents a broader conceptualization of the transition process which is intended to disentangle a sometimes ambiguous confluence of at least three factors. This disentanglement can then help us to structure explanations for some of the empirical trends that have emerged in Latin America, trends briefly explored in the subsequent two sections.

Democratic Transitions

The literature on democratic transitions usually posits a transition from authoritarianism to liberalization to some type of democracy, without assuming that successful consolidation has already occurred. Table 5.1 presents three overlapping typologies, by Linz, by O'Donnell and Schmitter, and by Mainwaring who has expanded the previous two similar dual typologies to three categories.

O'Donnell and Schmitter highlighted the differences between pacted transitions and transitions by regime collapse, concepts that overlap with Linz's *reforma pactada* and *ruptura por golpe*. In pacted transitions, leaders of the authoritarian regime retain a degree of power that allows them to extend guarantees to the outgoing regime and especially to the military prior to stepping down (military pacts). This situation, in turn, requires opposition leaders to seek a degree of unity among themselves (political pacts). To ensure support, or at least to avoid active resistance, opposition leaders often seek to provide economically dominant groups with assurances that radical programs of redistribution will not be enacted (socioeconomic pacts). As a consequence of the extensive web of guarantees conferred, these transitions were viewed as likely to encourage stability but to inhibit further democratization, particularly in the social and economic realms. As Przeworski emphasized, they leave a key "institutional trace," namely, the armed forces. For these and other reasons, the resulting democracies were sometimes considered to have emerged with "birth defects."[7] Mainwaring refined the typology somewhat by breaking down this category into two, depending upon the strength of the authoritarian government throughout the process (see Table 5.1).

It has been difficult to achieve consensus on the appropriate categorization of many country cases. Part of this has to do with the fact that some transitions were much briefer in time than others, and the longer the timespan the more the likelihood that different characteristics and interactive effects, including actions by mass actors as well as elite ones, become important. Another reason is that not all cases clearly contained formal features of "pacts" in all three areas. Although Uruguay in the 1980s did have a formal military pact that was impor-tant in providing assurances to the military and in reincorporating the left into democratic politics, it never had a formal political pact across the three major parties. In the Chilean case, a formal political pact across many of the opposition parties was crucial in the transition process in the late 1980s in the absence of any military pact; the opposition

Table 5.1 Typologies of Democratic Transitions

O'Donnell & Schmitter Linz	*Mainwaring*
Transition by regime collapse **Ruptura por golpe**	**Transition via regime defeat or rupture**

(Argentina, 1982–1983)

Pacted transition **Reforma pactada**	**Transition through extrication** (Authoritarian government weakened, but still able to negotiate crucial features of transition)

(Uruguay 1984; Chile 1990)
(Colombia 1958; Venezuela 1958)
(Peru 1980; Dominican Republic 1978)

	Transition through transaction (Authoritarian government initiates liberalization process, decisive actor throughout)

(Brazil until circa 1982)

also provided assurances they would not dramatically change the economic model. Sometimes, in the absence of formal, written documents, implicit or tacit pacts are assumed to have been made: Such is the case between the opposition represented by Tancredo Neves and the Brazilian military prior to the 1985 indirect election, based on meetings Neves held with ex-President Geisel and then with the minister of the army.

In the cases of transition by collapse, the likelihood of fuller, less restricted democracies appeared greater because of the inability of the armed forces to impose its conditions on the subsequent civilian government as they exited from power. Although this seemed to suggest less severe obstacles for advances in social and economic democracy, there also seemed to be greater risks of authoritarian reversals by a military forced to exit from power but not necessarily imbued with a democratic ethos or controllable by democratic forces.

These distinctions referred to different kinds of nonrevolutionary, elite led transitions. A more inclusive typology with four polar ideal-types presented in articles by Karl and by Karl and Schmitter (see note 1) addressed as well the differences between these "transitions from above" and those in which mass actors played a much more central, defining role. One of their major findings (also noted by Stepan and discussed by O'Donnell and Schmitter in their works referred to earlier), was that what they termed "transitions from below" (such as in Guatemala in 1946, Bolivia in 1952, Cuba in 1959, and Nicaragua in 1979) did not generate stable political democracies. Transitions from authoritarianism with extensive mass mobilization or political violence either led to authoritarian revolutionary regimes or to authoritarian reversals of radical democratic regimes. This was a significant empirical generalization which underscores the value of examining the mode or type of democratic transition as an explanatory factor for subsequent democratic evolution. Yet, as discussed by Stepan, the 1948 revolt in Costa Rica could be a partial exception to this finding, as it did result in a stable political democracy.[8] And, even if a reasonable scholarly consensus were achieved regarding categorization, it would still leave open discussion over the relative importance to be assigned to that factor over others regarding subsequent democratization trends.

What type of explanation does the transition literature articulate? The shorthand answer is one based on "path-dependency," an inter-mediate form of analysis between structural determinism (the past determines the future) and replacement (the present eliminates the past and determines the future).[9] This approach seeks to study how structural, institutional, and cultural constraints impose broad limits or shape the general nature of outcomes that are then determined by contingent choice, and how these, once made, have an independent impact on subsequent political, economic, and social trajectories.[10]

I am sympathetic to this approach to transitions and believe it can be accommodated both to reflect broader forces at work and to help draw relevant distinctions between seemingly similar transition cases. Although the works cited do not actually go this far and several of the authors in other writings have emphasized distinctly different themes, there is a risk of an undue emphasis on the mode of democratic tran-sition as *the* variable explaining subsequent democratization, reifying it as a "critical juncture" in a country's history when in fact it may not be.[11] And a misplaced emphasis may result in overlooking the nature of "missed opportunities" that a transition represented, or in missing critical elements engendered by the transition that have lasting consequences.

These issues can be addressed by conceptually disentangling, and also expanding, the mode of transition into three elements. Contingent choices congealed as decisions at a moment of transition reflect a confluence of three sets of factors in unequal mix in different cases: (1) the nature of the authoritarian regime, existing social and political forces, the international context and other structural, institutional, and cultural factors that helped determine the transition mode itself, some of which, themselves in a process of change, continue to have an influence on subsequent outcomes; (2) new institutional realities generated by the transition process itself; and, (3) opportunities or potentials opened up by the transition that could help move the country from transition to consolidation and that may or may not be realized.[12] Much of the literature specifically addressing the transitions collapsed the first two into one category and did not address the third set of factors at all. This had the consequence of downplaying the continuing post-transition impact of many of the factors included in the first set and of highlighting those in the second—especially the constraining political, military, and socioeconomic "pacts"—as the "mode." The different evolution and combinations of the three elements of this expanded conceptualization can help us to focus on why *differing modes of transition may not necessarily have opposing consequences* and why seemingly *similar modes of transition may not necessarily have the same effects.*

The first set of factors can itself be divided into those having a distinct impact on the institutional form of the transition and those having a continuing post-transition impact. The latter were of critical, and of embarrassingly obvious, importance for the period following transitions in the 1980s. Continuing factors of change—international and domestic—have had a profound effect on the possibilities for constructing legitimate government and have overwhelmed a contingent choice regarding a set of institutions or policy choices made during a transition period that might have otherwise survived. The debt crisis, which led to severe balance of payments problems, fiscal deficits, and generalized economic problems was clearly a factor that helped provoke the transition to democracy in several countries in the 1980s, for example in Argentina, Brazil, and Uruguay (though not Chile), and dramatic changes in the global political economy and the need to accommodate to these by drastic economic restructuring was and continues to be obviously central in complicating the possibilities for democratic consolidation. At the same time, as Linz has often noted, the legitimacy of governing institutions may permit democratic survival even in the face of serious economic crisis. Thus, just as important as economic legacies and continuing economic problems, if not more so, may be the evolving nature of the parties and the party system inherited from the country's democratic past and shaped by the most recent authoritarian experience.

Transitions are moments of institutional and sometimes constitutional change. Yet, institutional patterns are not necessarily fixed by the transition mode, both because they may be overwhelmed by inherited or new problems and because some kinds of transitions, particularly nonpacted ones, are open-ended in some of their political and institutional implications. Transitions, even "pacted" ones, embody not only "constraints" but also potential "opportunities" for political leaders to establish new modes and expectations of behavior and for new types of institutional rules to emerge, which, in turn could generate new long lasting patterns of democratic behavior. If these do *not* occur, we are left with complex counterfactual discussions regarding what the likely outcome under alternative scenarios could have been and assessing the relative weights of luck, the failure of agency, or the weight of structure in explaining the actual outcome.[13]

This scheme helps us to order explanations for why different kinds of transitions may ultimately have surprisingly similar outcomes. It also helps to do so with cases of seemingly similar transitions that generate different constitutional and institutional forms and patterns with implications for their subsequent democratic evolution.

Differing Modes of Transition, Similar Outcomes

The transitions in Argentina and Brazil, with brief references to Uruguay and Chile, allow us to illustrate in the context of this broader conceptualization of transitions how differing modes of transition, as these were initially construed, sometimes resulted in more similar outcomes than expectations based primarily on their mode of transition would lead us to expect. As suggested by the typologies noted above, cases in which the transition was very structurally constrained (pacted transitions) had different hypothesized outcomes than cases in which there was a greater margin of choice (transitions by regime collapse), all other things being equal. Although the Brazilian military regime suffered considerable erosion of control over the 1982–1985 period, and thus was not simply a "transition through transaction," it approximated a controlled pacted transition more closely than the other recent transition cases in the Southern Cone. In Brazil, the structural constraints on the democratic transition process of the 1980s were seemingly severe; as one author wrote: "There are reasons to be skeptical about the advantage of a conservative transition, despite it being *the only transition possible at that time.*"[14] Another argued that under the Brazilian military regime certain undemocratic practices became even further entrenched and that the politics of the transition process may have exacerbated these.[15] In Argentina, in contrast, although the military did not immediately devolve power to civilians following the Falklands/Malvinas debacle, they did so very shortly thereafter and under conditions that closely approximated what has been termed "regime collapse," appearing to open greater opportunities for fuller political democratization and fewer potential obstacles to social and economic reforms; at the same time, this implied greater risks for democracy because of the marginalization from political power of economically powerful groups and the military.[16] The cases of Uruguay and Chile both appeared to be cases of pacted transitions although their processes were not as controlled by the military nor as prolonged as in Brazil. Thus, they were intermediate between Argentina and Brazil, though more similar to the latter case (see Table 5.1).

If we accept the initial categorization of the countries by O'Donnell and Schmitter and by Mainwaring, the hypothesized consequences of their mode of transition would be that Brazil should be more stable but also more conservative due to a sustained possibility for a military veto and that Argentina should be the country with the greatest possibilities of making democratic advances but with the most danger of author-itarian reversion. Yet, expectations based primarily on the mode of transition did not appear to be borne out by subsequent events. In terms of democratic stability, the two countries with the most different kinds of elite led "transitions from above," Argentina and Brazil, looked more alike in the sense that they appeared less on the road to consolidation than either Uruguay or Chile. Nor were expectations regarding issues of democratic stability, civil-military relations, and social and economic policies borne out.

Brazil, far from being among the most stable countries in the region following its "conservative" transition, was fraught with political and economic instability. Certainly, some expectations were borne out. The military's continuing weight and influence were felt with regard to the fact that their self-proclaimed 1979 amnesty law was upheld and they maintained a major presence in the post-1985 cabinet. Following Tancredo Neves's demise before he could assume the presidency, President Sarney came to rely even more on the military as a key support group and the military lobbied extensively in the debates of the Constituent Assembly that enacted a new constitution. Yet, by the 1989 presidential elections, the political process led to a situation in which the leftist Workers' Party (Partido dos Trabalhadores, PT) and its candidate Luis Inacio da Silva (Lula) almost gained the presidency. Furthermore, under the administration of the winner of the 1989 elections, President Fernando Collor, the Brazilian military suffered several surprising reversals. Finally, the country remained in a severe socioeconomic crisis marked by low or negative growth, extraordinarily high levels of inflation, increasingly high levels of inequality, and an effective collapse of many key state institutions. Under Sarney and under Collor until his impeachment, Brazil appeared mired under a regime marked by the personalization of power and concentration of initiative in the executive, along with other features that O'Donnell captured with the term "delegative democracy."[17]

Why this "constrained" transition did not lead to a stable, if conservative democratic regime, can be analyzed in terms of the impact of certain key political continuities in the context of severe international constraints, as well as in terms of "missed opportunities." The features of the Brazilian transition process that analysts in the early 1990s have emphasized are political continuities such as the role of specific political leaders who played important roles under the previous military regime and the weak, fragmented multiparty politics in the context of presidentialism.[18] For another scholar, there were at least two "missed opportunities" that could have helped lead to a more stable and more democratic outcome. One was a product of Neves's death and its timing. Neves, chosen as president in the 1985 indirect elections, was at the center of an apparent tacit agreement with the military, even as he unified disparate opposition forces. As a result of his unfortunate death before he could assume office, Sarney became president. A much less efficacious political figure who represented considerably more continuity with the past military dictatorship, Sarney was required to renegotiate various agreements in a more complex and open process. Another opportunity revolved around the enactment of the 1988 constitution, in which the "final document reflected and reinforced the unstructured political process of elaborating it," rather than modifying or transforming it.[19] Neither transformative political leadership nor appropriate institutional rules resulted; although additional counterfactual analysis would be necessary to determine their likelihood, Neves might have exhibited the former and facilitated the latter.

Argentina also appeared at first to be bearing out some of the expectations that the initial transitions literature would lead us to expect. The first post-transition Alfonsín administration did appear to have a wider margin of maneuver with regard to the armed forces as it forced leaders of the previous military governments to submit to trials. However, the risks of the strategy in the context of the country's deteriorating economy also became apparent as the administration was confronted with serious military uprisings. Under the subsequent administration of President Menem, fear of continued military unrest (heightened by an uprising in December 1990) led the government to halt ongoing investigations and to pardon and release previously convicted military officers as well as those involved in the uprisings under the Alfonsín government. This pattern contrasted to that of the other three country cases in which military prerogatives in this area were largely preserved (although in Uruguay only by means of a complex process involving the defeat of a referendum on the subject).

Yet, the possibilities for creating a more participatory, democratic culture that the transition mode appeared to open up were not realized under President Alfonsín. Over time, rather than continuing to break new ground politically and establishing new patterns of accommodation with the opposition, Alfonsín emulated the historical Argentine pattern of exclusivist politics. For example, instead of seeking agreements with the democratic Peronist faction following the 1985 midterm elections, Alfonsín instead allowed himself to be tempted by the hopes that his Radical Party could become hegemonic in Argentine politics, a "Third Historical Movement": in this way, as Cavarozzi argues, "1986–7 turned out to be a missed opportunity."[20] Whether this was due more to political continuities and structural and institutional constraints or to a failure of leadership (of agency) "from above" would require more extensive analysis and cannot be resolved here. Yet, as the economy unraveled, Alfonsín's own popularity fell and the Peronists gained important victories in the 1987 midterm elections before sweeping into the presidency in 1989. Under President Menem, notorious examples of the abuse of presidential powers and the personalization of power took place, even as threats of authoritarian reversals by means of a military coup receded following the pardons. With the advantage of hindsight, it now appears that Argentina's more "open" transition process did not provide it with any of the hypothesized advantages, and rather than a fuller political democracy in the mid-1990s, its pattern is better captured by the term "delegative democracy." The depth of the country's socioeconomic crisis and the reassertion of "old" patterns of political behavior have meant that the perceived "opportunities" that the transition process opened up for Argentina were not realized.

As this discussion has underscored, past legacies and ongoing constraints, on the one hand, and potential "missed opportunities," on the other, may well overwhelm new institutional realities emphasized by the initial transitions literature. In viewing Argentina and Brazil as similarly crisis-ridden "delegative democracies," in contrast to either Chile or Uruguay, the precise nature of their previous authoritarian regime or the mode of their most recent democratic transition did not appear to be of particular predictive (or postdictive) power, in comparison to other historical features. These include the existence of "delegative" attributes in prior democratic episodes or interludes (themselves weak and episodic), and weak party systems, with an occasional strong party, in a presidentialist context. In this context, the confluence of socioeconomic and state crises mutually reinforced each other in a vicious cycle, and a potential opportunity for establishing a new pattern of democratic leadership and more effective constitutional and democratic rules was missed. Continuities from the past and urgent problems of the present, incorporated into the broader framework discussed in the introduction, more than institutional realities defined as a "mode of transition," appeared to be at least as important—and probably more important—in determining the evolution of democratic politics in these countries, as their differing transition modes did not have sharply opposing consequences.

Similar Modes of Transition, Different Outcomes

The previous section noted how continuing historical influences and contemporaneous factors, or missed opportunities, the first and third of the set of factors analytically distinguished in the first section, may sometimes overshadow the impact of the transition mode per se. At the same time, I believe that a careful analysis of the second set of factors, the new institutional realities created by the transition process, continues to be warranted and may provide insights into different countries' subsequent democratic evolution.

I will illustrate this by examining a pair of country cases with a similar transition process, Colombia and Venezuela. My argument is not that scholars expected the two countries to be totally similar because they had a similar transition; to my knowledge, none have. Rather, it is that over and above the differences to be expected based on past historical legacies and socioeconomic factors, certain key *variations* in the otherwise apparently similar mode of transition help to explain some of the subsequent differences in the countries' evolution.

One point many analysts have agreed upon is that Colombia and Venezuela had similar kinds of transitions involving pacts in the late 1950s.[21] The transitions from military rule in the late 1950s in Colombia and Venezuela, in fact, had some important similarities. In both cases, political pacts were signed among the opposition parties providing each other with mutual assurances that they would not seek to govern hegemonically. In both cases, a predominant party (the Liberals in

Colombia, Acción Democrática in Venezuela) purposefully underplayed its potential power in order to facilitate the transition. Assurances were also given to economic actors and to the Church that their interests would be respected. In that sense, both were conservative, "pacted" transitions from above that helped ensure that economically dominant groups would not feel threatened and turn to the military, simultaneously limiting the possibility that major social or economic reforms would be enacted, at least in the shortterm.

Venezuela became a consolidated democracy. In Colombia, a limited democracy survived but did not fully consolidate. Venezuela established a deeply rooted party system, a dense network of organizations in civil society, put down a guerrilla movement, and successfully incorporated guerrillas into the political life of the country in the late 1960s. These successes created broad legitimacy for democratic procedures and established democratic control over the armed forces; failed military uprisings in 1992 indicate a partial process of deconsolidation. In Colombia, in contrast, the political parties became more deeply factionalized throughout the 1960s and 1970s, with fewer ties to organized groups in society and increasing dependence upon clientelist ties to small electoral groups. An evident crisis of the regime and an incipient crisis of the state was growing in the late 1970s and early 1980s, marked by guerrilla actions compounded by the actions of powerful drug trafficking groups and extraordinarily high levels of violence.

One could attempt to explain the difference between these two countries in terms of nonpolitical factors. Indeed, Venezuela's greater revenues due to oil and its sharper boom-and-bust cycles, in contrast to Colombia's more modest and more moderate economic performance, must, in fact, be part of any explanation of their contrasting patterns of evolution. In addition, other historical legacies and attributes of their differing party systems not directly related to the transition are also important. Yet, "path-dependent" arguments related to the different institutional legacies of the apparently similar "pacted" transitions must also be considered.

In contrast to Venezuela, Colombia's rigid institutional agreement weakened the parties and encouraged increasing nonelectoral opposition over time. In Colombia, guarantees under the National Front agreement—constitutionally enshrined by a 1957 plebiscite—insured that neither Liberals nor Conservatives would be excluded from power but also blocked access to potential new parties. Party leaders agreed to complete parity in the three branches of government. Congress, the judiciary, departmental assemblies, and municipal councils would all automatically be half Liberal and half Conservative; cabinet posts, governorships and mayorships would also be divided equally between the two parties. Furthermore, most legislation would require a two-thirds majority for approval. Finally, because Conservatives could not agree on a candidate for the 1958 elections and because the presidency was such a major post, they agreed to alternation in the presidency from 1958 to 1974 (thus assuring the Conservatives the last presidency).

The agreement was enacted by elite negotiation and was intended to demobilize sectarian party followers and to end the rural violence. There was thus no interest in implementing other measures that might encourage increased participation. Immobilism induced by the restrictive National Front rules and fear of popular protests led most of the National Front governments to rule under state of siege regulations. Neither significant redistributive reforms nor dramatic strengthening of popular sector organizations took place. Thus, the nature of the country's democracy remained qualified throughout this period. The National Front period had the characteristics of a one-party and a multiparty, as well as of a two-party system. Because presidents were required to be of one designated party in each of the elections from 1958 through 1970, bipartisan agreement was necessary. This official National Front candidate thus headed a bipartisan government that appeared to be of a single party. Within each party, however, factions emerged opposed to the National Front. Because most legislation required a two-thirds majority for passage until 1968, the existence of these various factions necessitated extensive negotiation on the part of the president with what appeared to be a squabbling multiparty system. Throughout this period, however, and even into the late 1970s and 1980s, by which time many of the formal National Front requirements of coalition rule were lifted, the two traditional parties retained remarkably consistent percentages of the overall vote in elections. Nevertheless, sectarian identification with the two political parties by the populace declined significantly, the result of profound socioeconomic transformations including urbanization, industrialization, population growth, and increased literacy, as well as the limitations of the National Front agreement itself.

Over time, the centrality of the parties to the country's political life declined, even as they retained a near monopoly in the electoral arena. Nonelectoral forms of opposition emerged or were strengthened including labor confederations independent of the two parties, civic protest movements, and guerrilla movements. At the same time coalition rule remained attractive, for different reasons, to regional party leaders (access to patronage), major economic groups (access to policy-making), and international actors (insulation of decision-making). If any of the countries examined in this essay had a difficult constraining "birth defect" to overcome, it was Colombia. Indeed, with a partial exception in 1968, efforts to modify the country's political-institutional structure consistently failed until 1991.

Thus, in some good measure due to the constraining features of the National Front arrangement, Colombia was in considerable political turmoil by the 1980s. Successive administrations, beginning in the mid-1970s, were embroiled in questions of constitutional change, political reform, and response to guerrilla violence. Unrelated to these institutional issues, but vastly complicating these efforts was the emerging reality of drug trafficking, which weakened the state; embold-ened guerrilla groups and elements of the security forces alike; led to the assassination of popular sector leaders, leftist party activists, journalists and high government officials; and spurred sentiments of cynicism and despair. This period of stalemate, violence, and despair, however, was finally punctuated by the enactment in 1991 of a new constitution in which all remaining elements of coalition rule were dismantled. The constitution was prepared by a Constituent Assembly in which representatives of a recently reincorporated guerrilla group (the M-19 Democratic Alliance) had a major presence. The difficulty in modifying the institutional arrangements, and the dramatic, episodic, and discontinuous nature of the political change all give credence to the "path dependency" form of analysis.[22]

Venezuela's political pact among major parties in 1958 was neither as rigid or exclusive as Colombia's, nor did it form part of the country's constitution. However, the parties (excluding the Communist Party) did agree to a common program that sought to provide assurances to economic and Church elites. And, though AD handily won the 1958 elections, Betancourt (1958–1963) governed in conjunction with oppo-sition parties, collaborating particularly with Rafael Caldera of COPEI. As revolutionary guerrillas emerged, some from the disgruntled youth wing of the AD, Betancourt successfully portrayed himself as a coalition builder of the center and the right against this radicalized left. Yet, also unlike Colombia, rather than seeking to demobilize the country's population, the major Venezuelan parties maintained a vigorous institutional life. They actively sought to organize the country's growing electorate especially in urban areas where they were weak and to sustain a strong presence in labor and professional associations. In 1958, they instituted obligatory voting and electoral turnout has been nearly twice as high as in Colombia.

The 1968 and 1973 elections marked major turning points. Unlike Colombia, which found itself stalemated by coalition rule well into the 1980s, in 1969 COPEI formed a single party government, unhampered by any formal constitutional restriction. Eventually, Caldera was able to assure cooperation with AD in Congress on selected issues. Under Caldera, guerrillas were successfully reincorporated into the democratic process, and leftist parties were legalized. Targeted government expenditures facilitated by oil revenues, effective assurances regarding the physical integrity of former guerrilla leaders, and widespread legitimacy for democratic institutions in the country all facilitated the process. Finally, Caldera's administration set the stage for the effective dominance of the country's electoral landscape by AD and COPEI as these parties became "catchall" parties with overlapping social bases, ideological views, and policy positions. From the 1973 elections, which were won by AD's Carlos Andrés Pérez, the two parties received more than 80 percent of the vote, until the party's dramatic decline in 1993.

By 1989, it was apparent that Venezuela was in crisis. In 1992, following massive riots in 1989 in the wake of a structural adjustment program, Venezuela was rocked by two attempted military coups; then President Carlos Andrés Pérez, under investigation for corruption, was forced to resign in 1993 before his term was completed. As one analyst has written, two of the central factors that help explain this crisis appear unrelated to the nature of the "pacted" transition, although a third does, at least indirectly.[23] First, the country was reeling from a difficult process of economic restructuring following the boom and bust years of the oil bonanza and then the debt crisis. Second, underlying the economic and social discontent was a sense that the two political parties were led by corrupt cliques who had grown distant from their mass following, generating more of a government by parties (*partidocracia*) than by people (*democracia*). That is to say party leaders, due to their control over the party organization and the placement of names on lists for elected offices, held too much power over potential candidates. These candidates, then, sought to curry favor as much with the party leadership as with their potential electorate. Internal governance within the parties was far from a democratic process itself, even as the country's dramatic social transformations also helped generate the emergence of new social actors. The centralized, powerful Venezuelan parties represented a sharp contrast to the decentralized, factionalized and weak Colombian parties. And neither set of parties or type of party system could be directly attributed to the mode of transition. However, each was facilitated by the disparate institutional and electoral incentives generated by the seemingly similar kinds of transitions.

Finally, there was discontent with the seeming corruption, cronyism and self-serving mutual support that the two major parties provided for each other. When a willingness to work with the opposition and seek accommodation and compromise extends to a willingness to overlook and conceal abuses, the legitimacy of the regime can suffer. This is not a problem unique to democratic regimes that emanate from "pacted" transitions, as elements of it were apparent in Uruguay prior to the 1973 autogolpe and were at the center of political crises in Italy and Japan. Nor in the absence of the previous two issues was it likely to have rocked the Venezuelan regime to such an extent. Yet, in the context of socioeconomic crisis and military unrest, when corruption charges reached the president himself, Pérez was impeached, providing the country with a constitutional safety valve to the most serious crisis of confidence in the nation's fundamental institutions since the establishment of democracy in 1958. The extent and the permanence of the damage to the country's two major parties, AD and COPEI, were evident in the 1993 presidential elections.

As this comparison highlights, in addition to historical continuities and ongoing socioeconomic and political factors, considering the specific kinds of institutional rigidities and legacies that a mode of transition introduces are important and can help one to understand better why countries with seemingly similar modes of transitions may have different outcomes. The analysis in this section also presents the view—though more sustained comparative work would be required to make the case more convincingly—that the nature of the transition and its institutional legacies were more directly related to subsequent outcomes and crises in Colombia than in Venezuela.

Conclusion

In the spirit of understanding the complex interplay of continuity and discontinuity that democratic transitions represent for subsequent democratic evolution, this essay has provided an expanded three part conceptualization of transition processes focused on historical legacies and ongoing influences; institutional realities generated by the mode of transition; and potential opportunities to establish new leadership patterns and institutional rules that may or may not be realized. A comparison of Argentina and Brazil highlighted how the first and the last of these, historical and contemporary factors and the nature of possible "missed opportunities," could turn out to be more important than the characteristics and institutional realities of the mode of transition in understanding subsequent democratic evolution. In turn, a comparison of Colombia and Venezuela served to emphasize the importance of distinguishing across seemingly similar institutional inheritances from a period of transition to draw out their differing longer term implications.

More analysis would be required in each case to assess more convincingly what was the enduring impact of "pacts" or decisions made at the time of transition as constraints or defects especially in terms of the constitutional and institutional modifications that may have been introduced at the time, relative to the continuing legacy of institutional and party forms and party behavior and the impact of changing domestic and especially international socioeconomic forces. A part of that analysis should also involve counterfactual analysis of potential "missed opportunities" that moments of transition may have presented, especially regarding patterns of leadership and institutional rules, as old patterns of doing politics may reassert themselves in particularly inimical ways during periods of crisis. In these ways, we can seek to continue to advance work in the spirit of Juan Linz's scholarship which has often involved the thoughtful analysis of a "problem central to macropolitical sociological analysis: continuity and discontinuity in the political process."[24]

Notes

1. Alfred Stepan, "Paths toward Redemocratization: Theoretical and Comparative Perspectives," in Guillermo O'Donnell, Philippe C. Schmitter, and Laurence Whitehead, eds., *Transitions from Authoritarian Rule: Comparative Perspectives* (Baltimore: The Johns Hopkins University Press, 1986), p. 65. See also Guillermo O'Donnell and Philippe C. Schmitter, *Transitions from Authoritarian Rule: Tentative Conclusions about Uncertain Democracies* (Baltimore: The Johns Hopkins University Press, 1986); Scott Mainwaring, "Transitions to Democracy and Democratic Consolidation: Theoretical and Comparative Issues," in Scott Mainwaring, Guillermo O'Donnell, and J. Samuel Valenzuela, eds., *Issues in Democratic Consolidation: The New South American Democracies in Comparative Perspective* (Notre Dame: University of Notre Dame Press/Kellogg Institute, 1992); and for more recent articles, Terry Karl, "Dilemmas of Democratization in Latin America," *Comparative Politics* 23 (October 1990): 1–21; and Terry Karl and Philippe C. Schmitter, "Modes of Transition in Latin America, Southern and Eastern Europe," *International Social Science Journal* 128 (May 1991): 269–84.

2. Herbert Kitschelt, "Comparative Historical Research and Rational Choice Theory: The Case of Transitions to Democracy," *Theory and Society* 22 (June 1993): 413–27, quote on p. 413.

3. Marcelo Cavarozzi, "Beyond Transitions to Democracy in Latin America," *Journal of Latin American Studies* 24 (1992): 667; see also Adam Przeworski, *Democracy and the Market: Political and Economic Reforms in Eastern Europe and Latin America* (Cambridge: Cambridge University Press, 1991); and Frances Hagopian, "After Regime Change: Authoritarian Legacies, Political

Representation, and the Democratic Future of South America," *World Politics* 45 (April 1993): 464–500.

4. See Guillermo A. O'Donnell, "Delegative Democracy?" Helen Kellogg Institute for International Studies Working Paper 172, University of Notre Dame, March 1992.

5. One example is Dietrich Rueschemeyer, Evelyne Huber Stephens, and John D. Stephens, *Capitalist Development and Democracy* (Chicago: University of Chicago Press, 1992), although their analysis also places importance on the nature and evolution of political institutions and party systems.

6. For examples, see Juan Linz, "Crisis, Breakdown, and Reequilibration," in Juan Linz and Alfred Stepan, eds., *The Breakdown of Democratic Regimes* (Baltimore: The Johns Hopkins University Press, 1978); and "Transitions to Democracy," *The Washington Quarterly* (Summer 1990): 143–64.

7. Adam Przeworski, *Democracy and the Market.* Yet, based on the cases of Spain and Poland, Przeworski was also appropriately skeptical about how permanent the institutional "traces" would turn out to be; he was similarly skeptical with regard to the importance of the mode of transition, though he did not fully develop this theme (pp. 98–99). For a thoughtful critique of Przeworski's book which also underscores the need to consider structural, institutional, and normative factors, see Kitschelt, "Comparative Historical Research."

8. Stepan, "Paths toward Redemocratization," p. 82. For reasons I do not find totally convincing, Karl and Schmitter (in "Modes of Transition," p. 281) categorize the Costa Rican case as a "transition from above"; in this way, they do not need to seek to explain its anomalous status. As further evidence of the difficulties of and scholarly disagreements over categorization, their typology seeks to separate transitions "imposed" by authoritarian state incumbents from "pacted" ones, and thus contrary to O'Donnell and others they view Brazil as an "imposed" transition, but Spain and Uruguay (along with the earlier cases of Colombia and Venezuela) as "pacted" ones, while Chile and Argentina are placed in intermediate categories.

9. See David Stark, "Path Dependency and Privatization Strategies in East-Central Europe," *Working Papers On Transitions from State Socialism* 91-6, Cornell University, 1991.

10. On "path dependency" and the terms "structural determinism" and "replacement," see Stark, "Path Dependency"; see also Stephen Krasner, "Approaches to the State: Alternative Conceptions and Historical Dynamics," *Comparative Politics* 16, 2 (January 1984): 223–46; Douglass C. North, *Institutions, Institutional Change, and Economic Performance* (Cambridge: Cambridge University Press, 1990); and Kathleen Thelen and Sven Steinmo, "Historical Institutionalism in Comparative Politics," in Sven Steinmo, Kathleen Thelen, and Frank Longstreth, eds., *Structuring Politics: Historical Institutionalism in Comparative Analysis* (Cambridge: Cambridge University Press, 1992). Particularly valuable is the discussion on "critical junctures" in Ruth Berins

Collier and David Collier, *Shaping the Political Arena* (Princeton: Princeton University Press, 1991), especially pp. 27–39.

11. In "Modes of Transition," p. 269, Karl and Schmitter do state their belief in the assumption that the mode of transition may determine to a significant extent the type of democracy, its possibilities of consolidation, and long-range consequences for social groups, though they leave analysis of this assumption to future work.

12. These three factors are analogous to the mechanisms specified by Collier and Collier, *Shaping the Political Arena*, pp. 30–31, in their framework identifying "critical junctures." The first factor is analogous to their "constant causes," the second to their "mechanisms of reproduction," and the third to their "mechanisms of production." Yet, it is doubtful that democratic transitions, by themselves, meet the stringent requirements of a "critical juncture," that is, a juncture initiated by a major cleavage or crisis. Over this past decade, however, because democratic transitions have been combined with sustained socioeconomic crisis and state collapse leading to vast modifications in state-society relations as well as changes in political forms, many Latin American countries may in fact be in the midst of a "critical juncture."

13. Analogously, one may consider the implicit use of counterfactual analysis made in the study of democratic breakdowns; e.g., by Linz in his analysis of the potential role of a regime's "unsolvable problems," especially those that are the "work of its elites" (p. 51), or by many of the analyses of specific regime breakdowns by Linz and Stepan's collaborators in *The Breakdown of Democratic Regimes*.

14. Scott Mainwaring, "The Transition to Democracy in Brazil," *Journal of Interamerican Studies and World Affairs* 28 (Spring 1986): 174. Emphasis mine.

15. Frances Hagopian, "'Democracy by Undemocratic Means'? Elites, Political Pacts and Regime Transition in Brazil," *Comparative Political Studies* 23, 2 (July 1990): 147–70, cited from p. 154.

16. Guillermo O'Donnell, "Introduction to the Latin American Cases," in O'Donnell, Schmitter and Whitehead, eds., *Transitions from Authoritarian Rule: Latin America* (Baltimore: The Johns Hopkins University Press, 1986), pp. 8–9. For another valuable analysis which drew similar—but also appropriately qualified—inferences regarding the contrast between Argentina and Brazil, see also Eduardo Viola and Scott Mainwaring, "Transitions to Democracy: Brazil and Argentina in the 1980s," *Journal of International Affairs* 38, 2 (Winter 1985), especially p. 219.

17. See O'Donnell, "Delegative Democracy?"

18. See Scott Mainwaring, "Brazil: Weak Parties, Feckless Democracy," in Scott Mainwaring and Timothy R. Scully, eds., *Building Democratic Institutions: Parties and Party Systems in Latin America* (Stanford: Stanford University Press, 1994).

19. Thomas Bruneau, "Brazil's Political Transition," in John Higley and Richard Gunther, eds., *Elites and Democratic Consolidation in Latin America and Southern Europe* (Cambridge: Cambridge University Press, 1992), p. 273.

20. Marcelo Cavarozzi, "Patterns of Elite Negotiation and Confrontation in Argentina and Chile," in Higley and Gunther, *Elites and Democratic Consolidation*, p. 231. "Missed opportunities" resulting from political leaders that repeat past patterns of patrimonialist or exclusivist leadership rather than establish new patterns of democratic behavior in a context of socioeconomic crisis are also apparent in other transition cases. For the case of the administration of Salvador Jorge Blanco in the Dominican Republic, see Jonathan Hartlyn, "The Dominican Republic," in Abraham F. Lowenthal, ed., *Latin America and Caribbean Contemporary Record, Volume 5, 1985–1986* (New York: Holmes and Meier, 1988). A similar theme is discussed for Honduras in Mark B. Rosenberg, "Can Democracy Survive the Democrats?: From Transition to Consolidation in Honduras," in John Booth and Mitchell Seligson, eds., *Elections and Democracy in Central America* (Chapel Hill: University of North Carolina Press, 1989).

21. The arguments presented in this section appeared in a different form in Jonathan Hartlyn and Arturo Valenzuela, "Democracy in Latin America since 1930," in Leslie Bethell, ed., *The Cambridge History of Latin America, Volume VI, Part 2, Latin America since 1930: Economy, Society and Politics* (Cambridge: Cambridge University Press, 1994).

22. See also the related concept of "punctuated equilibrium" developed by Krasner in "Approaches to the State."

23. See Michael Coppedge, "Venezuela's Vulnerable Democracy," *Journal of Democracy* 4 (1993): 32–44.

24. Linz, "Crisis, Breakdown and Reequilibration," p. 92.

6

The Crisis of Presidentialism
in Latin America

Arturo Valenzuela

In this final decade of the twentieth century, the eyes of the world
focused on the former Soviet Union and Eastern Europe, witnessing a
succession of events with profound implications for the course of
human history. In a largely peaceful process, centrally planned socialist
regimes succumbed to economic and political stagnation, opening the
way for elections and the promise of democratic reform. With less
drama, Latin America also experienced change of historic dimensions.
The open and competitive presidential elections that Brazil and Chile
held in 1989 marked the first time that all the Ibero-American nations,
excepting Cuba, enjoyed the benefits of elected constitutional governments at the same moment.

There are grounds for cautious optimism about the future of
democracy in the Western Hemisphere, where the challenges of
economic and political reform are less daunting than in the old
continent and experimentation with representative institutions is of
longer standing. The very harshness of military rule in the 1970s and
1980s kindled a growing commitment by civilian elites and mass publics
to democracy and human rights as ends in themselves. Changes in the
global political environment and the growing consensus over free
market economic policies have led to a reduction in polarization and
conflict. Liberal democracy as a system of government is no longer
being challenged—from either the right or left—by alternative visions
for organizing the political community.

Yet, a fuller assessment of the progress of democracy in the
Americas that began with the end of military rule in Peru in 1980
suggests that the longterm prospects for representative government,
while generally positive, remain problematic. The 1991 coup in Haiti,

President Alberto Fujimori's autogolpe in Peru in 1992, and serious challenges to the constitutional order in Venezuela, Guatemala, and Paraguay in 1992, 1993, and 1996, respectively, are reminders of the fragility of democratic practices in the region.

Much recent scholarship dealing on the consolidation of democracy in Latin America and other developing countries has focused on the challenges involved in the implementation of stabilization and structural adjustment policies to correct economic imbalances and overcome the bankruptcy of statist policies. These policies, while generally successful in spurring industrialization and economic growth when first implemented in the immediate pre-War period, had by the 1970s spawned costly and inefficient state bureaucracies and protected markets that contributed to a recurring pattern of inflation and low growth. Although Chile and Mexico first pursued economic reforms under authoritarian regimes, for most of the continent the challenges of promoting free trade, open markets, and a downsizing of the state were undertaken by elected governments. To maintain longterm credibility, these governments face the daunting task of translating economic stability and export oriented growth strategies into policies that will address continued problems of poverty and inequality.

Although the economic and social dimensions of governance are important elements in analyzing the longterm prospects for democratic consolidation, more attention needs to be paid to the critical role of distinctly political factors, the central preoccupation in the work of Juan Linz. The most immediate challenge is for elected leaders to gain full authority over policymaking. This is difficult when, as is often the case, the armed forces succeeded in carving out considerable autonomy, claiming sole jurisdiction over internal military matters such as education, promotions, procurement and budgets, while exercising broad veto power over national security and domestic issues normally outside military purview. Fortunately, a decisive rejection of military movements in countries as disparate as Argentina, Venezuela, Guatemala, and Paraguay by both domestic groups and the international community, have made direct involvement of the military in the disruption of the constitutional order less likely than before.

The political challenges to democracy in the hemisphere stem less from overly intrusive military establishments than from the weakness of the institutions of democracy and the inadequate performance of elected governments. Authoritarianism left a legacy of weak and divided political parties and inefficient legislatures, a situation that often drives voters to look for salvation at the hands of populist leaders without experience or organizational support. Throughout the continent bloated, wasteful, and unaccountable state structures have suffocated economic growth and promoted governmental inefficiency. In the absence of strong judicial institutions, the rule of law is often precarious. Electoral systems based on proportional representation (PR) in large districts and with closed candidate lists controlled by party bosses have created a gulf between elected representatives and their constituents. Corruption has undermined trust in elected leaders, thus breeding a profound cynicism concerning politics and public affairs. In varying degrees, democracies in the region are all facing crises of representation, accountability, and efficacy. Citizens often feel that elected leaders and parties don't produce public policies that adequately interpret their hopes and expectations. Public officials are often viewed as distant and corrupt, unwilling to safeguard the public trust. Finally, in many instances democratic institutions and state structures lack the personnel, resources, and tools to respond adequately to the challenges of governance. The downsizing of the state does not mean that the state should lose its functions. On the contrary, the demands on state structures to adequately regulate markets while providing for critical societal functions such as education, health, and social service safety nets have increased significantly.

Many efforts are underway to address these conditions. Structural transformations of the state—including privatization, decentralization, and civil service reform—have been widely implemented. The outcry against corruption has led to the impeachment of presidents in Brazil and Venezuela, encouraging greater accountability of elected leaders. It has also led to the adoption of regionwide agreements to discourage corrupt practices in domestic and international transactions. Recent constitutional changes in countries such as Colombia, Chile, and Bolivia have sought to bring the state closer to the people by strengthening local governments and making state institutions more accountable in the administration and delivery of justice. Several countries have experimented with improvements in the electoral system to provide a closer link between voters and elected officials.

Institutional reformers and scholars have paid less attention, however, to a critical dimension that goes to the heart of democratic governability in Latin America and has significant implications for addressing the challenges of democratic representation, accountability, and efficacy. I refer to the implications for the success of democracy in Latin America of the institutional design of the presidential form representative democracy. In country after country, political systems based on the doctrine of the separation of powers have had difficulty generating the consensus needed to govern. Although Latin America emulated Europe in devising its electoral and judicial systems, it patterned its form of government after the United States, the homeland par excellence of presidentialism.

Presidentialism and Paralysis

The checkered history of democracy in the region has generally been attributed to cultural and economic factors, or else to the immaturity of political groups and leaders who have proven unable or unwilling to establish and respect democratic rules and procedures. Recently, however, intellectuals and institutional reformers have noted that the shortcomings of the presidential form of government have exacerbated governmental paralysis and ungovernability, contributing to the difficulties of democratic consolidation in the region.[1] The most dramatic manifestation of discontent with the presidential system occurred in Brazil, where a national plebiscite in April 1993 asked the people to choose whether to retain the presidential form of government or switch to European style parliamentary government. Although the parliamentary option was decisively defeated, surveys revealed that most educated Brazilians and much of the country's political class preferred it.[2]

Successful democratic government results from the translation of diverse societal options into majority options, either through the election of a majority party or the structuring of a majority coalition. Under parliamentarism the government is generated and sustained (or at least tolerated) by parliamentary majorities. Without at least tacit majority support a government falls, and new majority coalitions are sought or elections called. The fundamental weakness of presidential government is the frequent failure of presidents to secure cooperative legislative majorities, a problem that is particularly evident in multiparty or fragmented two party systems, and which badly aggravates the natural rivalries between branches of government. By contrast with parliamentary governments, presidential governments have no ready solution to the political impasse that arises when a president cannot command majority support in the legislature. Often the result is debilitating governmental paralysis, an outcome that is especially likely where presidentialism coexists with a multiparty system.

The framers of the U.S. constitution did not concern themselves with these problems. They were intent on balancing the interests of small states versus large ones and with instituting checks and balances to limit the power of the executive and curb the influence of passing majorities. They feared the quasiroyal power embodied in the executive and the tyrannical follies of immoderate majorities more than they feared governmental deadlock. The key to the system that they devised at the Philadelphia Convention was the doctrine of separation of powers, which created an executive independent of congressional majorities but beholden to them for the enactment of the administration's program and the appointment of its top officials. As Juan Linz has noted, presidentialism became a system of competing legitimacies, of built-in conflict between the executive and the legislature, each of which could claim to represent the will of the people.[3]

Presidentialism has been successful over a long period of time only in the United States. Many factors contributed to the consolidation of a regime based on the separation of powers, including the development of the Supreme Court as an arbiter between the other two branches, the firm tradition of civilian control of the military, and the practice of federalism (which centered power for generations at the state rather than the national level). Despite these factors, it is doubtful that presidentialism would have been as successful in the United States had it not been for something that was not foreseen by the U.S. founders, namely the development of distinct political parties organized in a two-party system.

It was the two party system that made it possible to construct political bridges across the institutional divide, providing presidents with the congressional majorities they needed to govern. As James Sundquist has noted, from the time of the expansion of mass parties in the Jacksonian era (1828–1836) until Eisenhower's second term (1956–1960), almost every U.S. president came into office with his party holding majorities in both houses of congress. The only exceptions to this pattern were the brief administrations of Zachary Taylor and his successor Millard Fillmore (1848–1852), and the failed administrations of Rutherford B. Hayes, James Garfield, and Grover Cleveland from 1876 to 1884. From the last decade of the nineteenth century until the middle of the twentieth century, a period during which the United States went from being a relatively isolated agricultural society to the world's leading industrial power, all presidents enjoyed majority support in both houses of the legislature on coming into office.[4]

Only in the second half of the twentieth century has this pattern changed, with the United States experiencing minority or divided government two-thirds of the time. This has contributed to governmental gridlock, with serious consequences for the nation's ability to act decisively in critical areas of domestic and foreign policy. It has not, however, provoked a crisis of governability, for the United States has been protected by resilient political institutions forged over generations at the national and state levels, by the moderate and pragmatic nature of its two party system, and by the underlying strength of the U.S. economy. The increased competitiveness and polarization of U.S. politics in the last decade of the twentieth century, in the aftermath of the end of the Cold War, raises serious doubts about the longterm success of a system of divided government even in the United States.

The nations of Latin America copied the institutional framework of the U.S. presidential system, but their legal traditions, political practices, and socioeconomic cleavages are far more similar to those of continental Europe than of the former British colonies of North America. Most Latin American countries remain highly centralized politically, providing the "winner-take-all" presidency a coveted source of patronage power. High courts are subject to executive control, hobbling them as institutional arbiters. Throughout the continent political parties evolved as complex organizations, reflecting deep ideological divisions stemming from conflicts over such issues as the dominant role of the Catholic Church in society, the competing claims of capital cities and far-flung regions, and the searing social conflicts between landowners and peasants and employers and workers. The result was a far less uniform and consensual political culture than that of the United States.

Multipartism and Majorities

These societal cleavages, coupled with the widespread adoption of proportional representation electoral systems, explain the greater tendency toward multipartism and fragmented two party systems in Latin America. In practice, multiparty or fluid two party systems are far less able to structure majority governments, and therefore tend to be beset by gridlock and governmental paralysis. Presidentialism is based on the assumption that the citizenry will naturally divide into two large blocks, each attempting to achieve a majority for its candidate. If the incumbent party fails, it is "thrown out" by the configuration of a new "majority." The "majoritarian" assumption may hold true for a few countries with broad societal consensus, where occasional shifts in the mix of policy preferences may lead to new majority coalitions, as "Republicans" replace "Democrats" or vice versa. But this state of affairs does not conform to the reality of most countries, where politics is more likely to be a matter of multiple, and at times highly antagonistic, options. Presidential regimes in multiparty contexts tend to be double minority systems, in which the president enjoys support from a mere plurality of the electorate while facing a legislature in which the presidential party lacks an absolute majority.

Of the fifty-three presidents elected in Latin America in the current phase of redemocratization which began in 1980, less than half—twenty to be exact—obtained absolute majorities. Thirty-three presidents (62 percent) were elected to office with only a plurality of the vote; seven of them actually trailed other candidates, only to be selected president in electoral or congressional runoffs.

In an attempt to remedy this problem of minority presidencies, all but one of the constitutions drafted in the 1980s and early 1990s (Guatemala, El Salvador, Colombia, Ecuador, Peru, Chile and Brazil; the exception was Paraguay) instituted the French system of *ballotage*, or second round, for presidential races. The objective was to ensure majority support for the president by requiring a runoff between the two candidates who obtain the highest vote shares in the initial balloting.

The second round does not resolve the problem however, since, by its very nature, the majority that the two candidate runoff produces is shaky and fleeting—more an artifact of the rules than a genuine voter consensus. In theory the two candidates facing each other in the second round are supposed to bargain with supporters of the losing candidates in order to assemble a viable majority coalition; in practice, they usually obtain that support by default without entering into any formal agreement. This was the case in Brazil and Peru, where presidential candidates Fernando Collor de Mello and Alberto Fujimori saw no need to create a formal alliance with the supporters of other candidates because their second round challengers, Luis Ignacio "Lula" da Silva and Mario Vargas Llosa, were so unacceptable to major segments of the electorate that they provoked massive "lesser of two evils" votes for Collor and Fujimori.

What is more, the second ballot may have a counterproductive effect, one that discourages the creation of maximum winning coalitions and reduction of the number of parties. Since parties need not combine (as they would have incentives to do in a race consisting of only one round), the system encourages multiple presidential candidacies: many parties can run candidates with reasonable hopes of making the second round. The battle to attain a spot in the second round can produce enough animosity and bitterness to make it difficult for the successful candidate to mend fences and build a governing coalition, a particularly serious problem in cases where competing candidates represent the same political persuasions.

More significantly, the institution of the runoff fails to address the fundamental problem of minority presidents—the lack of majority support in the legislature. Since legislators are elected at the time of the first presidential round, presidents can be left with extremely weak congressional support even if they obtain large majorities in the second round. Of the fifty-three presidents referred to above, twenty (or less than half) had majorities of their party or formal coalition in at least one house of congress at the beginning of their term. Only six of thirty-three presidents who had completed their terms by 1993 (18 percent) succeeded, however, in maintaining parliamentary majorities in both houses of congress throughout their terms. Furthermore, these six majority presidents were concentrated in only four countries (Colombia, Costa Rica, Honduras, and Paraguay) that also concentrated over half of the presidents with congressional majorities at the outset of their terms.

Contributing to the problem of minority presidencies is the contemporary phenomenon of "surge candidacies" made possible by the enormous reach of television. This term refers to candidates who sweep into office by capturing the voter's imagination, often without much organized party backing or any real congressional support. Collor de Mello in Brazil, Fujimori in Peru, Jorge Serrano in Guatemala, and Jean Bertrand Aristide in Haiti, all skyrocketed to prominence in the final stretch of presidential campaigning without substantial governmental experience or support of strong party organizations.

Brazil's Collor de Mello, who received 30.5 percent of the vote in the first round and 53 percent in the second round of the 1989 presidential race, saw his newly assembled Party of National Reconciliation obtain only five seats in the eighty-one member Senate and forty-one seats in the 502 member Chamber of Deputies in the 1990 congressional races. By contrast the PMDP, Brazil's largest party, whose presidential candidate obtained only 4.7 percent of the vote in the first round, had 21.7 percent of the seats in the Chamber of Deputies.

In Peru, Fujimori, who trailed Vargas-Llosa in the first round with 29.1 percent of the vote, surged to 62.5 percent in the second round balloting of June 10, but found that his party commanded only 16.9 percent of the vote in the lower house. The same was true for President Jorge Serrano in Guatemala whose percentage of the vote increased from 24 percent in the first round to 68 percent in the second round, but whose party won only 15.5 percent of the seats in the 116 member national congress. Indeed, the party of Serrano's defeated presidential rival, Jorge Carpio, obtained twice the number of parliamentary seats as the party of the new president. Aristide, by contrast with the other presidents mentioned, was elected on the first round with an overwhelming 67 percent. But, because he had no firm party base and entered the race only a month before the ballots were cast, his loose coalition, the National Front for Change and Democracy (FNCD), garnered only a third of the seats in the assembly.

The Tribune of the People?

Despite this reality, many new presidents seem to forget very soon after their inauguration that they were not the first choice of most voters. Having succeeded in attaining the presidency they come to believe that they embody the aspirations of all citizens. The trappings of the presidency blinds even the most modest politicians, and they come to see themselves as representing the nation as whole, above the querulous and fractious politicians in congress, whom they view as representing "special interests."

Yet few presidents have the political clout to match their idealized selfconceptions. If they lack majority support in the legislature, they soon discover that they are powerless to enact the most critical pieces of legislation in their program. Thus they are obliged either to cajole congressional leaders into granting congressional support or to try to govern in defiance of congress, with executive decrees as their main weapon.

Opposition leaders generally have few incentives to collaborate with the administration. Except in Uruguay, presidents cannot use the weapon of congressional dissolution to forge a congressional majority. Collaboration can bring the opposition a few ministerial and other government posts and some concessions on policy. Yet cabinet positions would not go to party leaders in congress, who are generally barred from holding an executive appointment, but to party leaders outside the legislature, many of whom are political rivals of the congressional chieftains.

Not that ministerial posts are particularly attractive anyway, for congressional opponents of the president soon realize that they can best improve their own and their parties' political fortunes by distancing themselves from incumbents and the trying task of governing societies afflicted by daunting socioeconomic problems. Nor will a popular president have much luck in attracting assistance. Support for the president's policies in the legislature would redound to the benefit of the chief executive, not to that of his temporary congressional allies. In minority presidential regimes a perverse logic sets in early as opposition forces soon perceive that their own political futures can best be assured with the political failure of the incumbent.

Indeed, because countries in Latin America (with the exception of the Dominican Republic and now Peru and Argentina) don't allow presidents to run for reelection, lameduck chief executives, even if they enjoy a majority in the legislature, soon face the prospect of losing support from congressional factions in their own party eager to maximize their own chances in the next presidential context. Often a presidents' most bitter intraparty rivals obtain legislative seats, while the president's closest allies are appointed to ministerial and cabinet posts. Presidentialism simply does not provide potent political incentives for coalition building and cooperation, even among members of the same party based in different branches of government.

Curiously, the reaction to the impasse of presidentialism in Latin America led over time to a sharp increase in presidential prerogatives and the use of executive decrees as legislatures abdicated their prerogatives or constitutional changes created "stronger" executives. But this trend only aggravated political conflict by reducing the legislature's role in the search for accommodation and compromise, undermining the only viable arena for coalition building. Indeed, as arbitrary uses of executive authority became more common, cooperation among parties and groups in congress became rarer as each worried mainly about its own autonomy and future electoral prospects. Political crises that a parliamentary regime would have resolved via the replacement of a prime minister, the structuring of a new working majority, or the calling of new elections, all too often tended to become fullblown constitutional crises under the conditions of presidentialism. Crises of government soon turned into crises of regime, often with military intervention.

The recent experience of Latin America shows the degree to which a country can become paralyzed when the president has little political support or loses the support he once had, unleashing a dangerous spiral that further weakens the incumbent and renders the country increasingly ungovernable. Raúl Alfonsín of Argentina, who enjoyed extraordinary levels of national support upon taking office in December 1984, chose to resign from office in July 1989, five months before the end of his term, because he had lost the ability to govern. In 1985, president Hernán Siles Suazo came to a similar decision when the parties that had initially supported him in congress decisively distanced themselves from him during a period of rising social unrest and hyperinflation.

Other failed presidents, such as Alan García of Peru, José Sarney of Brazil, and Vinicio Cerezo of Guatemala, opted to muddle through until the end of their terms, allowing their countries to move from crisis to crisis, leaving their successors with the practically impossible task of restoring order. Excepting extreme cases like those of Collor in Brazil and Carlos Andrés Pérez in Venezuela, where presidents are accused of criminal misconduct and subjected to high stakes impeachment proceedings, presidential forms of government have no constitutional solution for the problem of a president who has failed, yet has years in office still to go.

Impeachment for merely "political" reasons is not legitimate. Although Ernesto Samper of Colombia (1994–1998) escaped congressional impeachment, the conviction of several aides for criminal wrongdoing, and allegations of collusion with narcotraffickers, his presidency has plunged Colombia into the most serious crisis in fifty years. In sharp contrast, the leadership of the Conservative Party in Britain was able to dismiss a powerful sitting prime minister simply because she became a political liability to her own party's fortunes. A crippled president who cannot be charged with a crime or who fails to be impeached because of the absence of requisite congressional majorities, can drift for years like a hulk that has no rudder yet cannot be sunk.

In the current wave of democratization in Latin America, the most serious disruptions of the constitutional order have occurred in Haiti, Peru, and Guatemala. All three countries vary widely with respect to their institutional histories and complex factors explain the fragility of democracy and the course of events. Nevertheless in all three cases the absence of presidential majorities in congress, and the resulting sharp conflicts between executives determined to get their way and parliaments jealous of their constitutional prerogatives, was a critical factor in the final denouement.

President Jean Bertrand Aristide was overthrown by a military coup on September 30, 1991, only seven months after the first free election in the nation's history. With no tradition of democracy, the presence of a praetorian military establishment and a huge gulf between an overwhelmingly impoverished population and a small privileged elite, the prospects for democratic consolidation were daunting. Aristide's militant championing of the poor, which had made him overnight the most popular figure in the country, was viewed as a severe threat by an oligarchy accustomed to sharp repression of popular aspirations. In this environment, Aristide's chances of success were limited at best. The president, however, undermined his own chances by not understanding the degree to which he had to build bridges to elements of the political class, including leaders who, like him, had struggled against the Duvalier dictatorship. In particular, he viewed the mandate of the people as a sacred mandate that overrode any responsibility for seeking a middle ground with a legislature in which he had only minority support. It is instructive that his overthrow stemmed directly from an impasse with the legislature over the appointment of a prime minister that required, according to the Haitian constitution, ratification by the National Assembly. The resort of Aristide's supporters to mass demonstrations to press the president's case and his own threatening rhetoric fueled the fears of Haiti's elite and empowered antidemocratic forces who pressed the military to remove the president. Despite broad international condemnation and a crippling international embargo, it took a U.S. led international military force to restore President Aristide to office three years later.

Fujimori's presidential coup in Peru on 5 April 1992 is a also a vivid illustration of executive-legislative conflicts carried to the extreme. On taking office Fujimori made it clear that he was unwilling to work with congress, even disdaining his own Cambio 90 coalition. Drawing on authority granted him by Public Law 25327 he governed by issuing far reaching decrees in economic policy and national security.

Although the president was successful in implementing much of his program, he made a practice of lambasting the legislature and opposition political figures, many of whom had supported him in the second round. Fujimori's denunciations of the politicians escalated when the legislature, following its constitutional prerogatives, passed the Parliamentary Control of the President Act, seeking to reverse about a dozen of the 118 decree laws the president had enacted. Following the precedent set by President Gabriel Terra of Uruguay in 1933, Fujimori, with support of the military, rather than abiding by the congressional mandate or seeking a compromise with opposition political leaders, summarily shut down the courts and the legislature and suspended much of the constitution.

Fujimori's blatantly unconstitutional action received overwhelming domestic support for his dictatorial action. His attacks on the politicians and the legislature resonated favorably with a population disillusioned by the incompetence of previous civilian governments guilty of serious economic mismanagement and unable to cope with a growing and debilitating terrorist threat.

The president, however, was forced to reconsider his authoritarian blueprint and call new elections in face of the overwhelming negative reaction to his action by the international community. Nevertheless, Fujimori's bold action, and the subsequent arrest of the leader of the Shining Path insurrectionary movement, strengthened his own mandate and propelled him to victory when he stood for reelection. Although Fujimori has been successful in addressing many of Peru's economic and security issues, his actions have severely undermined the country's democratic institutions. Parties are weak and ineffective, the congress is reflexive, and the justice system has been widely criticized for its arbitrary and draconian measures. The armed forces, although strongly controlled by the president, have not evolved into the security forces appropriate for a democratic state.

In Guatemala, President Serrano, equally contemptuous of politicians and legislatures believed that he could emulate his Peruvian counterpart and garner significant popular support. In sharp contrast to the Peruvian case, however, civil society in Guatemala strongly condemned the president's ambitions and came to the defense of democracy. The international community, through the OAS and other channels, reacted decisively to reject the violation of the Guatemalan constitutional order. In the face of this overwhelming domestic and international opposition, the military withdrew its support for Serrano's scheme and he and his hapless vice president were forced to resign from office. Following the dictates of the Court of Constitutionality, the congress elected President Serrano's successor, restoring constitutional order.[5]

The most notable recent exceptions to the discouraging pattern of multiparty ungovernability in Latin America have been the administrations of Patricio Aylwin and Eduardo Frei Ruiz-Talge in Chile. In that country a broad multiparty coalition built a strong governmental alliance that distributed cabinet posts among coalition parties while retaining party discipline in the national congress. The success of the Chilean coalition, however, owes much to the continued success of the Chilean economy and the legacy of the common struggle to defeat General Augusto Pinochet at the polls in 1988, coupled with the continued presence of the latter as army commander until 1998. It is unlikely that Chile's multiparty system will keep working so smoothly into the indefinite future, particularly within the constitutional framework of exaggerated presidentialism inherited from the military regime. It is likely that growing rifts in the Concertación over the demand of the parties of the left to put forward one of their own as the coalition's presidential candidate in the presidential race of the year 2000 will break the strong majority consensus that has guided Chilean politics since the end of authoritarian rule.

Complex societies with multiparty or fragmented two party systems need to find reliable ways to elicit cooperation and encourage the formation of governing coalitions. In seeking to solve the problem of the missing majority, presidential systems must put aside the vain hope that simply switching to a two party configuration will provide presidents with the support they need. Military governments in countries as dissimilar as Uruguay, Chile, and Brazil attempted to transform the party systems of the past into Anglo-American style party systems, to no avail. The great preponderance of academic research, moreover, supports the proposition that it is exceedingly difficult to change the basic physiognomy of a party system that has been consolidated over several generations, or to create a particular kind of party system through constitutional engineering. It is also true that party systems last far longer than the particular societal divisions that may have generated them in the first place.

Even where the party system has not been fully consolidated, it might be unwise to install a majoritarian (i.e., first-past-the-post) electoral system for choosing the members of the legislature. Some Latin American countries with two party systems have also adopted PR, not in response to a demand for representation of societal diversity, but as a device to guarantee a measure of representation for the principal opposition party. Countries with two party systems like Uruguay, Costa Rica, and Colombia, experienced frequent civil wars during the nineteenth century as rival parties struggled not to be excluded from incumbency and its advantages. The adoption of PR, along with other practices such as constitutionally mandated representation for opposition parties, helped to mitigate the pernicious effects of winner-take-all politics and pave the way for consolidation of the concept of a "loyal" opposition. The tendency of majoritarian electoral systems to deny representation for minorities would generate significant opposition in Latin America, making it highly unlikely that countries with weak party systems would opt for a first-past-the-post formula.

Modest Proposals for Reform

Since political engineering is unlikely to bring fundamental changes in party systems, it follows that Latin American reformers should consider changes designed to make political institutions more "congruent" with political behavior. If presidentialism is retained, there are several reforms that might lessen its fragility. Scheduling congressional elections only in presidential election years would minimize the erosion of support that many presidents experience in off-year elections, though it would also deprive a minority president of the chance to campaign for greater congressional support. Requiring the electorate to vote for straight party lists for the presidency and the legislature would help to provide presidents with congressional allies in numbers roughly proportionate to the president's share of the vote and would also help presidents in two party systems to achieve congressional majorities. The adoption of such a measure, however, would not solve the problem of minority presidencies in multiparty contexts. Presidents could also be given the power to dissolve congress at least once during their tenure in office. Dissolution, however, does not guarantee that a president will obtain a majority in the new elections, so it leaves open the possibility that even more serious deadlock will occur.

Because runoff elections do nothing to provide minority presidents with majority support in the parliament, reformers might consider having congress select the president from the top two or three vote-getters in the first round. As the case of Bolivia illustrates, a president elected by congress is a president who knows the value and importance of compromise with political adversaries and who is keenly aware of the need to maintain viable congressional coalitions. Despite its poor longterm record of constitutional democracy, Bolivia has recently become one of Latin America's democratic success stories, in part because the election of the president by congress has encouraged the creation of working majority coalitions. It was the coalition government of the center-right Nationalist Revolutionary Movement (MNR) and the rightist National Democratic Action (ADN) that implemented in 1985 the successful macroeconomic stabilization program that broke the hyperinflationary spiral in Bolivia. And it was the coalition government of the ADN and the center-left Movement of the Revolutionary Left (MIR), generated by congressional agreement in 1989, which permitted the Paz Zamora government to maintain political stability while making some progress on economic and social problems. The success of the government of Gonzalo Sanchez de Lozada (1993–1997) in enacting, after a fitful start, widespread reforms for popular participation and capitalization, are a tribute to the continued vitality of congressionally generated majority coalitions. The contrast between Bolivia and Peru, countries that share many of the same daunting problems, could not be starker. Democratic politics of compromise and conciliation have enabled Bolivia to make difficult decisions without resorting to authoritarian tactics while at the same time consolidating democratic institutions.

The problem with congressional election of minority presidents is that the winning coalition, while likely to be more stable than one formed in the heat of a popular runoff, is still not guaranteed to last for the duration of an entire presidential term. In pre-1973 Chile, the use of a congressional runoff to select the president contributed to the formation of a coalition between Christian Democrats and the leftist Popular Unity grouping that brought Socialist Party leader Salvador Allende to the presidency in 1970. When the Christian Democrats later withdrew their support from Allende, his government did not fall but became unviable, and he resorted to the desperate strategy of attempting to rule by decree under conditions of increased political polarization. The legislative elections of 1973 could have resolved the impasse by either giving the opposition enough congressional strength to impeach the president or the government enough votes to enact its agenda in congress. The elections, however produced neither result, making a military coup far more inevitable. The short four year non-renewable term of the Bolivian presidency has contributed to that country's ability to retain the original presidential coalition. If Bolivia had the longer six year presidential term Chile has, it is more difficult to imagine the continuation of the ruling coalition.

A more extensive proposal for reform, one that has drawn considerable attention across Latin America, would establish parliamentary practices while maintaining presidentialism in the style of the French Fifth Republic. In France a popularly elected president enjoys significant powers, but governs together with a prime minister designated by the national assembly. Whatever its attractive features, however, this semipresidential formula does not resolve the fundamental problem: minority government in a multiparty context.

As the experience of the Fifth Republic in France shows, when the president has a majority in the national assembly, the political system functions like a strong presidential regime. When the president loses that majority, however, an inevitable tension develops between the president with his considerable constitutional powers, and the prime minister, the actual head of the government, who is responsible to the legislative majority. France has experienced such "cohabitation," for only a fraction of the duration of the Fifth Republic, and its viability has been heavily dependent on the personality of President François Mitterand. In a Latin American context, the French system could become a formula for repeated constitutional confrontations and juris-dictional disputes, exacerbating the problem of divided government. Juan Linz reminds us that the Weimar Republic in Germany was a semipresidential system, where the conflict between executive and parliamentary authority contributed to undermining the viability of an already fragile democracy.[6]

The Case for Parliamentarism

The problem, then, is how to achieve a stable democracy given Latin American political realities. Although it would be naive to imply that formal rules and procedures are paramount in explaining political outcomes, the rules of the game that are structured by differing institutional contexts play an important role in defining the fundamental incentives governing the political behavior of parties and politicians. What is required in Latin America is an institutional context that encourages the formation of coalitions among parties and groups, the search for governing or majoritarian consensus so essential for govern-ability, despite a highly variegated political society.

The logical option for countries with fragmented or multiparty systems where presidents can't count on structuring majority coalitions, is to move toward full-fledged parliamentarism. It is no accident that the vast majority of the world's stable democracies are parliamentary regimes. The United States boasts the only example of a presidential system successful over several generations.

The choice for Latin America, and indeed for Eastern Europe, should not be a parliamentary government of the assemblé variety, such as those of the Third and Fourth French Republics or of postwar Italy. A parliamentary formula for Latin America should incorporate many features of modern parliamentary practice, including the use of constructive votes of no confidence, constitutional tribunals, and electoral mechanisms that encourage genuine representation but not party fragmentation or the disproportionate influence of fringe parties.

Parliamentarism can promise Latin America three distinct advantages. In the first place a parliamentary government would reduce the enormous difficulty involved in building broad coalitions under conditions of winner-take-all voting and the uncertainties produced by second round elections, with their potential for undermining the basis for future coalition formation. Parliamentarism would also mitigate the recent Latin American phenomenon of surge candidacies who succeed in gaining office through access to the mass media but command little or no organizational base upon which to form a government.

Secondly, parliamentary government would encourage the formation of majority coalitions, providing strong incentives for MPs from different parties to band together lest they face the risk of losing their seats should an election be called. Rather than creating a sharp division between party leaders who seek the presidency or ministerial positions and those who go to the legislature, a parliamentary system would prompt top leaders to stand for election in individual districts and form governments from the ranks of elected officials.

By enabling key party leaders with seats in the legislature to move into coalition cabinets, the parliamentary system provides incentives and tools for structuring majority governments. Indeed, high rates of ministerial turnover may be an advantage in a multiparty context, satisfying the political ambitions of a broad range of leaders while providing them with real governmental experience. The typical Latin American phenomenon of party leaders confined to seats in weak legislatures, without the capacity for collaborating in the formation of a genuine majority coalition, is a significant barrier to the creation of successful democratic government.

It is misguided to argue that a parliamentary form of government would not work in Latin America because of the lack of maturity of the typical party system in the region. Parties and their leaders adjust themselves to the rules and incentives of the political game. Party discipline is a dependent variable, not an independent one.

Nor is it logical to argue that the problems of Latin America are far more acute than those of the European countries, making the adoption of parliamentary practices inappropriate. In Europe religious, ethnic, linguistic, and class conflicts have been far more devastating than in Latin America. Countries like Belgium or Holland, with historical divisions far deeper and more complex than those found in most of Latin America, have proven capable of using parliamentary practices to create relatively successful national governments.

Third and finally, the adoption of a parliamentary regime would eliminate the governmental paralysis and confrontation between the executive and legislative branches stemming in part from the lack of majority support for the president in parliament. The nation would not have to live with the rigidity of a fixed presidential term that can linger on long after the incumbent's majority support has evaporated. Latin American history is replete with examples of minority presidencies that prolong themselves beyond what is politically tolerable.

It is implicitly assumed in many circles that democratic rules and procedures are similar in design wherever they are found, that the institutional dimensions of representative government are constants, and that they will affect different societies in similar ways. These assumptions are simply not tenable. There is a great deal of variation in the formal and informal political architecture of democratic regimes and in the contexts in which they operate. Democracies require political institutions that work, peacefully channeling the natural divisions that are present in any society while producing public policies that respond to collective needs. Democracies also require strong and coherent parties, parties that represent citizen interests while being capable of formulating policy options.

Democratic governments must have the capacity to govern, which depends in turn on the structuring of a coherent majority party or coalition of parties capable of achieving majority support (or, at the least, majority tolerance). Different institutional arrangements are not neutral. They may be more or less appropriate in differing societal contexts, helping or hurting the prospects for democratic consolidation and governability. In Latin America, the debate over the appropriateness of a political system based on the doctrine of the separation of powers has just begun.

Notes

1. The most authoritative contemporary critique of presidentialism has been provided by Juan Linz. See his "Presidential or Parliamentary Democracy: Does it make a Difference?," in Juan J. Linz and Arturo Valenzuela, *The Failure of Presidential Democracy* (Baltimore: The Johns Hopkins University Press, 1994). I am greatly indebted to Linz for his insights, many of which are reflected in this chapter.

2. Bolivar Lamounier, ed., *Ouvindo o Brasil: Una Análise da Opinião Pública Brasileira Hoje* (São Paulo: IDESP Editora Sumaré, 1992), pp. 156–57. Support for parliamentary options has a long history in Latin America. See the speeches dating back to the 1940s by Federal Deputy Raúl Pilla in Brazil in Geraldo Guedes, *Raúl Pilla* (Brasília: Câmara dos Deputados, Perfis Parlamentares 16, 1980). For a discussion of parliamentary innovations in Latin America in the immediate postwar era, see William S. Stokes, "Parliamentary Government in Latin America," *American Political Science Review* 39 (June, 1945): 522–35.

3. See Juan J. Linz, "The Perils of Presidentialism," *Journal of Democracy* (Winter 1990): 62.

4. James L. Sundquist, "Needed: A Political Theory for the New Era of Coalition Government in the United States," *Political Science Quarterly* 103, 4 (Winter 1988–89): 617.

5. For general discussions of the Fujimori "coup" see Eduardo Ferrero Costa, "Peru's Presidential Coup," *Journal of Democracy* (January 1993), especially pages 28 to 40, and his edited volume *Proceso de retorno a la institucionalidad democrática en el Peru* (Lima: CEPEI, 1992). For a discussion of the Guatemalan incident see Francisco Villagrán de León, "Thwarting the Guatemalan Coup," *Journal of Democracy* (October 1993): 117–24. A valuable collection of essays on the international reaction in defense of democracy is Tom Farer, ed., *Beyond Sovereignty* (Baltimore: The Johns Hopkins University Press, 1996).

6. Ibid.

7

Juan Linz, Presidentialism, and Democracy: A Critical Appraisal

Scott Mainwaring and Matthew S. Shugart*

Since the 1960s, Juan J. Linz has been one of the world's foremost contributors to our understanding of democracy, authoritarianism, and totalitarianism. Although many of his contributions have had a significant impact, few have been as far reaching as his essay "Presidential or Parliamentary Democracy: Does It Make a Difference?" Originally written in 1985, the essay argued that presidentialism is less likely than parliamentarism to sustain stable democratic regimes. It became a classic even in unpublished form, and both among policy makers and scholars, it has already spawned a broad debate about the merits and (especially) the liabilities of presidential government. Now that the definitive version of the essay has appeared, we believe that a critical appraisal is timely. This task is especially important given that Linz's arguments against presidentialism have gained widespread currency.

This article reviews and critically assesses Linz's arguments about the perils of presidentialism. Although we mostly agree with several of Linz's criticisms of presidentialism, we disagree with one; we argue that presidentialism is less oriented toward winner-take-all results than Westminster parliamentary systems.[1] We argue that the superior record of parliamentary systems has rested partly on where parliamentary government has been implemented, and we claim that presidentialism

* We are grateful to Michael Coppedge, Steve Levitsky, Arend Lijphart, Timothy Scully, and two anonymous reviewers for helpful criticisms of earlier drafts of this article. This chapter appeared in *Comparative Politics* 29 (July 1997). It is reprinted with the permission of *Comparative Politics*.

has some advantages that partially offset its drawbacks. These advantages can be maximized by paying careful attention to differences among presidential systems; we recommend presidencies with weak legislative powers. Presidentialism also appears to be more viable with parties that are at least moderately disciplined, and it is especially problematic with highly fragmented multiparty systems. Finally, we argue that switching from presidentialism to parliamentarism could exacerbate problems of governability in countries with undisciplined parties. Even if Linz is correct that parliamentary government is more conducive to stable democracy,[2] a great deal rests on what kind of parliamentarism and presidentialism are implemented.

Before proceeding, we should define the regime types that we shall discuss. By presidentialism, we mean a regime in which 1) the president is always the chief executive and is elected by popular vote or, as in the United States, by an electoral college with essentially no autonomy with respect to popular preferences; and 2) the terms of office for the president and the assembly are fixed. Under pure presidentialism, the president has the right to retain ministers of his or her choosing regardless of the composition of the congress.

The Perils of Presidentialism: Linz's Argument

Linz bases his argument about the superiority of parliamentary systems partially on the observation that few long established democracies have presidential systems of government. He maintains that the superior historical performance of parliamentary democracies stems from intrinsic defects of presidential regimes. He analyzes several problems of presidential systems; here we discuss the five issues which we take to be most important.

First, in presidential systems, the president and assembly have competing claims to legitimacy. Both powers are popularly elected, and the origin and survival of each is independent from the other.[3] Since both the president and legislature "derive their power from the vote of the people in a free competition among well-defined alternatives, a conflict is always latent and sometimes likely to erupt dramatically; there is no democratic principle to resolve it."[4] Linz argues that parliamentarism obviates this problem because the executive is not independent of the assembly. If the majority of the assembly favors a change in policy direction, it can replace the government by exercising its no-confidence vote.

Second, the fixed term of the president's office introduces a rigidity that is less favorable to democracy than the flexibility offered by parliamentary systems, where governments depend on the ongoing confidence of the assembly. Presidentialism "entails a rigidity in the political process that makes adjustment to changing situations extremely difficult; a leader who has lost the confidence of his own party or the parties that acquiesced to his election cannot be replaced." Because the president cannot bolster his or her authority either through a vote of confidence or by dissolving the parliament to call new elections, presidential leadership can be weaker than that provided by some prime ministers. Presidential constitutions often manifest a contradiction "between the desire for a strong and stable executive and the latent suspicion of that same presidential power."[5] By virtue of their greater ability to promote changes in the cabinet and government, parliamentary systems afford greater opportunities for resolving disputes. Such a safety valve may enhance regime stability.

Just as presidentialism makes it difficult to remove a democratically elected head of government who no longer has support, it usually makes it impossible to extend the term of popular presidents beyond constitutionally set limits. Most presidential constitutions bar presidents from serving successive terms. Presidents therefore have relatively little time to pursue their projects and, as a result, are often tempted to try to accomplish too much in a short term.[6]

Third, Linz argues that presidentialism "introduces a strong element of zero-sum game into democratic politics with rules that tend toward a 'winner-take-all' outcome." In contrast, in parliamentary systems, "Power-sharing and coalition-forming are fairly common, and incumbents are accordingly attentive to the demands and interests of even the smaller parties." In presidential systems, the direct popular election is likely to imbue the president with a feeling that he or she need not undertake the tedious process of constructing coalitions and making concessions to the opposition. Moreover, "The danger that zero-sum presidential elections pose is compounded by the rigidity of the president's fixed term in office. Winners and losers are sharply defined for the entire period of the presidential mandate....The losers must wait at least four or five years without any access to executive power and patronage."[7]

Fourth, Linz argues that the style of presidential politics is less propitious for democracy than the style of parliamentary politics. The president's sense of being the representative of the entire nation may lead him or her to be intolerant of the opposition. "The feeling of having independent power, a mandate from the people...is likely to give a president a sense of power and mission that might be out of proportion to the limited plurality that elected him. This in turn might make resistances he encounters...more frustrating, demoralizing, or irritating than resistances usually are for a prime minister."[8] The absence in presidential systems of a monarch or a "president of the republic," deprives them of an authority who can exercise restraining power.

Finally, Linz claims that political outsiders are more likely to win the chief executive office in presidential systems, with potentially destabilizing effects. Individuals elected by direct popular vote are less dependent on and less beholden to political parties. Such individuals are more likely to govern in a populist, anti-institutionalist fashion.

A Critique of Linz's Argument

We agree with the main thrust of four of Linz's five basic criticisms of presidentialism. We concur that the issue of dual legitimacy is nettlesome in presidential systems, but we believe that his contrast between presidential and parliamentary systems is sometimes too stark on this account. To a lesser degree than in presidential systems, conflicting claims to legitimacy also exist in parliamentary systems. Conflicts sometimes arise between the lower and upper houses of a bicameral legislature, with each one claiming to exercise legitimate power. If both houses have the power of confidence over the cabinet, the most likely outcome when the houses are controlled by different majorities is a compromise coalition cabinet. In this case there is no dual legitimacy between executive and assembly, but between two chambers of the assembly. Such an arrangement could be troublesome if the two chambers were controlled by opposed parties or blocs. In a few parliamentary systems, including Canada, Germany, and Japan, upper houses have significant powers over legislation but cannot exercise a vote of no confidence against the government. In some the upper house cannot be dissolved by the government. Then there is a genuine dual legitimacy between the executive and (part of) the legislature. Thus dual democratic legitimacy is not exclusively a problem of presidentialism, though it is more pronounced with presidentialism. A unicameral parliament would avoid the potential of dual legitimacy under parliamentarism, but it sacrifices the advantages of bicameralism, especially for large, federal, or plural countries.[9]

Another overlooked potential source of conflicting legitimacy in a parliamentary republic is in the role of the head of state, who is usually called "president" but tends to be elected by parliament. The constitutions of parliamentary republics usually give the president several powers that are—or may be, subject to constitutional inter-pretation—more than ceremonial. Examples include the placement in the hands of the president of the exclusive discretion to dissolve parliament (as in Italy), the requirement of countersignatures of cabinet decrees (Italy), a suspensory veto over legislation (Czech Republic, Slovakia), the power to decree new laws (Greece for some time after 1975), and appointments to high offices, sometimes (as in the Czech Republic and Slovakia) including ministries. Linz argues that the president in such a system "can play the role of adviser or arbiter by bringing party leaders together and facilitating the flow of information among them." He also notes that "No one in a presidential system is institutionally entitled to such a role." He is quite right that political systems often face moments when they need a "neutral" arbiter; however, in order for the head of state to be more than a feckless position, it is necessary to make it "institutionally entitled" to other tasks as well. Linz correctly notes that "if presidents in pure parliamentary republics were irrelevant, it would not make sense for politicians to put so much effort into electing their preferred candidate to the office."[10]

Paradoxically, the more authority the head of state is given, the greater the potential for conflict, especially in newer democracies where roles are yet to be clearly defined by precedent. Hungary and especially Slovakia have had several constitutional crises involving the head of state, and in some Third World parliamentary republics such crises have at times been regime-threatening, as in Somalia (1961–1968) and Pakistan. Politicians do indeed care who holds the office, precisely because it has potential for applying brakes to the parliamentary majority. The office of the presidency may not be democratically legit-imated via popular election, but it typically has a fixed term of office and a longer term than that of parliament. By praising the potential of the office for serving as an arbiter, Linz implicitly acknowledges the Madisonian point that placing unchecked power in the hands of the assembly majority is not necessarily a good thing. Again, the key is careful attention to the distribution of powers among the different political players that are involved in initiating or blocking policy.

We also agree with Linz that the rigidity of presidentialism, created by the fixed term of office, can be a liability—sometimes a serious one. With the fixed term, it is difficult to get rid of unpopular or inept presidents without a system breakdown, and it is impossible (because it is constitutionally barred) in many countries to reelect a good president. However, there is no reason why a presidential system must prohibit reelection. Provisions against reelection have been introduced primarily to reduce the president's incentives to abuse executive powers to secure reelection. Despite the potential for abuse, reelection can be permitted— and we believe it should be in countries where there are reliable institutions to safeguard elections from egregious manipulation by incumbents.

Even if reelection is permitted, we are still left with the rigidity of fixed term lengths. One way of mitigating this problem is to shorten the presidential term so that if a president loses support dramatically, she or he will not be in office for as long a time. For this reason, we believe that a four year term is usually preferable to the longer mandates that are common in Latin America.

The argument about the flexibility of replacing cabinets in parliamentary systems is two-edged. In a parliamentary system, the prime minister's party can replace its leader or a coalition partner can withdraw its support and usher in a change of government short of the coup that might be the only way to remove a president who lacks support. We agree with Linz that cabinet instability need not lead to regime instability and can offer a safety valve. Yet crises in many failed parliamentary systems, including Somalia and Thailand, have come about precisely because of the difficulty of sustaining viable cabinets. Presidentialism raises the threshold for removing an executive; opponents must either wait out the term or else countenance undemocratic rule. There may be cases when this higher threshold for government change is desirable, as it could provide more predictability and stability to the policymaking process than the frequent dismantling and reconstructing of cabinets that afflicts some parliamentary systems.

Theoretically the problem of fixed terms could be remedied without adopting parliamentarism by permitting—under certain conditions— the calling of early elections. One way is to allow either the head of government or the assembly majority to demand early elections for both branches, as is the case under newly adopted Israeli rules. Such provisions represent a deviation from presidentialism, which is defined by its fixed terms. Nevertheless, as long as one branch cannot dismiss the other without standing for reelection itself, the principle of separation of powers is still retained to an extent not present in any variant of parliamentarism.

We take issue with Linz's assertion that presidentialism induces more of a winner-take-all approach to politics than does parliamentarism. As we see it, parliamentary systems do not afford an advantage on this point. The degree to which democracies promote winner-take-all rules depends mostly on the electoral and party system and on the federal or unitary nature of the system. Parliamentary systems with disciplined parties and a majority party offer the fewest checks on executive power, and hence promote a winner-take-all approach more than presidential systems.[11] In Great Britain, for example, in the last two decades a party has often won a decisive majority of parliamentary seats despite winning well under 50 percent of the votes. Notwithstanding its lack of a decisive margin in popular votes, the party can control the executive and the legislature for a protracted period of time. It can even use its dissolution power strategically to renew its mandate for another five years by calling a new election before its current term ends.

Because of the combination of disciplined parties, single member plurality electoral districts, and the prime minister's ability to dissolve the parliament, Westminster systems provide a very weak legislative check on the premier. In principle, the MPs of the governing party control the cabinet, but in practice they usually support their own party's legislative initiatives regardless of the merits of particular proposals because their electoral fates are closely tied with that of the party leadership. The norm is that a disciplined majority party leaves the executive virtually unconstrained between elections.[12] Here more than in any presidential system, the winner takes all. Given the majority of a single party in parliament, it is unlikely that a no-confidence vote would prevail, so there is little or no opposition to check the government. Early elections occur not as a flexible mechanism to rid the country of an ineffective government but at the discretion of a ruling majority using its dissolution power strategically to renew its mandate for another five years by calling a new election before its current term ends.[13]

Presidentialism is predicated upon a system of checks and balances. Such checks and balances usually inhibit winner-take-all tendencies; indeed, they are designed precisely to limit the possibility that the winner would take all. If it loses the presidency, a party or coalition may still control congress, allowing it to block some presidential initiatives. If the president's own legislative powers are reactive only (a veto, but not decree powers), an opposition-controlled congress can be the prime mover in legislating, as it is in the United States and Costa Rica, the two longest standing presidential democracies. Controlling congress is not the biggest prize and it usually does not enable a party or coalition to dictate policy, but it allows the party or coalition to establish parameters within which policy occurs. It can be a big prize in its own right if the presidency has relatively weak legislative powers. Moreover, compared to the Westminster parliamentary systems, most presidential democracies offer greater prospects of dividing the cabinet among several parties. This practice, which is essentially unknown among the Westminster parliamentary democracies, is common in multiparty presidential systems. To get elected, presidents need to assemble a broad interparty coalition, either for the first round (if a plurality format obtains) or for the second (if a two round, absolute-majority format obtains). Generally, presidents allocate cabinet seats to parties other than their own in order to attract the support of these parties or, after elections, to reward them for such support. Dividing the cabinet in this manner allows losers in the presidential contest a piece of the pie.

The norm in multiparty presidential systems is similar to that in multiparty parliamentary systems: a coalition governs, cabinet positions are divided among several parties, and the president typically must retain the support of these parties to govern effectively. Thus, most parliamentary systems with single member district electoral systems have stronger winner-take-all mechanisms than presidential systems. It is specifically the combination of parliamentarism and a majority party that produces these winner-take-all-results. This situation of extreme majoritarianism under parliamentarism is not uncommon; it is found throughout the Caribbean and some parts of the Third World. In fact, outside Western Europe, all parliamentary systems that have been continuously democratic from 1972 to 1994 have been based on the Westminster model (see Table 1). Thus Linz is not right when he states that an absolute majority of seats for one party does not occur often in parliamentary systems.[14] In presidential systems with single member plurality districts, the party that does not win the presidency can control congress, thereby providing an important check on executive power.

Linz's fourth argument is that the style of presidential politics is less favorable to democracy than the style of parliamentary politics. This argument rests in part on his view that presidentialism induces a winner-take-all logic; we have already expressed our skepticism about this claim. We agree with Linz that the predominant style of politics differs somewhat between presidential and parliamentary systems, but we would place greater emphasis on differences of style that stem from constitutional design and the nature of the party system.

Finally, we agree with Linz that presidentialism is more conducive than parliamentarism to the election of a political outsider as head of government, and that this process can entail serious problems. But in presidential democracies that have more institutionalized party systems, the election of political outsiders is the exception. Costa Rica, Uruguay, Colombia, and Venezuela have not had an outsider political president in recent decades, unless one counts Rafael Caldera of Venezuela in his latest incarnation (1993–). Argentina last elected an outsider president in 1945, when Perón had not yet built a party. In Chile, political outsiders won the presidential campaigns of 1952 and 1958, but this was the exception rather than the norm. The most notable recent cases of elections of political outsiders—Fernando Collor de Mello in Brazil (1989) and Alberto Fujimori in Peru (1990)—owe much to the unraveling of the party systems in both countries, and in Fujimori's case also to the majority runoff system that encouraged widespread party system fragmentation in the first round.

Table 1. Independent countries that were continuously democratic, 1972–1994

Income level	Pop. size	Parliamentary	Presidential	Other
Low/lower-middle	Micro			
	Small	Jamaica Mauritius	Costa Rica	
	Medium/Large		Colombia Dominican Republic	
Upper-middle	Micro	Nauru Barbados Malta		
	Small	Botswana Trinidad and Tobago		
	Medium/Large		Venezuela	
Upper	Micro	Luxembourg		Iceland
	Small	Ireland New Zealand Norway	Cyprus	
	Medium/Large	Australia Belgium Canada Denmark Germany Israel Italy Japan Netherlands Sweden United Kingdom	United States	Austria Finland France Switzerland

All regimes in the "other" column are premier-presidential, except for Switzerland.

Countries that have become independent from Britain or a British Commonwealth state since 1945: Jamaica, Mauritius, Nauru, Barbados, Malta, Botswana, Trinidad and Tobago, Cyprus, Israel

Assessing the Record of Presidentialism

Linz is correct that most of the long-established democracies in the world have parliamentary systems. Presidentialism is poorly represented among the long established democracies in the world today. This fact is apparent in Table 1, which lists countries that have established a long continuous democratic record according to criteria of Freedom House.

Freedom House has been rating countries on a scale of 1 to 7 (with 1 being best) on political rights and civil rights since 1972. Table 1 lists all thirty-three countries that were continuously democratic from 1972 to 1994. We considered a country continuously democratic if it had an average score of three or better on political rights throughout the period 1972–1994.[15] Additionally, the scores for both political and civil rights needed to be four or better in every annual Freedom House survey for a country to be considered continuously democratic.

Of the thirty-three long established democracies, only six are presidential despite the prevalence of presidentialism in many parts of the globe. Twenty-two are parliamentary and five fall into the "other" category. However, as we show in this section, the superior record of parliamentarism is in part an artifact of where it has been implemented.

Table 1 provides information on three other issues: income level, population size, and British colonial heritage. These categories are important because each may play a role in a society's likelihood of sustaining democracy. It is widely recognized that a relatively high income level is an important background condition for democracy.[16] In classifying countries by income levels, we followed the guidelines of the World Bank's *World Development Report 1993*: low is under $635 per capita GNP; lower-middle is $636 to $2555; upper-middle is $2556 to $7910; and upper is above $7911. We collapsed the bottom two categories.

Table 2 summarizes the income categories of countries in Table 1. Most of these long established democracies (twenty-eight of thirty-three) are in upper-middle or upper income countries. But among the low to lower-middle income countries, there are actually more presidential (three) than parliamentary (two) systems. Fifteen of the parliamentary democracies are found in Europe or other high-income countries such as Canada, Israel, and Japan. It is likely that these countries would have been democratic between 1972 and 1994 had they had presidential constitutions. So some of the success of parliamentary democracy is accidental: in part because of the evolution of constitutional monarchies into democracies, the region of the world that dem-

Table 2. Income Levels of Continuous Democracies, 1972–1994 (number of countries in each category)

Per capita GNP in U.S. $	Parliamentary	Presidential	Other
0–2555	2	3	0
2556–7910	5	1	0
Over 7911	15	2	5
Total	22	6	5

ocratized and industrialized first is overwhelmingly populated with parliamentary systems.

Very small countries may have an advantage in democratic stability because they typically have relatively homogenous populations in ethnic, religious, and linguistic terms, thereby attenuating potential sources of political conflict. We classified countries as micro (population under 500,000), small (500,000 to 5,000,000), and medium to large (over 5,000,000), using 1994 population data.

Table 3 groups our thirty-three long established democracies by population size. Here, too, parliamentary systems enjoy an advantage. None of the five micronations that have long established democracies has a presidential system.

The strong correlation between British colonial heritage and democracy has been widely recognized. Reasons for this association need not concern us here, but possibilities mentioned in the literature include the tendency to train civil servants, the governmental practices and institutions (which include but cannot be reduced to parliamentarism) created by the British, and the lack of control of local landed elite over the colonial state.[17] Nine of the thirty-three long established democracies had British colonial experience. Among them, eight are parliamentary and one is presidential. Here, too, background conditions have been more favorable to parliamentary systems.

It is not our purpose here to analyze the contributions of these factors to democracy; rather, we wanted to see if these factors correlated with regime type. If a background condition that is conducive to democracy is correlated with parliamentarism, then the superior record of parliamentarism may be more a product of the background condition than the regime type.

Table 4 shows twenty-four additional countries that had been continuously democratic by the same criteria used in Table 1, only for a shorter time period (at least ten years). Together, Tables 1 and 4 give us a complete look at contemporary democracies that have lasted at least ten years.

Table 3. Population Size of Continuous Democracies, 1972–1994 (number of countries in each category)

Population	Parliamentary	Presidential	Other
Under 500,000	4	0	1
500,000 to 5,000,000	7	2	0
Over 5,000,000	11	4	5
Total	22	6	5

There are three striking facts about the additional countries in Table 4. First, a large number of microstates that became independent from Britain in the 1970s or 1980s appear, and all of them are parliamentary. All seven presidential democracies but only three of the sixteen parliamentary democracies are in medium to large countries. Table 5 provides this breakdown.

Using the combined data for Tables 1 and 4, all sixteen democracies (mostly island nations) in our sample with populations under one-half million are parliamentary as are eight of ten democracies with populations between half a million and five million. On the other hand, there are no presidential systems among the microstates; many are exeptionally large countries, such as Argentina, Brazil, and the United States.

Second is the substantial increase in the number of presidential democracies, most of which are in the lower and lower-middle income categories, and all of which are in Latin America. Table 6 summarizes the income status of the newer democracies listed in Table 4. Clearly not all of parliamentarism's advantage stems from the advanced industrial states. Even in the lower to upper-middle income categories, there are more parliamentary systems (twenty-one if we combine Tables 1 and 4, compared to eleven presidential systems). However, every one of the parliamentary democracies outside of the high income category is a former British colony. The only other democracies in these income categories are presidential, and all but Cyprus are in Latin America.

Thus, if the obstacles of lower income (or other factors not considered here) in Latin America continue to cause problems for the consolidation of democracy, the number of presidential breakdowns could be large once again in the future. More optimistically, if Latin American democracies achieve greater success in consolidating this time around, we will have a substantial number of presidential democracies in the future.

Table 4. Independent countries that were democratic for at least ten years (but less than twenty-three) as of 1994

Income Level	Population Size	Parliamentary	Presidential	Other
Low/lower-middle	Micro	Belize (1981) Dominica (1978) Kiribati (1979) St. Lucia (1979) St. Vincent (1979) Solomons (1978) Tuvalu (1978) Vanuatu (1980)		
	Small	Papua New Guinea (1975)		
	Medium/Large	India (1979)	Bolivia (1982) Brazil (1985) Ecuador (1979) El Salvador (1985) Honduras (1980)	
Middle	Micro	Antigua and Barbuda (1981) Grenada (1985) St. Kitts-Nevis (1983)		
	Small			
	Medium/Large	Greece (1974)	Argentina (1983) Uruguay (1985)	Portugal[a] (1976)
Upper	Micro	Bahamas (1973)		
	Small			
	Medium/Large	Spain (1977)		

Numbers in parentheses give the date when the transition to democracy took place or the date of independence for former colonies that were not independent as of 1972.

Notes
a. Portugal has a premier-presidential system.

Countries that have become independent from Britain or a British Commonwealth state since 1945: Belize, Dominica, Kiribati, St. Lucia, St. Vincent, Solomons, Tuvalu, Vanuatu, Papua New Guinea, India, Antigua and Barbuda, Grenada, St. Kitts-Nevis, Bahamas.

Table 5. Population Size of Continuous Democracies, 1985–1994 (number of countries in each category)

Population	Parliamentary	Presidential	Other
Under 500,000	12	0	0
500,000 to 5,000,000	1	0	0
Over 5,000,000	3	7	1
Total	16	7	1

Similarly, if British colonial heritage or small population size is conducive to democracy, parliamentarism has a built-in advantage simply because Britain happened to colonize many small island territories. As a rule, British colonies had local self-government, always on the parliamentary model before independence.[18] Further, if other aspects of Latin American societies (such as extreme inequality across classes or regions) are inimical to stable democracy, then presidentialism has a built-in disadvantage.

In summary, presidentialism is more likely to be adopted in Latin America and in Africa than in other parts of the world, and these parts of the world have had more formidable obstacles to democracy regardless of the form of government. On the other hand, parliamentarism has been the regime form of choice in most of Europe and in former British colonies (a large percentage of which are microstates), where conditions for democracy may be generally more favorable. Thus there are reasons to be cautious about the observed correlation between constitutional form and democratic success.

Advantages of Presidential Systems

Presidential systems afford some attractive features that can be maximized through careful attention to constitutional design. These advantages have not received sufficient attention in the burgeoning literature on presidentialism.

Greater choice for voters

The competing claims to legitimacy are also the flipside of one advantage. The direct election of the chief executive gives the voters two electoral choices instead of one — assuming unicameralism, for the

Table 6. Income Levels of Continuous Democracies, 1985–1994 (number of countries in each category)

Per capita GNP in U.S. $	Parliamentary	Presidential	Other
0–2555	10	0	0
2556–7910	4	5	1
Over 7911	2	2	0
Total	16	7	1

sake of simplicity of argument. Having both executive and legislative elections gives voters a freer range of choices. Voters can support one party or candidate at the legislative level but another for the head of government.

Electoral Accountability and Identifiability

Presidentialism affords some advantages for accountability and identifiability. Electoral accountability describes the degree and means by which elected policymakers are electorally responsible to citizens, while identifiability refers to voters' ability to make an informed choice prior to elections based on their ability to assess the likely range of postelection governments.

The more straightforward the connection between the choices made by the electorate at the ballot box and the expectations to which policymakers are held, the greater the electoral accountability. On the principle of maximizing direct accountability between voters and elected officials, presidentialism is superior to parliamentarism in multiparty contexts because the chief executive is directly chosen by popular vote. Presidents (if eligible for reelection) or their parties can be judged by voters in subsequent elections.

One objection to presidentialism's claim to superior electoral accountability is that in most presidential systems, presidents may not be reelected immediately, if at all. Where this is the case, the electoral incentive for the president to remain responsive to voters is weakened, and electoral accountability suffers. Bans on reelection are deficiencies of most presidential systems, but not of presidentialism as a regime type. Direct accountability to the electorate exists in some presidential systems, and it is always possible under presidential government. If, as is often the case, the constitution imposes a ban on immediate reelection but allows subsequent reelection, presidents who aspire to regain their office have a strong incentive to be responsive to voters and thereby face a mechanism of electoral accountability. Only if a president 1) can never be reelected and 2) will become a secondary (or non-) player in national and party politics after his or her term are incentives for accountability via popular election dramatically weakened. Even where immediate reelection is banned, voters can still directly hold the president's party accountable. Under parliamentarism, on the other hand, with a deeply fragmented party system, the lack of direct elections for the executive inevitably weakens electoral accountability, for a citizen cannot be sure how to vote for or against a particular potential head of government.

In multiparty parliamentary systems, even if a citizen has a clear notion of which parties should be held responsible for the shortcomings of a particular government, it is often not clear whether voting for a certain party will increase the likelihood of excluding another party from the governing coalition. Governments often change between elections and even after an election, parties that lose seats are not infrequently invited to join governing coalitions.

Strom used the term "identifiability" to denote the degree to which the possible alternative executive-controlling coalitions were discernible to voters before an election.[19] Identifiability is high when voters can assess the competitors for control of the executive and can make a straightforward logical connection between their preferred candidate or party and their optimal vote. Identifiability is low when voters cannot predict easily what the effect of their vote will be in terms of the composition of the executive. This may be the case either because post-election negotiations will determine the nature of the executive, as occurs in multiparty parliamentary systems, or because a large field of contenders for a single office makes it difficult to discern where a vote may be "wasted" and whether voting for a "lesser-of-evils" might be an optimal strategy.

Strom's indicator of "identifiability" runs from 0 to 1, with 1 indicating that in 100 percent of a given nation's post–World War II elections the resulting government was identifiable as a likely result of the election at the time voters went to the polls. The average of his sample of parliamentary nations in Western Europe from 1945 until 1987 is .39, meaning that most of the time the voters could *not* know what government they were voting for. Yet under a parliamentary regime, voting for an MP or a party list is the only way voters can influence the choice of executive. In some parliamentary systems, such as Belgium (.10), Israel (.14) and Italy (.12), a voter could rarely predict the impact of a vote in parliamentary elections on the formation of the executive. The formation of the executive is the result of parliamentary negotiations among many participants. For this reason, the calculus for the voter as to how most effectively to support a particular executive can be virtually unforeseeable.

In presidential systems with a plurality one-round format, identifiability is likely to approach 1.00 in most cases because voters cast ballots for the executive, and the number of significant competitors is likely to be small. Cases in which majority runoff is used to elect the president are different, as three or more candidates may be regarded prior to the first round as serious contenders. When plurality is used to elect the president and when congressional and presidential elections are held concurrently, the norm is for "serious" competition to be restricted to two candidates even when there is multiparty competition in congressional elections. Especially when the electoral method is not majority runoff, presidentialism tends to encourage coalition-building *before* elections, thus clarifying the basic policy options being presented to voters for executive elections and simplifying the voting calculus.

Linz has responded to the argument that presidentialism engenders greater identifiability by arguing that voters in most parliamentary systems can indeed identify the likely prime ministers and cabinet ministers.[20] His logic is that, because the parliament and cabinet are a "nursery" for leadership, by the time any individual is approaching leadership status, he or she is well-known to voters. While his rejoinder is valid on its face, Linz is using the term, identifiability, in a different manner from Strom or us. He is speaking of voters' ability to identify personnel, rather than government teams, which, as we have noted, may not be at all identifiable.

Congressional Independence in Legislative Matters

Because representatives in a presidential system can act on legislation without worrying about immediate consequences for the survival of the government, issues can be considered on their merits rather than as matters of "confidence" in the leadership of the ruling party or coalition. In this specific sense, assembly members exercise independent judgment on legislative matters. Of course, it is precisely this independence of the assembly from the executive that can generate the problem of immobilism. This legislative independence is particularly problematic with highly fragmented multiparty systems, where minority presidents are the rule and legislative deadlock more easily ensues. However, where presidents enjoy substantial assembly support, congressional opposition to executive initiatives can promote consensus-building and can avoid the possibility of ill-considered legislation being passed simply to prevent a crisis of confidence. The immobilism feared by presidentialism's detractors is merely the flip side of the checks and balances desired by the U.S. Founding Fathers.

Congressional independence can encourage broad coalition-building because even a majority president is not guaranteed the unreserved support of partisans in congress. In contrast, when a prime minister's party enjoys a majority, parliamentary systems exhibit highly majoritarian characteristics. Even a party with less than a majority of votes can rule almost unchecked if the electoral system "manufactures" a majority of seats for the party. The incentive not to jeopardize the survival of the government pressures members of parliament whose parties hold executive office not to buck cabinet directives. Thus presidentialism is arguably better able than parliamentarism to combine independence of legislators with an accountable and identifiable executive. If one desires that the consensual and often painstaking task of coalition-building should be undertaken on each major legislative initiative, rather than only on the formation of a government, then presidentialism has an advantage.

Variations among Presidential Systems

Linz's critique is based mostly on a generic category of presidential systems; he does not sufficiently differentiate among kinds of presidentialism. As Linz acknowledges, the simple dichotomy, presidentialism versus parliamentarism, while useful as a starting point, is not sufficient to assess the relative merits of different constitutional designs.

Presidentialism encompasses a range of systems of government, and variations within presidentialism are important. In this section, we discuss three dimensions along which presidential systems vary in important ways. The dynamics of presidential systems change considerably according to how powerful the president is constitutionally, how disciplined the parties are, and how fragmented the party system is.

Presidential Powers

The dynamics of presidential systems vary according to presidents' formal powers. Some constitutions make it easier for the president to dominate the political process, while others make it more difficult.

One way to think of presidential legislative powers is the relationship of the exercise of power to the legislative status quo.[21] Powers that allow the president to attempt to establish a new status quo may be termed proactive powers. The best example is decree power. Those that allow the president to defend the status quo against attempts by the legislative majority to change it may be termed reactive powers.

The veto is a reactive legislative power in that it allows the president to defend the status quo by reacting to the legislature's attempt to alter it. The veto does not permit the president to get more of whatever policy the bill addresses, but it does enable the president to block change. Provisions for overriding presidential vetoes vary from a simple majority, in which case the veto is very weak, to the almost absolute veto of Ecuador, where no bill other than the budget can become law without presidential assent (but congress can demand a referendum on a vetoed bill).

In a few constitutions, the president may veto specific provisions within a bill. In a true partial veto—also known as an item veto—the president may promulgate the items or articles of the bill with which he or she agrees, while vetoing and returning to congress for reconsideration only the vetoed portions. A partial veto strengthens presidents vis-à-vis congress by allowing them to block the parts of a bill they oppose while passing those parts they favor; the president need not make a difficult choice of whether to accept a whole bill in order to win approval for those parts he or she favors.

Several presidents have the right of exclusive introduction of legislative proposals in certain policy areas. Often this exclusive power extends to some critical matters, most notably budgets, but also military policy, the creation of new bureaucratic offices, and laws concerning tariff and credit policies. This is another reactive power: If the president prefers the status quo to any outcome he or she deems likely to win the support of a veto-proof majority in congress, he or she can prevent any changes simply by not initiating a bill.

A proactive power lets the president establish a new status quo. If the president can sign a decree that becomes law the moment that it is signed, he or she has effectively established a new status quo. Relatively few democratic constitutions allow presidents to establish new legislation without first having been delegated explicit authority to do so.[22] Those that do confer this authority potentially allow the president to be very powerful.

Decree power alone does not let the president dominate the legislative process—she or he cannot emit just any decree, confident that it will survive in congress—but it lets her or him powerfully shape it and obtain legislative outcomes that congress on its own would not have passed. Even though a congressional majority can usually rescind such a decree, the president can still play a major role in shaping legislation for three reasons: 1) unlike a bill passed by congress, a presidential decree is already law—not a mere proposal—before the other branch has an opportunity to react to it; 2) presidents can overwhelm the congressional agenda with a flood of decrees, making it difficult for congress to consider measures before their effects may be difficult to reverse; and 3) a president can use the decree power strategically, at a point in the policy space at which a congressional majority is indifferent between the status quo and the decree.

Legislative decree authority differs from regulatory authority. Nearly all presidents or their ministers can issue regulatory (not legislative) decrees to implement existing legislation. (In the United States, for the most part, the regulatory function falls to independent agencies established by acts of congress—such as the Interstate Commerce Commission.) Administrative decree authority is also different from the legislative power we are referring to. Nearly all presidencies have executive authority to rearrange functions within the bureaucracy, create interagency task forces or ad-hoc commissions, and perform similar administrative functions. Emergency power is also distinct from presidential decree powers, and in most countries emergency powers are narrowly circumscribed. Finally, there are decree-laws that—in contrast to those that we have discussed as a constitutional prerogative—require prior delegation by congress before they can be issued. The delegation law usually must indicate specific policy areas in which decrees may be issued and provide for a deadline after which the decree authority expires unless it is extended by another act of congress. Delegated decree power is substantially different from constitutionally entrenched legislative decree power.

Of course, a comparison of constitutional powers does not convey information about how powerful presidents actually are in different contexts. The relationship between constitutional provisions and actual presidential powers depends on the nature of the parties and party system. In Mexico, for example, the president has relatively limited constitutional authority. But given his control over the PRI and the PRI's overwhelming legislative majorities until 1988, the president had great *de facto* powers, and for decades the legislature rubber stamped virtually all presidential initiatives.

A case can be made that presidential systems generally function better if the president has relatively limited powers. In a presidential system, weakening the presidency means primarily weakening its powers over legislation. When the congress is powerful relative to the president, situations in which the president is short of a majority in the congress need not be crisis-ridden. If the president has great legislative powers, the ability of the congress to debate, logroll, and offer compromises on conflictual issues confronting the society is constrained. The presidency takes on enormous legislative importance and the incumbent has formidable weapons with which to finetune legislation and limit consensus-building in the assembly. In this respect it is probably no accident that some of the most obvious failures among presidential democracies have been systems with strong presidential powers.

Presidentialism and Party Discipline

Linz properly argues that parliamentary systems function better with disciplined parties. We believe that some measure of party discipline also facilitates the functioning of presidential systems. Parties in presidential systems need not be extremely disciplined, but indiscipline makes it more difficult to establish stable relationships among the government, the parties, and the legislature. Presidents must be able to work with legislatures, for otherwise they are likely to face inordinate difficulties in governing effectively. Moderate party discipline makes it easier for presidents to work out stable deals with congress.

Where discipline is weak, party leaders can negotiate a deal only to have the party's legislative members back out of it. Presidents may not even be able to count on the support of their own party. Under these conditions, presidents are sometimes forced to rely on ad hoc bases of support, frequently needing to work out deals with individual legislators or faction leaders rather than negotiating primarily with party leaders who can deliver the votes of their copartisans. This can be a difficult situation for presidents, and it encourages the widespread use of patronage to secure the support of individual legislators.

With more disciplined parties, presidents can negotiate primarily with party leaders, which reduces the number of actors involved in negotiations and hence simplifies the process. Party leaders can usually deliver the votes of most of their parties, so there is greater predictability in the political process.

How to encourage greater party discipline in countries where it is lacking? Party discipline depends significantly on how candidates are selected and on who controls the order of electoral tickets. If a central party organization controls candidate selection, legislators have incentives to toe the party line; otherwise, they risk losing their candidacy the next time around. Conversely, where primary elections prevail or where candidate selection is decentralized, the central organization has less control over legislators, other things equal.

In a similar vein, if the party (especially the national party organization) controls who gets elected, as occurs with a closed list system under proportional elections, politicians have strong incentives to follow the party leadership; otherwise, they jeopardize their own position on the party list. Conversely, where members are elected because of their own resources and efforts, as in systems in which candidates of the same party must compete against one another, politicians are less dependent on their party. Under these conditions, party discipline is likely to be weaker.

Party Systems and Presidentialism

Linz notes that the problems of presidentialism are compounded in nations with deep political cleavages and numerous political parties. This argument could be taken further: the perils of presidentialism pertain largely to countries with deep political cleavages, numerous political parties, or both. In countries where political cleavages are less profound and where the party system is not particularly fragmented, the problems of presidentialism are attenuated. Many presidential democracies either have deep political cleavages or many parties, and hence Linz's arguments about the problems of presidentialism are often pertinent. But some presidential systems have less indelibly engraved cleavages and less party system fragmentation. In these cases, presidentialism often functions reasonably well, as cases such as the United States, Costa Rica, and Venezuela suggest. This point is important, for it suggests that one way of easing the strains on presidential systems is to take steps to avoid high party system fragmentation.[23]

Significant party system fragmentation can be a problem for presidentialism because it increases the likelihood of executive-legislative deadlock. With extreme multipartism, the president's party will not have anything close to a majority of seats in congress, so he or she will be forced to rely on a coalition. Interparty coalitions tend to be more fragile in presidential systems for two reasons.[24]

First, whereas in parliamentary systems, party coalitions generally take place after the election and are binding for individual legislators, in presidential systems they often take place before the election and are not binding past election day. The parties are not co-responsible for governing, even though members of several parties often participate in cabinets. Governing coalitions in presidential systems can differ markedly from electoral coalitions, whereas in parliamentary systems the same coalition responsible for creating the government is also responsible for governing. Several parties may support the president during the electoral campaign, but this does not ensure their support once he or she assumes office. Even though members of several parties often participate in cabinets, the parties are not responsible for the government. Parties or individual legislators can join the opposition without bringing down the government, so a president can end his or her term with little support in congress.

Second, in presidential systems, the commitment of individual legislators to support an agreement negotiated by the party leadership is often less secure than it is in most parliamentary systems. The extension of a cabinet portfolio does not necessarily imply party support for the president, as it usually does in a parliamentary system. In contrast, in most parliamentary systems, individual legislators are more or less bound to support the government unless their party decides to drop out of the governmental alliance. MPs risk bringing down a government and losing their seats in new elections if they fail to support the government.[25]

The problems in constructing stable interparty coalitions make the combination of extreme multipartism and presidentialism problematic and help explain the paucity of long established multiparty presidential democracies. At present, Ecuador, which has had a democracy only since 1979—and a troubled one at that—is the world's oldest presidential democracy with more than 4.0 effective parties. Only one country with this institutional combination, Chile from 1932 to 1973, has sustained democracy for at least twenty-five consecutive years. This combination is manageable, but not optimal.

Where party system fragmentation is moderate (say, under 4.0 effective parties), building and maintaining interparty coalitions is easier. The president's party is certain to be a major one that controls a significant share of the seats. This situation mitigates the problem of competing claims to legitimacy because many legislators are likely to the president's copartisans. Conflicts between the legislature and the executive tend to be less grave than when the overwhelming majority of legislators is pitted against the president.

The problems of the fixed term of office are also mitigated by limited party system fragmentation. The fixed term of office is particularly pernicious when the president cannot get legislation passed. This problem is much more likely when the president is in a distinct minority situation. It is no coincidence that the oldest and most established presidential democracies—the United States, Costa Rica, and Venezuela—have two or two-and-one-half party systems. Six of the seven presidential democracies that have lasted at least twenty-five consecutive years (Uruguay, Colombia, and the Philippines in addition to the three already mentioned cases) have had under three effective parties,[26] Chile being the sole exception. Extreme multipartism does not doom presidential democracies, but it does make their functioning more difficult.

Electoral Rules for Presidentialism

Other things equal, presidential systems function better with electoral rules or sequences that avoid extreme multipartism. Party system fragmentation can be limited by any one of a number of mea-sures—and it is best to avoid draconian steps that might lead to the exclusion of politically important groups, for such an exclusion could undermine the legitimacy of the political system.[27]

Having both an executive and an assembly come before the voters allows the presidential election to be structured so as to maximize accountability and the assembly election so as to permit broad repre-sentation. Party system fragmentation can be limited, even with proportional representation, by either of two factors: (1) most impor-tant, by having concurrent presidential and legislative elections and by having a single round plurality format for electing the president; (2) by establishing a relatively low district magnitude or a relatively high threshold for congressional elections.

Holding assembly elections concurrently with the presidential election results in a strong tendency for two major parties to be the most important even if a very proportional electoral system is used, as long as the president is not elected by majority runoff.[28] The presidential election is so important that it tends to divide voters into two camps, and voters are more likely to choose the same party in legislative elections than when presidential and legislative elections are non-concurrent.

If assembly elections are held at different times from presidential elections, fragmentation of the assembly party system becomes much more likely. If assemblies are elected more frequently than presidents, then there necessarily are midterm elections. Presidents often have sharply diminished legislative support after midterm elections. In some cases the party systems for congress and president are so divergent that presidents' parties have only a small minority of legislators. We caution, therefore, that with presidentialism, concurrent elections are preferable.

The increasingly common majority runoff method for electing presidents has the advantage of avoiding the election of a president who wins a narrow plurality but who would easily lose to another candidate in a face to face election. Majority runoff is appealing because it requires that the eventual winner obtain the backing of more than 50 percent of the voters. However, the runoff system also encourages fragmentation of the field of competitors for both presidency and assembly. Many candidates enter the first round with the aim of either finishing second and upsetting the front runner in the runoff or else "blackmailing" the two leading candidates into making deals between rounds. A candidate like Alberto Fujimori in Peru or Stanislaw Timynski in Poland can come out of nowhere and deny a first-round victory to the frontrunner and even come from behind and win the second round. For the countries Shugart and Carey analyzed, in majority runoff systems the eventual winner garnered on average just under 40 percent of the first-round vote, while the runner-up averaged only 25 percent. The plurality rule, on the other hand, encourages only two "serious" contenders for the presidency in most cases. In plurality systems, the averages for winners and runners-up were nearly 50 percent and 35 percent. Other mechanisms besides straight plurality can guard against the unusual but potentially dangerous case of a winner earning less than 40 percent of the vote. Such mechanisms include requiring 40 percent for the frontrunner or a minimum gap between the top two finishers instead of requiring an absolute majority to avoid a runoff, or employing an electoral college in which electors are constitutionally bound to choose one of the top two popular vote winners.

If the president is elected so as to maximize the possibility of two-candidate races and a majority (or nearly so) for the winner, the assembly can be chosen so as to allow the representation of partisan diversity. Extreme fragmentation need not result if only a moderately proportional system is used and especially if the assembly is elected at the same time as the president and the president is *not* elected by majority runoff. Proportional representation can permit the representation of some important minor parties without leading to extreme fragmentation.

Switching from Presidential to Parliamentary Government: A Caution

Convinced that parliamentary systems are more likely to sustain stable democracy, Linz implicitly advocates switching to parliamentary government. We are less than sanguine about the results of shifting to parliamentary government in countries with undisciplined parties. Undisciplined parties create particularly daunting problems in parliamentary systems.[29] In countries with undisciplined parties, switching to parliamentary government could exacerbate rather than ameliorate problems of governability and instability, unless party and electoral legislation were simultaneously changed to promote greater discipline.

In parliamentary systems, the government depends on the ongoing confidence of the assembly. Where individual assembly members act as free agents, unfettered by party ties, the governmental majorities that were carefully crafted in postelection negotiations easily dissipate. Free to vote as they please, individual legislators abandon the government when it is politically expedient to do so. Under these conditions, the classic Achilles heel of some parliamentary systems, frequent cabinet changes, is likely to be a problem.

Linz counterargues that presidentialism has contributed to party weakness in some Latin American countries, so that switching to parliamentary government should strengthen parties by removing one of the causes of party weakness. Moreover, analysts might expect that the mechanism of confidence votes would itself promote party discipline, since remaining in office would hinge upon party discipline. We do not dismiss such claims, but in the short term, switching to parliamentary government without effecting parallel changes to encourage greater party discipline could prove problematic. The French Fourth Republic showed that parliamentary government in and of itself need not encourage the formation of disciplined parties. It also showed the perils of undisciplined parties in a parliamentary democracy even in the context of an advanced industrial nation, as governments were toppled with considerable frequency.

Any switch to parliamentary government, therefore, would need to carefully design a panoply of institutions to increase the likelihood that it would function well. In presidential and parliamentary systems alike, institutional combinations are of paramount importance.[30]

Conclusion

While we greatly admire Linz's seminal contribution and agree with parts of it, we believe that he understated the importance of differences among constitutional and institutional designs within the broad category of presidential systems, and in doing so overstated the extent to which presidentialism as a regime type is inherently flawed, regardless of constitutional and institutional arrangements. Presidential systems can be designed to function more effectively than they usually have. We have argued that providing the president with limited legislative power, encouraging the formation of parties that are reasonably disciplined in the legislature, and preventing extreme fragmentation of the party system enhance the viability of presidentialism. Linz clearly recognizes that not any kind of parliamentarism will do; we are making the same point about presidentialism.

Under some conditions, the perils of presidentialism can be attenuated, a point that Linz generally underplays. It is important to pay attention to factors that can mitigate the problems of presidentialism because it may be politically more feasible to modify presidential systems than to switch to parliamentary government. We have also argued that presidentialism, particularly if it is carefully designed, has some advantages over parliamentarism. In our view, Linz does not sufficiently consider this point. Moreover, on one key issue—the alleged winner-take-all-nature of presidentialism—we question Linz's argument. The sum effect of our arguments is to call more attention to institutional combinations and constitutional designs and to suggest that the advantages of parliamentarism may not be quite as pronounced as Linz argued. Nevertheless, we clearly share the consensus that his pathbreaking article was one of the most important scholarly contributions of the past decade, and that it deserves the ample attention among scholars and policy makers that it has already received.

Notes

1. We follow Arend Lijphart's understanding of a Westminster (British) style democracy. See his *Democracies: Patterns of Majoritarian and Consensus Government in Twenty-One Countries* (New Haven: Yale University Press, 1984), especially pp. 1–20. For our purposes, the most important features of a Westminster democracy are (1) single party majority cabinets; (2) disciplined parties; (3) something approaching a two party system in the legislature; (4) plurality single member electoral districts.

2. Adam Przeworski et al. find that parliamentary democracy is indeed more conducive to sustaining democracy. See "What Makes Democracies Endure?," *Journal of Democracy* 7 (January 1996): 39–55.

3. Matthew Shugart and ˙John Carey, *Presidents and Assemblies: Constitutional Design and Electoral Dynamics* (New York: Cambridge University Press, 1992), chapter 2.

4. Juan J. Linz, "Presidential or Parliamentary Democracy: Does It Make a Difference," in Linz and Arturo Valenzuela, eds., *The Crisis of Presidential Democracy: The Latin American Evidence* (Baltimore: Johns Hopkins University Press, 1994), p. 7.

5. Ibid., pp. 9–10; Linz, "The Perils of Presidentialism," *Journal of Democracy* 1 (Winter 1990): 55.

6. Linz, "Presidential or Parliamentary Democracy," p. 17.

7. Ibid., p. 18; Linz, "The Perils of Presidentialism," p. 56.

8. Linz, "Presidential or Parliamentary Democracy," p. 19.

9. Lijphart, *Democracies,* chapter 6.

10. Linz, "Presidential or Parliamentary Democracy," pp. 46, 47.

11. Donald L. Horowitz, "Comparing Democratic Systems," *The Journal of Democracy* 1 (Fall 1990): 73–79; and George Tsebelis, "Decision Making in Political Systems: Veto Players in Presidentialism, Parliamentarism, Multicameralism and Multipartyism," *British Journal of Political Science* 25 (1995): 289–325.

12. This statement rests on the assumption that the party itself remains united. If it does not, it may oust its leader and thereby change the prime minister, as happened to Margaret Thatcher in Britain and Brian Mulroney in Canada. Such intraparty crises of leadership are, however, the exception rather than the rule in majoritarian (Westminster) parliamentary systems.

13. A possible exception in Westminster systems occurs with the occasional minority government, which is more common than coalition government in such systems. But even then, early elections are as likely to be called by the government in attempt to convert its plurality into a majority as they are to be called as a result of a vote of no confidence. Kaare Strom, *Minority Government and Majority Rule* (Cambridge: Cambridge University Press, 1990).

14. Linz, "Presidential or Parliamentary Democracy," p. 15.

15. Using an average of three on both measures would have eliminated three countries (India and Colombia in Table 1 and Vanuatu in Table 3) that we consider basically democratic, but that have had problems with protecting civil rights, partly because of a fight against violent groups.

16. Robert A. Dahl, *Polyarchy: Participation and Opposition* (New Haven: Yale University Press, 1973), pp. 62–80; Kenneth Bollen, "Political Democracy and the Timing of Development," *American Sociological Review* 44 (August 1979): 572–87; Seymour Martin Lipset, "The Social Requisites of Democracy Revisited," *American Sociological Review* 59 (1994): 1–22.

17. Larry Diamond, "Introduction: Persistence, Erosion, Breakdown, and Renewal," in Larry Diamond, Juan J. Linz, and Seymour Martin Lipset, eds., *Democracy in Developing Countries: Asia* (Boulder: Lynne Rienner, 1989); Myron Weiner, "Empirical Democratic Theory," in Myron Weiner and Ergun Ozbudun, eds., *Competitive Election in Developing Countries* (Washington: American Enterprise Institute, 1987); Dietrich Rueschmeyer, Evelyne Huber Stephens, and John D. Stephens, *Capitalist Development and Democracy* (Chicago: University of Chicago Press, 1992).

18. Some British colonies later adopted presidential systems and did not become (or remain) democratic. However, in many cases, democracy was ended (if it ever got underway) by a coup carried out by the Prime Minister and his associates. These were not breakdowns of presidential democracies, but of parliamentary proto-democracies. Typical was the case of Seychelles. That most of these countries have not evolved back into democracy cannot be attributed to presidentialism.

19. Strom, *Minority Government and Majority Rule.*

20. Linz, "Presidential or Parliamentary Democracy," pp. 10–14.

21. Matthew Shugart, "Strength of Parties and Strength of Presidents: An Inverse Relationship," forthcoming.

22. In Latin America, only the Argentine, Brazilian and Colombian presidents have the ability to issue new laws by decree on practically any policy area.

23. Przeworski, et al., "What Makes Democracies Endure?", found that the combination of presidentialism and a high degree of party system fragmentation was not propitious to stable democracy.

24. Arend Lijphart, "Presidentialism and Majoritarian Democracy: Theoretical Observations," in Linz and Valenzuela, eds., *The Crisis of Presidential Democracy.*

25. The key issue here is whether or not parties are disciplined, and nothing guarantees that they are in parliamentary systems. Nevertheless, the need to support the government serves as an incentive to party discipline in parliamentary systems that is absent in presidential systems. See Leon Epstein, "A Comparative Study of Canadian Parties," *American Political Science Review* 58 (March 1964): 46–59.

26. The number of effective parties is calculated by squaring each party's fractional share of the vote (or seats), calculating the sum of all of the squares, and dividing this number into one.

27. Arturo Valenzuela, "Party Politics and the Crisis of Presidentialism in Chile: A Proposal for a Parliamentary Form of Government," in Linz and Valenzuela, eds., *The Failure of Presidential Democracy: The Case of Latin America,* pp. 91–150.

28. Shugart and Carey, *Presidents and Assemblies;* Mark P. Jones, *Electoral Laws and the Survival of Presidential Democracy* (Notre Dame: University of Notre Dame Press, 1995).

29. Giovanni Sartori, "Neither Presidentialism nor Parliamentarism" in Linz and Valenzuela, eds., *The Crisis of Presidential Democracy.*

30. James W. Ceaser makes a similar argument in "In Defense of Separation of Powers," pp. 168–93 in Robert A. Goldwin and Art Kaufman, eds., *Separation of Powers – Does It Still Work?* (Washington, D.C.: American Enterprise Institute, 1986).

8

The Evolution of Latin American Party Systems

Michael Coppedge

In the aftermath of Independence, almost all of the new nations of Latin America were divided by the same cleavage—liberals versus conservatives. Conservatives were more likely to be *peninsulares*, to own land, to defend the Church's property and corporate privileges, and to favor a strong central government and state regulation of trade. Liberals were more likely to be *criollos*, to engage in commerce or the professions, to resent the Church's property and privileges, and to favor a weaker federal government that allowed free trade. The relative salience of these issues varied from country to country, and in a few cases some of the positions were reversed, but for the most part this was the basic cleavage of Latin American politics, even if the Liberals and Conservatives were called by different names in some countries.

Contemporary Latin American party systems, however, no longer reflect this original or traditional cleavage except in Colombia and Uruguay.[1] Class cleavages are reflected in Chile and to a partial degree in Argentina; Venezuela, Mexico, and Costa Rica contain a cleavage between a large multiclass party and the opposition to it; and most of the other countries (Brazil, Peru, Bolivia, Ecuador) have such volatile party systems that it is difficult to identify what the principal cleavage might be.[2] These party systems differ greatly in other respects as well. In some, the political culture welcomes the pluralism of party competition while in others, each of the major parties considers itself the sole legitimate representative of the people or the national interest. In some, parties are poorly institutionalized and relatively unimportant to the political process; in others, parties have acquired such strength and importance that the political system is criticized as being a *partidocracia* rather than a *democracia*.

This paper explains why contemporary Latin American party systems are so diverse in spite of their common point of departure in the nineteenth century conflict between liberals and conservatives. While a full explanation of the many minor differences in party systems—the nature of the smaller parties, major parties' success in particular elections, etc.—would require a detailed political history of each country, the most obvious and most interesting differences—which cleavage divides the major parties, how legitimate the role of the opposition is, and how well institutionalized the parties are—can be explained by just two factors. The first is the nature of the political order (if any) that was achieved before the expansion of political participation to the middle and lower classes. This order (or disorder) left a legacy of cleavages, culture, and institutions that shaped the environment in which aspiring party leaders built organizations, defined issues, and competed for votes once that crucial threshold had been passed. The second factor is the timing of the expansion of participation, which constrained the possibilities for recruiting supporters at the time the new mass parties were being founded.

This explanation is supported by a brief comparative political history of eleven Latin American countries. It is similar to Lipset and Rokkan's comparison of cleavage structures and party systems in Western Europe in the set of questions it addresses, its historical focus, and its emphasis on crucial thresholds and the possibilities for alliances among social groups.[3] As Robert Dix has observed, the history of Latin America differs from that of Western Europe in several ways that require a modification of their explanatory framework before applying it to Latin America. First, Latin America lacked two cleavages that were present in several Western European countries: one between Catholics and Protestants, and another between a national and a subnational culture with a different language or religion. Thus there is little need to account for the origins of exclusively Protestant, Catholic, ethnic, or regional parties in Latin America.[4] Second, political instability in Latin America has interrupted both democracy and party development, creating a discontinuous pattern of evolution.[5]

Dix further argues that Latin America differs from Western Europe in that parties are typically catchall parties rather than "class-mass" parties. In this generalization there is some truth, but more error. Only eleven of the twenty-three parties Dix mentions by name fit his full definition of a catchall party. While it is true that many of the others possess a few catchall-like characteristics, the desire to identify a "Latin American type" of party leads Dix to downplay important differences in the parties of the region. And rather than explain these differences, as Lipset and Rokkan did, Dix merely attributes them to "the vagaries of political history."[6] This essay makes those vagaries less vague.

Substantively, however, this essay has more in common with Juan Linz's study of the party system of Spain than it does with Lipset and Rokkan's survey of other European countries.[7] As Linz noted, the Spanish party system of the nineteenth and early twentieth centuries did not fit Lipset and Rokkan's model. The nineteenth century was interrupted too often by civil wars, the "dynastic" Liberal and Conservative parties failed to organize a mass base of support, dictatorship undid what little party development had taken place by the 1920s, and the first attempt at mass democracy ended in polarization and civil war. Anyone familiar with Latin American history will immediately see parallels.

It should not be surprising that such strong parallels exist; rather than insisting on classifying Spain as a relatively backward European country, perhaps we should think of it as a relatively advanced Latin American one, the most advanced of twenty countries formed by the breakup of the Spanish Empire. In that spirit, this paper is an attempt to describe the dynamics of the alternative universe of party evolution to which the Spanish case belongs. Offering a broader range of possibilities than the countries of northern Europe, it is a universe in which radical discontinuities and lagging social development have a dramatic impact on what kinds of parties develop, when they develop, and whether they develop at all.

Overview

Before attempting to explain the characteristics of a party system, it is prudent to consider whether there is a party system there to be explained. A party system, at least in the sense intended in this essay, is more than a collection of parties; it is a collection of parties of a certain kind: parties that 1) are organized well enough to survive the loss of their most important leader, and 2) are able to rely on a core of strong party identifiers in the electorate, and therefore are not likely to disappear from one election to the next. A system of such parties is characterized by a fairly constant set of parties, whose share of the vote varies within roughly predictable limits. By this criterion, not all Latin American democracies have party systems; some merely have poorly institutionalized parties with a tenuous and fickle base of support. The first question to answer, therefore, is: what conditions are necessary for the development of party organizations and party loyalties?

One of the claims of this essay is that party systems became established only in countries where it was expected, at the time that mass parties were first being formed, that the new parties would play an important role in government. This expectation provided the necessary incentive for party leaders to invest their energies in building party organizations and recruiting a loyal base of support. Once these efforts bore fruit, partisan identification was passed down through families and friends by processes first described by Converse and thoroughly documented since then.[8] In these countries, organizations were able to outlast the founding generation of leadership, so parties became institutionalized.

Whether or not this crucial expectation existed was a function of that country's history up to that point. One favorable scenario, present in Chile, Costa Rica, Colombia, and Uruguay, occurred when embryonic parties, formed by elites before the expansion of electoral participation to the middle and lower classes, already played an important role in recruiting candidates, distributing patronage, and organizing the work of congress. This situation gave rise to the expectation that mass parties would perform similar functions. A second favorable scenario, present only in Venezuela, occurred when the country had no experience with democracy or parties whatsoever before participation was expanded. In this situation, the public's idealistic illusions about the role of parties in a democracy remained intact, untarnished by direct experience with sordid politicking, long enough for parties to become established.

If, however, embryonic parties had been too ephemeral, inconsistent, divided, or dependent on a regime or a founding leader to play an important role in the past, in the context of either a stable regime or general instability, then the public naturally expected that new parties would be similarly weak. This was the situation in Brazil, Ecuador, and Peru. Argentina and Mexico are intermediate cases, and Bolivia is an exception due to the extreme disruptions of the Chaco War, which divided the old aristocratic regime from the new era of mass politics. A companion argument to be advanced here is that some of the regimes preceding mass participation passed certain characteristics on to the emerging party systems—especially tendencies toward pluralism or hegemony.

Provided that there is party system, the next question is *which* cleavages does it reflect? The second claim of this essay is that the answer to this question depends in part upon what happened to the old cleavages that predated mass participation. Among the cases examined here, there were four different outcomes. In Colombia and Uruguay, the civil wars of the nineteenth century lasted so long that the middle and lower classes came to identify strongly with the traditional parties even before electoral participation was opened to them, so that this cleavage between liberals and conservatives became institutionalized in the competitive embryonic party system. In Chile the suffrage expanded gradually, allowing both sides to be successful at recruiting supporters among the new voters, but eventually this old cleavage lost its relevance to a greatly expanded electorate, and the old parties, facing marginalization, eventually merged.

In Argentina, Costa Rica, Mexico, and Venezuela, the liberals won on the battlefield long before the age of mass politics. Eventually the problem of how to incorporate the rising classes created a new cleavage, but in the meantime, political conflict consisted of nothing more than personal rivalries among elites within the liberal consensus. In the countries that never managed to establish party systems, the fate of the liberal vs. conservative cleavage is irrelevant. If it survived, it was eventually lost in the shuffle of other parties; if it was resolved, there was still instability from another source that prevented it from having any lasting impact on party formation.

Still, we cannot explain which cleavages a party system reflects until we know how the new cleavages came to be reflected by parties. The third claim of this essay is that parties reflect the issues that were most salient in society at the time that the parties were recruiting their initial base of support, and that these periods of new party growth coincide with the years of dramatic expansion of electoral participation. This claim is a logical extension of Converse's widely accepted model of increasing party identification.[9] If voters tend to inherit the party loyalties of their parents and become more partisan as they grow older, then the only way a new party can enter the system and grow is to appeal to voters who have not already formed a loyalty to an existing party. When political space is full, it is harder for new parties to enter the system.[10] New parties can grow only at the margins, picking up a few apathetic voters here, a few defectors there, a share of the voters who have just come of age, and some of the swing vote in any given election. Until some sort of crisis undermines voters' loyalties to their parties, the only way for a new party to grow suddenly and rapidly is for there to be a dramatic increase in the size of the electorate, which creates a large pool of uncommitted, first-time voters. This argument does not deny that there are swing voters and defectors; it assumes only that such crises are absent and these party switchers either cancel each other out or are few enough in number to make only marginal changes in the level of support a party receives. The comparative history presented below shows that over and over, in country after country, the established parties that survive today first grew large during periods in which electoral participation was expanding rapidly.

It is also logical for the content of this cleavage to reflect the important issues at the time of expanded participation, if one considers the matter from the perspective of aspiring party leaders. If participation is expanding gradually, the potential rewards for organizing are meager in comparison to the effort expended, so there is little incentive to start a new party. But if participation expands dramatically, comparatively little effort can bring in a great return, so many "political entrepreneurs" attempt to found parties. One of them is bound to succeed—the one who does the best job of defining the party's appeal in terms that resonate with the most salient concerns of the new voters; the one, in other words, who is most closely aligned with the cleavage of the day.

The pace of expansion also suggests how pragmatic or ideological a new party will be. The larger the pool of new voters, the more diverse they are likely to be, and the broader the party's appeal will have to be in order to take full advantage of this opportunity for growth. This would account for the narrowly ideological appeal of parties in Chile, where participation expanded gradually, as contrasted with the major multiclass or catchall parties of Venezuela and Bolivia, where participation exploded in 1945 and 1952, respectively.

A Conceptual Caveat

It is tempting to equate the expansion of participation with a relatively simple phenomenon, such as the extension of the suffrage or phases of incorporation of the middle class, followed by the working class, and then peasants. Such an approach would promise enticing (and familiar) hypotheses concerning middle-class parties, labor parties, and populism. The reality, however, is much too complex for that kind of analysis.

In the first place, the suffrage was not restricted or extended by class criteria, but by property, income, literacy, age, and sex. Property and income would coincide roughly with class, but not perfectly; literacy would only somewhat; and age and sex cut straight across classes. Each extension of the suffrage, therefore, released a heterogenous (with respect to class) group of new voters into the system, and the parties consequently recruited a heterogenous base of support. This is an important reason why it is hard to identify any party with a particular social class.

Second, there is more to participation than suffrage. Participation is also a question of the *ability* and *desire* to vote, on *one's own terms*. Therefore, in addition to simple extension of the suffrage, one needs to take into account: 1) the enforcement of voter eligibility, both denying it to those who are eligible and granting it to those who are not; 2) turn-out: sometimes an expansion of participation is manifested as a sudden increase of turnout sparked by some event—the secret ballot, an attractive candidate—that signals to many previously apathetic eligibles that now their vote will *matter*; and 3) intimidation of voters: voters who are intimidated into voting for a party do not form a genuine party loyalty to it. Results of such elections therefore do not necessarily reflect party loyalties faithfully.

Colombia and Uruguay

The analysis properly begins with two cases in which the traditional parties and cleavages of the nineteenth century survived into the twentieth—Colombia and Uruguay. The Liberals and Conservatives have dominated Colombian politics in this century, sharing more than 90 percent of the vote in every election before 1990 except 1970 and 1974.[11] Party politics in Uruguay has been dominated historically by the Colorado Party and the National Party (the Blancos). Before the emergence of the Frente Amplio in 1971, these two parties shared 90 percent of the vote.[12]

Both of these party systems reflect cleavages held over from the nineteenth century. The Colombian Liberals' ideals were anticlericalism, federalism, and free trade, while the Conservatives defended the Church and favored centralization and protectionism, although "these disputes became interwoven with personal, familial, and regional rivalries."[13] The only cleavage clearly expressed by the Uruguayan parties is an urban-rural one, since the Colorados have been disproportionately strong in Montevideo, and the Blancos in much of the interior, in line with their respective strengths in the last century. However, the Colorados also have had a mild tendency to be more anticlerical, statist, and strong among ethnic Italians and French (as opposed to Spanish), and therefore more classically liberal, than the Blancos.[14]

The origin of these parties is no mystery. The Liberals and Conservatives began as warring alliances of *caudillos* and their peasant militias dating from at least 1850, which frequently struggled for control of the central government in the nineteenth century.[15] Gradually, with numerous setbacks along the way, they transformed their competition into a struggle for votes, and in the process became political parties. Similarly, the Blancos and Colorados began as militias led by two *caudillos* of the 1830s and 1840s—Manuel Oribe and Fructuoso Rivera. Rivera's men were called Colorados because of the red armbands they wore, and Oribe's were called Blancos because of their white arm-bands.[16] All observers agree that these militias, organized even before a unified nation-state of Uruguay definitely existed, evolved over the course of the nineteenth and early twentieth centuries into the principal political parties of modern-day Uruguay.

What needs to be explained is why the cleavage expressed by these traditional parties survived when similar cleavages in most other Latin American countries were erased or displaced by other cleavages. There are two reasons—one common to both cases, and one that is peculiar to each case.

The common reason is that the two sides were more evenly matched in Colombia and Uruguay than in the rest of Latin America, and therefore they fought longer—into the twentieth century. In most other countries of the region, the fighting between liberals and con-servatives ended by the 1870s, usually because of a liberal victory. In Colombia, the Liberals dominated from 1863 to 1880, but the Conservatives regained control during the Regeneración of 1880–1910. After 1910 the Conservatives gradually opened their system to electoral participation by Liberals, which allowed the Liberals to dominate from 1930 to 1946, but not on a permanent basis, for the Conservatives returned to power in 1946 to 1953. And in 1948, *la violencia* began, ex-tending the violent struggle between the traditional parties at the local level into the National Front period (1958–1974), when a powersharing pact between the two parties finally brought their partisan war to an end (while other groups continue to fight other battles). Clearly, the Liberal vs. Conservative civil war lasted longer in Colombia than anywhere else in Latin America.

The Colorados in Uruguay, with the help of the British, French, and the Brazilians, gained control of Montevideo by 1851, but Blancos, entrenched in the interior and buttressed by Argentine support, could not be completely subdued, and continued to rise against the Colorados frequently the rest of the century.[17] In 1865, the Colorados recognized Blanco control of four interior departments, but fighting broke out again and by 1897 the Blancos had control of six departments.[18] Peace came only in 1904, when Colorado President José Batlle y Ordóñez won a relatively decisive victory over the Blancos after an eight month civil war and the Blancos agreed to end the fighting in exchange for a perma-nent share of power in a reorganized state.[19] While Colorado observers have interpreted Batlle's offer to share power with the Blancos as a purely magnanimous gesture, it was not a completely free choice. The Blancos may have been temporarily defeated in 1904, but they were still strong enough to recover and challenge future Colorado governments.

It was the Blancos' potential to renew the civil war endlessly that led Batlle to propose a powersharing arrangement.

In Colombia it was the prolonged and intense fighting that forged the public's strong identification with the two traditional parties and prevented other parties from displacing them. According to Kline there were more than fifty insurrections between 1853 and 1885, and eight civil wars totaling eleven years in the nineteenth century.[20] The "War of a Thousand Days" in 1899–1902 took 100,000 lives. As the fighting continued and more and more Colombians of all classes lost property, relatives, or their own lives, it became a feud between two national families, Liberals and Conservatives. Party loyalties were firmly rooted long before electoral participation was expanded. When that finally happened (1910–1936 for men, 1954 for women), Colombians naturally voted for their side in the feud. *La violencia* later reinforced these loyalties.

In Uruguay the fighting was not as bloody and did not involve as many people directly. To be sure, much of the population formed attachments to one side or the other during the decades of virtually constant civil war, whether or not they had any opportunity to vote for Blancos or Colorados in an election. In a country with fewer than one million inhabitants, it was hard for people to avoid taking sides in that kind of environment, especially during periods of prolonged tension, such as the nine year siege of Montevideo (1842–1851), when even the Italian and French immigrant communities formed militias to defend the city against the Blanco assault.[21]

However, the traditional parties would not have remained as dominant in Uruguay as they did in Colombia if it had not been for the early expansion of electoral participation, while the rivalry between the two camps was still fresh. Universal suffrage for males eighteen and older came in 1918, and at the same time the secret ballot was adopted and elections became indisputably fair. (Female suffrage followed in 1934 but, as elsewhere, had little impact on party formation.) Virtually everyone, therefore, who could possibly be called upon to vote for a party was given the vote at a time when the rivalry between Blancos and Colorados, the most salient cleavage during the previous two or three generations, was still fresh. It is quite understandable that most of them formed loyalties to those two parties and that those loyalties have changed only marginally since that time.

The manner in which party loyalties were formed also accounts for the relatively weak and factionalized party organizations in these two countries. With a large population of party faithful virtually guaranteed to support their party in elections (as well as an opposing camp that they could not hope to win over), there was little reason for politicians in either country to invest their time, energy, and wealth in developing a strong, disciplined party machinery. Their chief competitors were other politicians in their own party. Therefore, they devoted themselves to organizing their own cliques of personal loyalists, who form the basis for the factions that still permeate the traditional parties today.

Chile

The modern Chilean party system is often considered the most "European" system in Latin America. This is probably because it is a multiparty system that reflects two ideologically charged cleavages that are commonly found in European party systems—the Catholic-secular cleavage and the class cleavage.[22] There are two reasons for this pattern. First, the two cleavages were the most salient ones during the three periods of Chilean history in which political participation was expanding and party identities were being formed—1891–1915, 1917–1925, and 1958–1965. The second reason is that the political order that was achieved before the expansion of participation was pluralistic, and therefore any new parties that came into existence were simply added on to the previous party system. The traditional parties and traditional cleavages continued to exist alongside the new ones.

It is this second reason—the early achievement of a pluralistic political order—that sets Chile apart from the rest of Latin America. While Chile was institutionalizing parliamentary parties in a stable aristocratic republic, the rest of the region was consumed by *caudillismo* and civil wars lasting into the 1870s and beyond. Chile's unusual geography helped it escape a similar fate, for in a long, narrow coastal country, it was harder for a rebellious *caudillo* to establish a stronghold, and easier for the central government to assert its control over the national territory, especially since the bulk of the population was concentrated in the central valley. It also helped that the largely European population was united by the very real common threat of attack from the southern Araucanians, who were not completely subjugated until 1883. Chilean stability was further fostered by the wisdom of Diego Portales (whose 1833 constitution laid the groundwork for a strong central state) and the leadership of the successor to his de facto presidency, Manuel Bulnes, who brought the Portalian state into being. Bulnes succeeded in his undertaking because of the prestige he had won as the victorious general in the war against the Peru-Bolivia Confederation in 1839, and because of a generally prosperous economy.

Portales and Bulnes headed the conservative *pelucones* faction which, although it controlled the government until 1851, never completely excluded the faction of liberal *pipiolos* from the parliament. The political class was so small and so intertwined by marriage and economic interests that political conflict took on the character of a friendly competition rather than a life-or-death struggle. Bulnes himself married the daughter of a *pipiolo*, and the proportion of the members of parliament who were related by ties of blood, marriage, or *compadrazgo* began extraordinarily high and increased from 1834 to 1888.[23] The need for cooperation among different factions also increased during these years, as the original factions in the parliament fragmented repeatedly. The *pelucones* divided into clerical Conservatives and anticlerical Nationals in 1851, and the *pipiolos* divided into Liberals and Radicals when the latter favored coalition with President Montt's Nationals and the former opposed it. By 1871 the legitimacy of political opposition was recognized, understandable given the fact that factionalism had forced three of the four embryonic parties into the opposition by that year.

These parties remained parliamentary parties without a mass base of support before the civil war of 1891. The suffrage was extremely restricted in the beginning—limited to literate males twenty-five years and older who met income and property requirements. Only 0.01 percent of the population voted in the election of 1864.[24] The Radical Party promoted some extension of the suffrage believing that it stood to gain from middle-class participation, and the Conservative party at times cooperated, believing that the lower classes would side with the Conservatives on clerical issues. But these occasional measures, such as the elimination of the income requirement in 1885, had little effect, due to the presidents' determination to administer elections in their own favor.

Control of elections was one of the issues that caused the civil war between the presidency and the Congress in 1891.[25] One of the powers that was stripped from the presidency in the aftermath was the power to administer elections. This did not mean that elections became fair, only that the abuses were decentralized. Nevertheless, in some areas, particularly in the larger cities and the northern nitrate fields, Radicals had enough local strength to oversee elections and make sure that their candidates were elected. While electioneering in this era had more to do with buying votes than with persuading voters, it required an extra-parliamentary party organization, so the Parliamentary Republic of 1891–1925 became the context for the first expansion of participation, and therefore the first formation of mass party loyalties. The Radicals grew from twenty local assemblies in 1888 to 100 in 1919; in order to broaden their base of support, the Conservatives began organizing departmental assemblies after 1900, and the Liberals followed suit in 1906–1907.[26]

Participation expanded slowly, however. Even by 1915, only 5 percent of the population was eligible to vote in the congressional elections of that year.[27] Since participation expanded slowly and selectively, at the discretion of the traditional parties running elections in the departments they dominated, new parties did not emerge. Instead, the new voters formed loyalties to the traditional parties (including the Radical Party, which did become more important) and the old Catholic-secular cleavage was preserved. New parties were not added to the system until a new social group began to participate in electoral politics.

This new social group was, of course, the working class of miners, railway and port workers, and industrial labor. Their numbers increased rapidly after 1883, when Chile acquired rich nitrate fields from Peru and Bolivia in the War of the Pacific, attracting foreign investment and spurring the development of infrastructure. They became an increasingly large and militant force but shunned electoral and parliamentary politics during the early years, preferring to take direct action. The governments of the Parliamentary Republic, however, consistently met their strikes with brutal repression, which encouraged some leaders to try other avenues. At the same time, some elites began searching for ways to channel working-class discontent into more peaceful avenues. These complementary desires came to a head in 1917–1919 when the First World War disrupted nitrate exports and caused greater labor disruption than ever in the north, and brought down greater repression than ever.

Hoping to avert another such disaster, progressive Liberals and Radicals formed a Liberal Alliance that appealed for working-class support in the elections of 1918 and captured a majority in the Chamber of Deputies for six months. The leader of this majority, Arturo Alessandri, was then elected president with the support of Radicals, Democrats, and progressive Liberals in 1920. These successes encouraged labor leaders to support leftist political parties, and when they did, they found that the pluralist political institutions that had been built up by the elites were surprisingly open to them. The principal labor federation, the Workers' Federation of Chile (Federación Obrera de Chile—FOCh), in 1921 formalized ties to the Socialist Workers Party (Partido Obrero Socialista—POS) which in 1922 became the Communist Party (Partido Comunista de Chile—PCCh) and won representation in both houses of Congress. By 1924–1925, organized labor was committed to the electoral path to power.[28]

The parties that were formed when participation expanded during these last years of the parliamentary Republic carry their imprint to the present day. They are well organized, since the supremacy of Congress rewarded party discipline and effective electoral machines. They also reflect the cleavage of the day which was, without any doubt, the Social Question, that is, what to do about the inequality and class conflict that had been intensified by industrialization. This is why the Chilean party system expresses the class cleavage so clearly.

The rate of participation was still rather low, however. Even though the 1925 constitution abolished the property and income restrictions and lowered the voting age to twenty-one, the literacy requirement was still in place and was a substantial obstacle. Only 10–19 percent of the population was eligible to vote before 1958.[29] Several things happened in the 1950s, however, that dramatically expanded participation. First, female suffrage was granted in 1952, and women began streaming into the electorate in the late 1950s and early 1960s. Second, increasing numbers of peasants left the large agricultural estates and migrated to the large cities where they were finally free to vote for someone other than the *patrón's* candidate. Third, literacy rates were increasing—up to 75 percent in 1950—which contributed to the expansion of the electorate until the literacy requirement was abolished in 1972.[30] And finally, the secret ballot was introduced in 1958, making it possible for the peasants who were still on the large estates (and probably many others) to vote according to their consciences and form their own party identities for the first time.

Some of the existing parties flowed into this new political space, especially the Communist and Socialist parties, which grew gradually. But the party that benefited most dramatically was the one that best reflected the cleavage of those years—the Christian Democrats. Frightened by the extremism and atheism of the rising left in a Cold War environment, alienated by the traditional right's lack of compassion in the face of glaring poverty, and disgusted by the Radicals' tiring lack of principles, many Chileans, including many of the newly enfranchised, were looking for a Third Way, and Eduardo Frei promised one. His Christian Democracy did not add a new cleavage to Chilean politics so much as redefine an old one, the Catholic-secular cleavage, which was made to carry the Church's progressive social aims and oppose the secularism of the left rather than that of the Radicals and Liberals. By 1965, the PDC was the largest party in the Chamber of Deputies. It became a disciplined and well-organized party like the others, perhaps even more than the others, driven by its belief that it could become the majority party of Chile.[31]

Three decades later, there has been less change in the Chilean party system than one might expect after a sixteen year military interregnum. This should not be surprising. By 1973, Chile's parties were well established and their supporters identified with them strongly (though less with the Radicals). These partisan identities change on a timescale of generations, not years, and Pinochet, for all his tenacity, was not in power long enough to erase them completely. One should expect only incremental change in such a party system, barring any great expansion of participation, and that kind of expansion has been impossible since the 1960s when elections and registration became fair and universal adult suffrage was achieved.[32]

Costa Rica

In recent years, Costa Rica has appeared to have a nearly two-party system in which the nominally social democratic Party of National Liberation (PLN) is pitted against the Social Christian Unity Party (PUSC). The PLN is definitely a strong, well-institutionalized political party. The PUSC, however, formally became a party only in 1984; before that, it was a series of coalitions built from smaller, largely personalist parties. The two-party label is therefore misleading. It would be more accurate to say that Costa Rica has an old party system nested inside a new one, for the PLN is the product of the Revolution of 1948–1949; the parties that make up the PUSC belong to an earlier tradition of party formation rooted in the politics of the nineteenth century.

The first phase of party organization in Costa Rica occurred during the Liberal Republic, a long period of stable civilian rule (1890–1948) interrupted only by a brief dictatorship in 1917–1919. Electoral participation expanded from a tiny minority of the coffee elite in the 1830s to 10–15 percent of the population in 1928.[33] A variety of measures made this expansion possible. Every government of the period is credited with expanding education and therefore increasing literacy; mutual-aid societies were organized after 1875, and multitrade guilds between 1890 and 1902, and both involved their members in politics; the franchise was extended between 1905 and 1914; presidents began to be elected directly in 1914, and peasants were allowed to run for municipal council; unionization spread among the still small working class in the 1920s; a National Election Council was established in 1925; the secret ballot was adopted in 1928; and voting became obligatory in 1936.

It is difficult to tell which of these measures had the greatest impact, or even whether participation expanded gradually or suddenly, but in this case, the pace of expansion had little consequence for the formation of party identities because the available parties did not inspire strong loyalties, except to personalities who failed to routinize their charisma. The only party that lasted throughout the Liberal Republic was the Republican Party, which was "a loosely organized electoral platform for liberal elite politicians...held together more by patronage than by program."[34] After 1930, the party's orientation depended on which charismatic figure happened to be leading it at the time. In 1936, conservative, antilabor León Cortés Castro gained control to serve the coffee barons. Rafael Calderón Guardia, who succeeded him as party leader, was his political opposite: a populist supported by reformist Catholics, organized labor, and the Communist Party.[35] This odd alliance of Catholics, labor, and the left survived into the 1960s but it is significant that they were known as Calderonistas, not Republicanos.

Personalism dominated the Liberal Republic because Costa Rica was so thoroughly liberal and there were no other significant cleavages. In a country that inherited few colonial interests, relative social equality, and a consensus in favor of promoting coffee exports, conservatism never had much of a foothold. Its last gasp was the clerical Catholic Union Party, which did not survive past the 1890s, despite an open society and free elections. Liberal reforms had been begun by nominally Conservative presidents Carrillo (1835–1842) and Mora (1849–1859), and finished by the Liberal Constitution of 1871 and the liberal "dictatorship" of Tomás Guardia (1870–1882).[36] In the midst of liberal consensus, the most important conflicts were personal rivalries. By the time new cleavages developed in society, the expectation that parties were little more than personalist vehicles hindered efforts to institutionalize strong parties with a mass base of support. The Reformist Party of the 1920s, for example, managed to mobilize a mass following but it disintegrated after 1924 when its founder Jorge Volio was coopted by an offer of the vicepresidency in a Republican administration.[37]

It took a revolution to make it possible for a different kind of party to become established in Costa Rica. That revolution occurred in 1948, when José Figueres and a rebel army of students, middle-class professionals, and organized workers took advantage of an electoral dispute between Calderón and publisher Otilio Ulate to start a civil war, seize power, and enact a series of deep social reforms for 18 months.[38] Figueres' National Liberation Junta (Junta de Liberación Nacional) became the National Liberation Party (Partido de Liberación Nacional, PLN) in 1951, during a rapid expansion of participation caused not by changes in eligibility but by increased motivation to participate due to the credible promises of fair elections following the establishment of the Supreme Electoral Tribunal in 1949 and the polarization of the civil war years. Voter turnout increased from 12.4 percent of the population in 1948 to 21.0 percent in 1953 and 29.7 percent in 1962.[39] The PLN has remained the most important party in the country ever since, to such a degree that the principal cleavage in Costa Rican politics since 1948 has been between the PLN's supporters and its adversaries.

Argentina

There are a number of fundamental differences between Argentina and the cases discussed so far that need to be highlighted at the beginning because they make for a very different style of party politics. First, Argentina has a true federal system. Most Latin American republics have had federalism on paper but in Argentina the provincial governors are powers to contend with and provinces guard their autonomy jealously, even to the point of having different electoral laws and provincial political parties. Second, the Argentine Congress has never been as important a body as the legislatures of Chile, Costa Rica, or Uruguay. Instead, presidents have always been accustomed to exercising broad executive powers, whether or not Congress approves, and sometimes whether or not their actions are constitutional. (Effective implementation of presidential decrees is, of course, another matter.) Third, the "corporate interests" of society—the military, the Church, cattlemen, financiers, and more recently, industrialists and organized labor—have from the beginning eclipsed political parties and Congress as agents of influence. Decisions are much more the result of informal negotiations between these interests and the president than of bargaining between the president and Congress.

All three of these characteristics—federalism, executive dominance, and corporate representation—have caused parties to be weaker in Argentina than in the cases discussed above. They are weaker in an organizational sense, being parties with at least a federal structure internally, and often an aura of separate but affiliated provincial parties considered part of their movement. This structure has promoted chronic factionalism among both Radicals and Peronists, culminating in several profound party splits. They are also weaker in the sense that party loyalties have been more focused on the party founders—Irigoyen and Perón—and less on the party itself, than in Chile, Costa Rica, Uruguay, or Colombia.

The Argentine party system has also been shaped by the regime that held power for a generation before the expansion of electoral participation. From 1880 to 1916, Argentina was governed by the leaders of single group, the National Autonomous Party (Partido Autonomista Nacional, PAN), which was not a true electoral party as much as it was the bureaucratic machine of a string of presidents who handpicked their own successors and their governors, who in turn handpicked congressmen and senators and had them ratified in tightly controlled elections with extremely limited participation.[40] Partly due to the regime's ability to coopt, and partly due to a strong cross-class consensus in favor of promoting the export economy, the PAN had virtually no electoral opposition. While this single party regime could not last forever, its success during at least twenty-five years fixed a powerful notion into the political culture of Argentina. This notion is that national consensus is possible, which means that opposition is at best misguided and at worst malicious, and in any case, illegitimate. Political organizations that have arisen since the PAN's *unicato* have therefore striven for complete hegemony even when that meant ignoring the rights of the opposition.

Thus the Radicals and the Peronists both deny that they are political parties and instead claim to represent the entire nation; the conservative regime of 1930–1943 engaged in fraud (except in 1940) to prevent the Radicals from winning; the Peronists amended the electoral law and the constitution in the late 1940s to deprive the Radicals of a fighting chance at elections; the Radicals acquiesced in the proscription of the Peronists from 1955 to 1973; and the military felt justified in banning all parties from 1976 to 1983 in the interest of national unity.

Because of these manipulations intended to achieve hegemony for one group or another, electoral results in Argentina have not always reflected party loyalties faithfully. It is only since truly competitive and unfettered elections began to be held in 1983 that election results confirmed what was obvious to most: that most Argentines are loyal to one of two political tendencies—radicalism or Peronism. These tendencies do not coincide perfectly with parties, because the parties have often been divided into different factions and have been organized as separate parties in some provinces. But the predominant loyalties to radicalism and Peronism have not changed greatly since the late 1940s. These are the loyalties to be explained here.

Radicalism took root in the first expansion of political participation, following the Sáenz Peña Law of 1912. Technically, the party had been founded in 1891, and its founders—Leandro Alem and Hipólito Irigoyen—had become active in politics as early as 1877, when they split from the PAN to form the shortlived Republican party (Partido Republicano).[41] But the Radical Civic Union (Unión Cívica Radical, UCR) did not succeed in winning a mass base of support in these early years. In fact, it was party policy to *abstain* from elections between 1892 and 1912, since Hipólito Irigoyen preferred to seek power through armed insurrections in 1890, 1893, and 1905 (all of which were defeated). The PAN had not recruited a mass base of loyalties either, since elections were simply unimportant to its dominance.

When President Roque Sáenz Peña decreed universal (eighteen years and older) male suffrage in 1912, and backed it up with permanent registration, the secret ballot, obligatory voting, and guaranteed representation of the minority party, political space was suddenly wide open, and the UCR moved rapidly to fill it between 1912 and 1930. In anticipation of an electoral opening, the party had begun organizing in 1906, so it had a head start on the other fledgling parties. This was one reason for its success in winning the support of the huge mass of new voters.

The other reason was that the UCR was most closely aligned with the cleavage of the day. All previous cleavages had been erased by the *unicato*. Upon Independence the nascent struggle between conservatives and liberals (called Demócratas at first) was quickly overwhelmed by a deeper struggle over federalism vs. centralism and over control of the Buenos Aires port revenues. The *unitario* advocates of centralism were defeated militarily by 1832, and Buenos Aires established its dominance over the interior provinces in 1861 when Mitre's Liberals defeated Urquizas' Federalists in the Battle of Pavón. After that, the only remaining issue was a hairsplitting dispute among Liberals over whether the province or the city of Buenos Aires should dominate the federation, and that issue was resolved when Julio Roca federalized the capital city in 1880.

The absence of cleavages made a long period of stability and economic growth possible, but it also cleared the way for the next emerging cleavage to polarize politics, and that cleavage swept away the PAN regime. That emerging cleavage pitted the oligarchy of ranchers producing for export against the middle class and small working class that had been created by decades of economic development and a flood of immigration. Their aspirations were diverse, but they had one demand in common—an end to political domination by the large landowning elite. The UCR had unassailable credentials as an intransigent opponent of the regime and issued an uncomplicated call for fair elections, broad suffrage, and honest administration. Typical of its platform was José Cantillo's claim that "the only program of the UCR is the restoration of the constitution and freedom of suffrage."[42] As the candidate appealing best to the least common denominator, Irigoyen in 1916 won the first presidential contest he entered, with 51.5 percent of the vote.

Peronism coincided with the second great expansion of participation, in the late 1940s. Although universal manhood suffrage had been achieved in 1918, there was still political space open for a new party because much of the population either had not identified strongly with radicalism the first time around, or had lost that identification in the intervening years. Many of the people who had voted for the UCR before 1930 did so more as a protest vote against the Conservatives than because of any positive identification with the party. Snow writes:[43]

> In spite of the electoral success of the Radicals after the adoption of the Sáenz Peña Law, it seems quite possible that many of the votes cast for UCR candidates were primarily a reaction against the Conservative rule which appeared to many to benefit only the upper classes. The UCR had very little competition for the vote of the middle and lower classes....In many areas there was virtually no choice for the voters who wanted to see the Conservative removed from office—the UCR offered them their only hope.

It is also very true that many of the UCR's middle-class supporters, who had voted it into power trusting its promises of moral renovation and honest administration, became disillusioned by the nepotism, corruption, and mediocre leadership of the Radical governments and were open to appeals by other parties by 1930.[44] Others may have despaired of a Radical return to power during the Patriotic Fraud years (1930–1943), when elections were stolen from the UCR repeatedly.

Another potential base of support was to be found among immigrants and their descendants. While most immigration occurred in the nineteenth century, the first generation preferred direct action to electoral participation, and citizenship was required for suffrage.[45] Consequently, 55–60 percent of the adult male population was ineligible to vote even in 1912.[46] Since the percentage of the total population that was eligible to vote increased only gradually between 1912 and 1930, from 13 to 17 percent, there can be little doubt that there were a substantial number of first- and second-generation immigrants who had yet to form partisan loyalties by the end of the Radical Republic.

But participation exploded during Perón's first term as president (1946–1951). Before 1946, never had as much as 20 percent of the population voted in an election; in 1951, suddenly 45 percent of the population voted, a 137 percent increase in five years.[47] The extension of the suffrage to women in 1947 was probably responsible for doubling participation, but the remaining 37 percent increase can only represent the mobilization of previously inactive voters.

Peronism quickly occupied this newly available political space. Perón took advantage of his powers as minister of labor and president to attract as many supporters as possible. Many were won over, for example, by his "Aguinaldo Decree" during the presidential campaign of 1946, when he granted most of the workforce a 5–20 percent salary increase and an annual Christmas bonus equal to one month's pay.[48] Sticks were used along with the carrots, too. Union leaders who refused to affiliate with Perón's organizations in return for generous wage increases and benefits were removed by the labor ministry and replaced by new leaders loyal to Perón.[49] In this way, Perón accomplished a nearly complete takeover of organized labor, which remains predominantly Peronist to this day.

The appeal of Peronism is not now, and was not then, limited to organized labor. While the probability of being a Peronist is higher at the lower income levels, Peronism is well represented in all classes and sectors of Argentine society.[50] The original Peronist coalition, therefore, could not have been united by any common economic interest. Many Peronists were, rather, attracted by the personality of Juan Domingo Perón and by his vague rhetoric of *justicialismo*, which blended elements of anti-imperialism, national solidarity, and social justice. Only vague rhetoric and personal charisma could have held together the diverse coalition that remained to be politicized in Argentina. The reliance on personal appeals also prevented the formation of a strong party organization. Since Perón's exile in 1955, and especially since his death in 1974, Peronism has been a deeply, sometimes violently, divided movement.

Still, Peronism and radicalism survive as political tendencies with which the bulk of the Argentine electorate identifies. No major new parties have arisen since the late 1940s, and it is unlikely that any will soon, as Peronism and radicalism have almost completely filled the available political space.

Mexico

In view of the tremendous differences between the Argentine and Mexican party systems today, it is perhaps surprising to note that these two countries evolved along similar paths prior to the expansion of participation. In both countries, the liberals won the civil wars following Independence and established a hegemonic civilian regime that lasted more than a generation. In Argentina, it was the PAN's *unicato*; in Mexico, it was Díaz's Porfiriato (1876–1911).

Two legacies of this resolution of the liberal-conservative conflict were the same in Mexico as they were in Argentina. First, the cleavages of the nineteenth century were erased from Mexican political life. The original conservative vs. liberal cleavage aligned monarchists, centralists, protectionists, and defenders of the Church's property and authority against republicans, federalists, free traders, and anticlericals.

The dream of a monarchy died abruptly when Iturbide's delusions of grandeur bankrupted the government in 1822.[51] The conflict over the Church's property fizzled out as both sides expropriated it and sold it off to pay for the civil wars. The period of liberal dominance known as La Reforma then restricted the Church's authority over marriages, burial, and other rites, and enacted hard-to-reverse liberal economic and social policies.[52] The federalism vs. centralism issue became moot until Díaz, by force and cooptation, was able to establish the authority of the national government in the entire territory of the nation. Porfirio Díaz inherited a nation whose cleavages had been scoured away by civil war, an important reason why he was able to maintain order for the next thirty-five years and preside over a long period of economic recovery and growth.

Another consequence of the Porfiriato that parallels the Argentine case is the desire for hegemony and intolerance of opposition. Díaz faced virtually no opposition for many years; the PRI until recently expected the same. Of course, Mexico's leaders actually achieved hegemony, while for the various Argentine aspirants hegemony had to remain an unfulfilled dream. The reason for this difference is that the Porfiriato ended in a revolution, while the *unicato* ended in a relatively smooth transition to a fairly democratic regime. The causes of the Mexican Revolution were many and complex, but in comparison with Argentina one cause stands out: the Díaz regime was not institutionalized enough to have routinized presidential succession. The PAN's rule was stable, and had solved this question by allowing the incumbent to choose his successor, subject to ratification in a pro forma election. The expanded suffrage only modified an established practice. The Mexican regime was also stable, but it was a personal dictatorship. When Díaz abandoned the presidency, his regime collapsed, and the power vacuum was filled by civil war.

The consequences of the Revolution for the Mexican party system were profound. After more than a decade of fighting, the forces of Calles and Obregón emerged from the rubble to establish virtually uncontested control over the country. Any groups that had not been completely subjugated by military force, such as organized labor and a few regional caudillos, were soon coopted. Because it was thoroughly in control, the "Revolutionary Family" was able to use state resources to create an official party (PNR, the PRM, and finally the PRI of 1946 to the present) that was from its founding the dominant party in Mexico.

"Participation" was expanded preemptively in Mexico, into an overwhelmingly poor and uneducated population. Only a tiny middle class had even asked for effective suffrage; the mass of the population had not, though many of them had asked for land, wage increases, or the spoils of war. The official party formulated its appeal to reach all of these groups, and succeeded in obtaining their votes, but elections have never been fair enough to inspire genuine party loyalty in much of the electorate. What party loyalty the PRI enjoys had different origins. First, the intense fighting of the Revolution, which cost 1,000,000 lives, created strong loyalties within the Sonoran clique that eventually prevailed and later launched the official party. Second, a different kind of loyalty was generated by Lázaro Cárdenas' land reform, interventions in labor disputes, and expropriations of the railroads and the foreign oil companies. Thus the PRI (until 1988) possessed enough genuine loyalty to make its victories plausible, even if its margin of victory was not. But a true party system has not yet taken shape in Mexico and cannot take shape until the PRI is willing to accept its own electoral defeat. Only then will voters form loyalties to other parties.

Venezuela

The evolution of the Venezuelan party system is simple to explain, for there were no significant parties before the 1940s. The absence of parties was due to the absence of meaningful elections in which parties might participate; in their place was a dynasty of military dictators who maintained an unbroken line of Andean hegemony from 1899 to 1945. The dictator who ruled the longest, Juan Vicente Gómez (1908–1935), controlled opposition by banning it altogether: potential opponents were imprisoned, exiled, or murdered, so parties did not have a chance to form during his twenty-seven year rule. His successor, General López Contreras, experimented briefly with liberalization, but when it led to a general strike in 1936, he renewed the repression. General Medina Angarita (1940–1945), however, was more committed to liberalization, and it was during his government that party (and union) organizing really began. Organizational activity therefore took place in an organizational vacuum, which meant that virtually the entire adult population was open to the appeals of the party that best expressed the cleavage of the moment—the yearning for democracy.[53]

The chance to make those appeals came in 1945, when the Democratic Action party (Acción Democrática, AD) joined with junior military officers to seize power from General Medina. They established a Revolutionary Junta that expanded suffrage completely all at once: men and women, literate or not, propertied or not, were given the vote. They were also given two chances to exercise their suffrage—constituent assembly elections in 1946, and presidential and legislative elections in 1947. AD won both votes overwhelmingly. Like the UCR in

1916, it had the advantage of championing the winning side of a new cleavage, in an environment wiped clean of old cleavages:[54]

> The peasant, who by the simple act of joining Acción Democrática found himself able to call the Jefe Civil or Comisario 'compañero,' believed that in reality the country was divided between the Partido del Pueblo [AD], the party of the people who wore sandals, and those who had traditionally governed.

According to Bunimov-Parra, AD identified itself with democracy with such great success that in the elections of 1946 and 1947, a vote for AD was considered a vote for democracy and a vote for anyone else was a vote for a return of the old dictatorships.[55]

Having grown up under a hegemonic regime, the leaders of AD sought to establish their own hegemony. Working in an organizational vacuum and from a position of power, AD's leaders quickly came close to achieving hegemony. But their very success created a new cleavage dividing AD's supporters from those who feared that Venezuela had escaped from a military dictatorship only to be ruled by a party dictatorship. The Catholic Church and other opponents of AD funneled support to one party, COPEI, which was able to occupy much of the remaining political space before it was filled up by other parties. During this period of initial party organization (1945–1948, known as the Trienio), COPEI had a definite conservative and Catholic mentality, but really the nature of the opposition party was defined in reaction to AD's bid for dominance from which to secularize the state and impose radical social reforms. Even though both parties became very pragmatic, moved toward the center, and learned to seek consensus, and the original cleavage between them meant little, they became the largest parties by far and shared 80–90 percent of the vote from 1973 to 1989.[56] Thus it was the cleavage of the Trienio that survived. One could also say that the legacy of hegemony persisted for, even though AD had to share power with other parties, the "establishment" parties *jointly* established their hegemony over political life at the expense of most nonparty organizations, leading to charges of *partidocracia*.

Volatile Party Systems

The seven countries discussed to this point are the only major ones in which party systems have become institutionalized. In the other major countries of Latin America—Peru, Bolivia, Brazil, and Ecuador—party loyalties are not as firm and not as widespread and as a result, election results are often marked by discontinuities: victories by electoral novices, devastating defeats for parties that had seemed to be important, and a high turnover in the roster of parties winning representation in Congress. The only consistent explanation for this common trait is a negative one: these countries lacked the advantageous experiences undergone by the other seven countries before the expansion of participation to the middle and lower classes. Unlike Chile and Costa Rica, they lacked a period of institutionalized protoparty competition immediately prior to expansion. Unlike Argentina, Mexico, and Venezuela, no stable hegemonic regime had been in power in that crucial period. And unlike Colombia and Uruguay, the wars between liberals and conservatives either did not take place or ended too long before the expansion of participation to permit the survival of the traditional cleavages.

These countries that failed to institutionalize some kind of political order before the expansion of participation were not prepared to handle the new cleavage and the result was that the problem of how to incorporate the new social groups merely complicated the search for order. In the ensuing cycle of democratic and authoritarian governments, the incentives for organizing permanent political parties were negligible, hopelessly complicating discussions of which cleavages are expressed in party systems that change so rapidly.

Peru

Peru is an apt illustration of the pattern described above. Peruvian history is the story of a fruitless search for stability:[57]

The country's longest period of uninterrupted rule (constitutional or otherwise), the Aristocratic Republic, lasted for only nineteen years (1895–1914). During the twentieth century, the common pattern has been alternation between constitutional and de facto rule every five to twelve years. Overall, between independence in the early 1820s and 1985, approximately two-thirds of Peru's presidents have been military, ruling for almost 100 of those 160 years.

The first mass participation occurred in 1931 when Luis Sánchez Cerro, riding a wave of popularity after ending eleven years of dictatorship under Augusto Leguía, defeated Víctor Raúl Haya de la Torre of the APRA in a presidential election. The election was relatively fair, and turnout was 20 percent of the adult population, double the level of participation in any previous election.[58] If regular elections had continued and the suffrage had continued to expand, 1931 might have been the beginning of a party system. But Haya repudiated the election results (apparently without cause); Sánchez Cerro exiled all of APRA's congressmen; APRA seized Trujillo, killing sixty army officers; the army retaliated by killing 1,000 to 2,000 Apristas; and an Aprista assassinated Sánchez Cerro in 1933. This was not an auspicious beginning for mass party politics.

It was, rather, the beginning of a fifty year feud between APRA, on the one hand, and the oligarchs and the military on the other. The results of the 1936 election were annulled because of a strong showing by APRA, the party was banned altogether from 1948 to 1956, and coups were staged in 1962 and 1968 partly to prevent Haya from becoming president. This was not the ideal environment for the development of an electoral party but the atmosphere of violence and persecution did create strong loyalties to APRA, much the same as the intense fighting in Colombia created deepseated loyalties to Liberals and Conservatives.

It is hardly surprising that other parties were not encouraged to recruit loyal followers, especially in view of the fact that the suffrage remained relatively restricted until very late. Illiterates could not exercise the right to vote until 1980. Less than half of a sample of Peruvian urban residents, and 5–6 percent of a sample of peasants, considered themselves party members, compared to two-thirds of a similar sample of lower-class Chileans.[59] The low levels of party identification show up in extreme electoral volatility. AP, for example, which is the vehicle of two-time president Fernando Belaúnde Terry, dropped from 45.4 percent of the presidential vote in 1980 to 7.3 percent in 1985. APRA itself dropped from 53 percent in 1985 to 22 percent in 1990. Most notorious, however, is the case of President Alberto Fujimori, who won 29 percent of the vote in the first round of the 1990 elections and 56 percent in the runoff, even though he was completely unknown six weeks before.

Bolivia

Bolivia might have had a chance at developing a party system if the Chaco War had not intervened. Oligarchic parties had been developing during a long and relatively stable period of civilian rule from 1884 to 1932. The suffrage was restricted to 2–3 percent of the population and elections were won by the best-armed group (though usually without fighting), but under the successive rule of the Conservatives, Liberals, and Republicans, Congress and the elite protoparties inside it came to play an important role in government.[60]

This system came crashing down in the wake of the Chaco War which President Salamanca foolishly provoked to strengthen his support in Congress. When the war left 65,000 dead for no good reason, the traditional parties were completely discredited and any legacies of the past regime were wiped away, ushering in two decades of great instability and political ferment, for the war had also taken many mestizos and Indians from their homes and led them to question the arrangements under which they had been living. This was a time when many new parties were founded, but it was unfortunately an environment that did not encourage aspiring party leaders to take the electoral path to power. The MNR, for example, founded in 1941, plotted to take power by force with the assistance of junior military officers.[61]

Their plot succeeded in 1952. It was during the MNR-led Bolivian Revolution that electoral participation expanded dramatically, from 120,000 voters in 1951 to 958,000 in 1952, and the timing of this expansion explains why the MNR is the only party from that period that survives today. However, today's MNR is a shadow of its former self, after chronic fragmentation during the Revolution and proscription and cooptation by a string of mostly military governments between 1964 and 1982. This inherently unstable environment has not only not provided the necessary incentives for party organization, it has at times violently discouraged party organization. Participation is still very low; only 17 percent of the total population voted in 1980 despite the fact that illiterates have been eligible to vote since 1952.[62]

Ecuador

Ecuador has been, over the last century and a half, the most consistently unstable country in Latin America. Periodic fighting between liberals and conservatives lasted almost into the twentieth century, but ended long before the expansion of participation, which came very late. Illiterates were not enfranchised until 1978 and did not actually vote until 1984. The Liberals won the civil war of 1895–1896, after which the Conservatives never governed again, but the Liberals did not establish order. Rather, they fought among themselves, especially during the 1911–1916 civil war between Eloy Alfaro and Leonidas Plaza. After 1925, the military began intervening on its own in politics, with the result that there were twenty-seven governments between 1925 and 1948.[63] There was a brief oasis between 1948 and 1961, when three elected presidents served out their terms, but the overwhelming fact of Ecuadorian politics has been instability and, therefore, political parties have hardly organized.

Instead of party politics there is a politics of personality, epitomized by the career of José María Velasco Ibarra, a charismatic orator elected president in 1933, 1944, 1952, 1960, and 1968—and allowed to finish his term only once. Velasco had no real party, only a varying coalition of opportunistic groups who supported his presidential candidacies, hoping to share in the spoils of office, and who then deserted him and disbanded after the election. It is common for congressmen to change their party affiliation after the election. These practices are so well-known that some parties are known as "taxi parties"—hired for a ride to the presidential palace and then vacated to serve as a vehicle for someone else.[64] Velasco was not the only president to be abandoned by the parties who supported his candidacy: Jaime Roldós lost seventeen of his twenty-nine CFP congressmen to an opposition faction within a year of taking office, and Febres Cordero suffered from similar political isolation.

Brazil

Brazil is probably the best-known example of a poorly institutionalized party system. Politicians negotiate their candidacies with several parties or alliances of parties, then switch parties after they are elected; legislative discipline is unknown; and the party system changes dramatically from one election to the next.[65] This reality is somewhat surprising in view of the fact that the country enjoyed forty-one years of stability during the Old Republic (1889–1930), when an aristocratically dominated political system became fairly institutionalized. The reason why this promising start did not culminate in established mass parties was that there was little true expansion of participation either during the Old Republic or immediately after it. Expanded participation was postponed by a government that in the interim sabotaged party development for decades to come—Vargas and his Estado Novo.

Technically, suffrage had been extended to literate males over twenty-one already in 1891, but with elections administered by state oligarchs in a system in which it was understood that the presidents from São Paulo and Minas Gerais would look the other way, it was ludicrous to contemplate winning power in an election; therefore parties did not organize during the Old Republic. The rising middle class in São Paulo began to clamor for the secret ballot by 1930, so Vargas granted it in 1933, along with voting rights for eighteen to twenty-one year-olds and women; and then proceeded to ban parties and elections four years later.[66] Effective suffrage, therefore, came into being only in 1945, when Vargas was forced to step down and hold elections.

Before stepping down, however, Vargas asked his governors to organize the PSD, and his Labor Minister to organize the PTB. These two parties won all but one of the elections held between 1945 and 1964, but they did not make much of an effort to organize in a way that would establish strong party loyalties. That is, they paid little attention to platforms, programs, promises, or to recruiting cadres who would recruit likeminded supporters throughout the nation. Instead, the PSD simply asked the governors to get out the vote in the traditional clientelistic style of the *coroneis*, while the PTB relied on its network of coopted official labor leaders to mobilize their union members. People who voted for these parties did so to support their local leader, not because of any identification with the party or its symbols.

The electoral laws of the Second Republic, some inherited from the Old Republic and some adopted in 1945, encouraged crossparty alliances and the independence of candidates from parties, and rewarded small regional parties.[67] This was the immediate reason for the fragmentation and indiscipline of the party system. These laws guaranteed that any other parties that developed would have predominantly regional strengths, like the PSP and even UDN.

There was a deeper cause, however, for both the electoral rules and the paternalistic cooptation practiced by the PTB and PSD. Both were deliberate strategies adopted by the upper class to prevent genuine participation by the lower classes. As long as these new groups were either under the tutelage of state-sponsored organizations or atomized into localities easily manipulated by the local bosses, the vested interests of the upper class were safe. It was when some labor groups dared to assert their autonomy and Goulart began to talk about mobilizing the peasants that the military put an end to the Second Republic and its party system.   Needless to say, twenty-one years of authoritarian government did little to further the development of a party system. In 1965, the military forced the politicians it found acceptable into an artificial two-party mold but when the mold was lifted in 1979, they discovered that the solution had not gelled. Since then, the party system has veered erratically from extreme fragmentation to PMDB dominance to the rise of the PT and the near demise of the PMDB. After the overnight emergence of President Collor, one wonders whether party leaders will ever have any incentive to build grassroots organizations; it is so much easier to appeal directly to the voters on television.

Summary

Figure 8.1 summarizes the main points of the argument detailed in the preceding pages. The principal distinction to be made among the party systems of Latin America is between the established systems — Colombia, Uruguay, Chile, Costa Rica, Argentina, Mexico (with some qualifications), and Venezuela — and the chaotic systems — Peru, Ecuador, Bolivia, and Brazil. A necessary condition for the creation of an established party system was the institutionalization of some kind of political order prior to the expansion of electoral participation to the middle and lower classes. Where this order was either never achieved, as in Peru and Ecuador, or destroyed just prior to the expansion of participation, as it was by the Chaco War in Bolivia and the Estado Novo in Brazil, the environment was too unsettled to make the organization of political parties a worthwhile enterprise. Moreover, these systems were repeatedly unbalanced by the demands of the newly activated social groups, so the cycle of instability continued. The elite political culture was infused by a fear of the masses and by personal rivalries among elite leaders, mediated by military force.

Elsewhere, order was achieved in time, but the different ways in which order was achieved affected the kinds of party systems that subsequently evolved. In the Argentine *unicato*, the Mexican Porfiriato, and the dynasty of Andean dictators in Venezuela, the heirs of nineteenth century liberalism established their hegemony. It became possible to establish parties in these countries but they carried with them the legacy of a hegemonic political culture, whether it was the hegemony of party vs. party (Argentina and Mexico) or parties vs. society (Venezuela). Liberals and Conservatives (or their Colorado and Blanco equivalents) were more evenly matched in Colombia and Uruguay, but loyalty to the two sides permeated the population during the long civil wars so completely that it became possible for the elites eventually to channel their conflict into electoral competition without the danger of losing power to the middle or lower classes. The traditional cleavage was thereby preserved (and enforced, to the exclusion of third parties for decades) in the party system, although it was composed of parties that never felt the need to organize at the grass roots, due to the strong preexisting loyalties in the population. In Chile and Costa Rica, the wars did not last long enough to instill liberal or conservative loyalties in the larger population; instead, for various reasons elites learned to handle their conflicts peacefully among themselves, before mass participation began. Embryonic parties came to play

Figure 8.1 The Evolution of Party Systems in Latin America

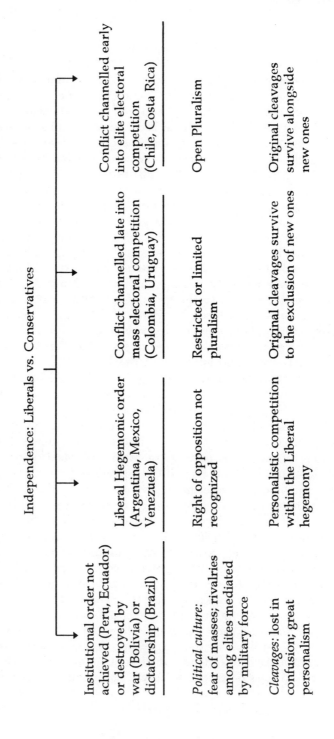

Independence: Liberals vs. Conservatives

Institutional order not achieved (Peru, Ecuador) or destroyed by war (Bolivia) or dictatorship (Brazil)

Political culture: fear of masses; rivalries among elites mediated by military force

Cleavages: lost in confusion; great personalism

Liberal Hegemonic order (Argentina, Mexico, Venezuela)

Right of opposition not recognized

Personalistic competition within the Liberal hegemony

Conflict channelled late into mass electoral competition (Colombia, Uruguay)

Restricted or limited pluralism

Original cleavages survive to the exclusion of new ones

Conflict channelled early into elite electoral competition (Chile, Costa Rica)

Open Pluralism

Original cleavages survive alongside new ones

Institutional development: chaotic: few organized parties; clientelistic networks	Organizations are either officialist (Mexico, Argentina) or non-existent (Venezuela)	Strong party loyalties without effective organizations	Institutionalized elite organizations
		BEFORE EXPANSION OF POLITICAL PARTICIPATION	
		Colombia: loyalties established by violent civil war, 1830–1960s → Liberals vs. Conservatives	*Costa Rica:* sudden expansion in 1948–1962 → PLN, a multiclass alliance
		Uruguay: early (1918) expansion on heels of civil war freezes loyalties → Colorados vs. Blancos	
		AFTER EXPANSION OF POLITICAL PARTICIPATION	
Peru, Ecuador, Bolivia, Brazil: participation aggravates preexisting problems, so chaos continues, undermining incentives for organizing political parties. Low levels of party identification	*Argentina:* two-step expansion; 1912–1930 → UCR 1946–1951 → Peronism		Chile: gradual expansion → multiparty system reflecting old Catholic-secular and new class cleavages
	Venezuela: sudden expansion; 1945–1948 → AD, COPEI		
	Mexico: sudden expansion through revolution → PRM/PNR/PRI, but political space not yet full		

an important role in political life, which created the expectation that mass parties would also.

This institutional and cultural context was only a necessary condition for the establishment of a party system (except in Colombia, where the extreme violence of the civil wars was sufficient to establish party loyalties). Sufficient conditions for the creation of new parties existed only when the suffrage was broadened and the newly enfranchised were moved to vote and free to do so on their own terms. These conditions emerged at different times and rates in different countries. In Chile, it was a gradual, phased process that led to the formation of many rather small parties that added the class cleavage to the old Catholic-secular cleavage. In Argentina, it was a two-step process, first creating the Radical Civic Union in the wake of the Sáenz Peña law of 1912, and then the Justicialist Party during the mobilizing excitement of Perón's first term as president. In Uruguay, participation expanded very rapidly after 1918, but since it took place less than a generation after the end of the civil wars, it had the effect of freezing the traditional cleavage between Blancos and Colorados. In Costa Rica and Venezuela, participation expanded very suddenly also, but long after the resolution of the liberal-conservative conflict. This led to the creation of large multiclass or catchall parties (PLN and AD) and soon afterward, a major opposition party galvanized by the threat of one-party dominance (PUSC and COPEI). In Mexico, the sudden social mobilization during the Revolution also led to the formation of a broad multiclass (middleclass/labor/peasants) party, but because it was formed so early in the country's social development, and during a tumultuous time when the need for order predominated, it was both possible and desirable for the PNR/PRM/PRI to favor controlling mobilization over genuine participation in fair elections with the result that much of the Mexican electorate has not yet formed a party loyalty.

Notes

1. Robert Dix and McDonald and Ruhl add Paraguay and Honduras to the list of party systems in which the traditional cleavage is preserved. See Robert H. Dix, "Cleavage Structures and Party Systems in Latin America," *Comparative Politics* (October 1989): 23–27 and Ronald H. McDonald and J. Mark Ruhl, *Party Politics and Elections in Latin America* (Boulder: Westview Press, 1989).

2. It should be understood that this essay seeks to explain only the *major* cleavages represented in Latin America's party systems, i.e., the pivotal issues that divide the *major* parties in each country. The "major" parties are meant to be the two or three largest parties which together win at least two-thirds of the vote.

3. Seymour Martin Lipset and Stein Rokkan, "Cleavage Structures, Party Systems, and Voter Alignments." in Lipset and Rokkan, *Party Systems and Voter Alignments: Cross-National Perspectives* (New York: The Free Press, 1967), pp. 1–64.

4. While there are many examples of parties with regional strengths or weaknesses (the Mexican PAN, most parties in Brazil, the Ecuadorean CFP), the only purely regional parties are found in Argentina, and they have always been too small to justify consideration here. Recently there have been presidential candidates who have had a notably Protestant Evangelical base of support (Fujimori in Peru, Ríos Montt and Serrano in Guatemala), but they do not yet constitute political parties as such. Only since the 1980s have noteworthy indigenous parties emerged, and only in Bolivia and Ecuador.

5. Dix, "Cleavage Structures and Party Systems," pp. 23–27.

6. Ibid., p. 26.

7. Juan J. Linz, "The Party System of Spain: Past and Future," in Lipset and Rokkan, *Party Systems and Voter Alignments: Cross-National Perspectives*, pp. 197–282. This paper would not have been possible without Juan Linz, not only because he encouraged and directed my own interest in the development of parties and other democratic institutions, but also because he taught or worked with many other scholars whose publications on Latin America were essential references for this study — Catherine Conaghan, Charles Gillespie, Luis Eduardo González, Jonathan Hartlyn, Bolívar Lamounier, Daniel Levine, Scott Mainwaring, and Arturo Valenzuela.

8. Philip E. Converse, "Of Time and Partisan Stability," *Comparative Political Studies* 2, 2 (July 1969): 139–71.

9. Converse, "Of Time and Partisan Stability."

10. Juan J. Linz, "Political Space and Fascism as a Late-Comer," in Stein Ugelvik Larsen, Bernt Hagtvet, and Jan Peter Myklebust, eds., *Who Were the Fascists?* (Bergen: Universitetsforlaget, 1980), pp. 153–89.

11. This remains true in the 1990s, except that the M-19 enjoyed a brief burst of success in the constituent assembly election of 1990 and both traditional parties are being challenged by regional splinters.

12. That share dropped to 82 percent in 1971, 78.8 percent in 1984, and 69 percent in 1989, making it now effectively a 3.5-party system by the Laakso-Taagepera Index. The emergence of the Frente is compatible with the general argument defended here, since even well institutionalized party systems change marginally over the years. The most important characteristic to be explained is why the Uruguayan party system remained unchanged for so long.

13. McDonald and Ruhl, *Party Politics and Elections in Latin America*, p. 78.

14. Luis Eduardo González, "Los partidos políticos y la redemocratización en Uruguay," *Cuadernos del "CLAEH"* 37, 1 (1986).

15. Jonathan Hartlyn, *The Politics of Coalition Rule in Colombia* (Cambridge: Cambridge University Press, 1988).

16. McDonald and Ruhl, *Party Politics and Elections in Latin America*, p. 92.

17. George Pendle, *Uruguay*, 3rd ed. (Oxford: Oxford University Press, 1963), pp. 24–26.

18. Ronald H. McDonald, "Party Factions and Modernization: A Comparative Analysis of Colombia and Uruguay," in Frank Belloni and Dennis Beller, eds., *Faction Politics: Political Parties and Factionalism in Comparative Perspective* (Santa Barbara and Oxford: ABC-Clio, 1978).

19. The Blancos agreed to Batlle's offer to share administrative responsibilities with a nine member *Consejo Nacional de Administración* elected in a way that guaranteed the Blancos a third of the seats. See Pendle, *Uruguay*, pp. 33–34.

20. Harvey F. Kline, *Colombia: Portrait of Unity and Diversity* (Boulder: Westview, 1983), chapter 2.

21. Pendle, *Uruguay*, p. 25.

22. According to Arend Lijphart, the greater the number of cleavages, the more fragmented the party system. Thus it is no accident that Chile's two cleavages are found in a multiparty system. See his *Democracies: Patterns of Majoritarian and Consensus Government in Twenty-One Countries* (New Haven: Yale University Press, 1984), pp. 147–49.

23. Brian Loveman, *Chile: The Legacy of Hispanic Capitalism*, 2d ed. (New York: Oxford University Press, 1988), p. 159.

24. McDonald and Ruhl, *Party Politics and Elections in Latin America*, p. 19.

25. Harold Blakemore, "Chile from the War of the Pacific to the World Depression, 1880–1930," in Leslie Bethell, ed., *The Cambridge History of Latin America, Volume V, c. 1870–1930* (Cambridge: Cambridge University Press, 1986).

26. Karen L. Remmer, *Party Competition in Argentina and Chile: Political Recruitment and Public Policy, 1890–1930* (Lincoln: University of Nebraska, 1984), pp. 67–77.

27. McDonald and Ruhl, *Party Politics and Elections in Latin America*, p. 192.

28. Charles Bergquist, *Labor in Latin America: Comparative Essays on Chile, Argentina, Venezuela, and Colombia* (Stanford: Stanford University Press, 1986).

29. McDonald and Ruhl, *Party Politics and Elections in Latin America*, p. 192.

30. John J. Johnson, *Political Change in Latin America: The Emergence of the Middle Sectors* (Stanford: Stanford University Press, 1958), p. 89.

31. Arturo Valenzuela, *The Breakdown of Democratic Regimes: Chile* (Baltimore: The Johns Hopkins University Press, 1978).

32. In 1972, the voting age was reduced to eighteen and the literacy requirement was abolished. Neither change expanded participation greatly since only a small fraction of the population was between eighteen and twenty-one and literacy rates had long since been high enough to make the literacy requirement a minor obstacle.

33. This estimate is based on Ameringer's statement that half of the adult male population could vote by 1928. See Charles D. Ameringer, *Democracy in Costa Rica* (New York: Praeger, 1982).

34. McDonald and Ruhl, *Party Politics and Elections in Latin America*, p. 170.

35. Ibid., pp. 170–71.

36. Ciro F. S. Cardoso, "Central America: The Liberal Era, c. 1870–1930," in Leslie Bethell, ed., *The Cambridge History of Latin America*.

37. McDonald and Ruhl, *Party Politics and Elections in Latin America*, p. 170.

38. Robert J. Alexander, *Organized Labor in Latin America* (New York: The Free Press, 1965), p. 215.

39. John A. Booth, "Costa Rica: The Roots of Democratic Stability," in Larry Diamond, Juan J. Linz, and Seymour Martin Lipset, eds., *Democracy in Developing Countries, Volume 4: Latin America* (Boulder, CO: Lynne Rienner, 1989), pp. 396–97.

40. Peter G. Snow, *Argentine Radicalism: The History and Doctrine of the Radical Civic Union* (Iowa City: University of Iowa Press, 1965), p. 6.

41. Snow, *Argentine Radicalism*, p. 5.

42. Ibid., p. 30.

43. Ibid., p. 30.

44. Ibid., pp. 34, 44–45.

45. Remmer, *Party Competition in Argentina and Chile*, pp. 106–109.

46. Liliana de Riz, and Catalina Smulovitz, "Instituciones y dinámica política. El presidencialismo argentino," Documento CEDES/37 (Buenos Aires, 1990).

47. Figures in the last two sentences are from McDonald and Ruhl, *Party Politics and Elections in Latin America*, p. 160.

48. Snow, *Argentine Radicalism*, p. 61.

49. Gary W. Wynia, *Argentina in the Postwar Era: Politics and Economic Policymaking in a Divided Society* (Albuquerque: University of New Mexico Press, 1978), pp. 43–45.

50. McDonald and Ruhl, *Party Politics and Elections in Latin America*, p. 163.

51. Monarchy was resurrected in 1863–1867 under the Emperor Maximilian, but only with a push from the French, and it failed as soon as French troops were withdrawn.

52. Some would say that the nineteenth century religious cleavage survived to spur the *cristero* revolt and the emergence of the PAN. I would say the old cleavage was effectively resolved, and a new religious cleavage was created during the Revolution by the Northern generals and Cárdenas, whose radical secularism broke with the prevailing understanding between Church and State.

53. Daniel H. Levine, *Conflict and Political Change in Venezuela* (Princeton: Princeton University Press, 1973). It also meant that the parties' organizational efforts were unimpeded by preexisting nonpolitical organizations. This is why parties came to penetrate social groups so thoroughly, prompting complaints about *partidocracia*.

54. Boris Bunimov-Parra, *Introducción a la sociología electoral venezolana* (Caracas: Editorial Arte, 1968), p. 248.

55. Bunimov-Parra, *Introducción a la sociología electoral venezolana*, pp. 246–48.

56. Other research suggests that AD and COPEI would have been nearly as successful even in the elections of 1963 and 1968, when the party system was much more fragmented, if AD had not suffered three internal splits in the early 1960s. See Michael Coppedge, *Strong Parties and Lame Ducks: Presidential*

Partyarchy and Factionalism in Venezuela (Stanford: Stanford University Press, 1994), chapter 3.

57. Cynthia McClintock, "The Perils of Presidentialism? Insights from the Peruvian Case," in Juan J. Linz and Arturo Valenzuela, eds., *The Failure of Presidential Democracy* (Baltimore: The Johns Hopkins University Press, 1995), p. 337.

58. Ibid., p. 379n.

59. Ibid., p. 355.

60. Herbert S. Klein, *Bolivia: The Evolution of a Multi-Ethnic Society* (New York: Oxford University Press, 1982).

61. Christopher Mitchell, *The Legacy of Populism in Bolivia: From the MNR to Military Rule* (New York: Praeger, 1977).

62. McDonald and Ruhl, *Party Politics and Elections in Latin America*, p. 230.

63. David W. Schodt, *Ecuador: An Andean Enigma* (Boulder: Westview Press, 1987), chapter 3.

64. The intended meaning of "taxi" parties is that they are so small that they can hold their conventions in a taxi, but the implication that they are parties for hire is equally apt. Catherine Conaghan, "Party Politics and Democratization in Ecuador," in James M. Malloy and Mitchell A. Seligson, eds., *Authoritarians and Democrats: Regime Transition in Latin America* (Pittsburgh: University of Pittsburgh Press, 1987).

65. Scott Mainwaring, "Brazilian Party Under-development in Comparative Perspective," *Political Science Quarterly* 107 (Winter 1993): 677-707.

66. Bolívar Lamounier, "Brazil: Inequality Against Democracy," in Larry Diamond, Juan J. Linz, and Seymour Martin Lipset, eds., *Democracy in Developing Countries, Volume 4: Latin America.*

67. Mainwaring, "Brazilian Party Underdevelopment."

9

Regionalism and Federalism
in Brazil, 1889–1937

Joseph L. Love

As one of Juan Linz's early students, I became interested in two of his
longterm and closely related interests — regionalism and center-peri-
phery relations. His essay, "The Eight Spains," regionalizing Spain by
economic and sociological characteristics, had a formative impact on my
dissertation. More broadly, my generation at Columbia University had
the privilege of taking Linz's seminar on authoritarianism three years
before the publication of "An Authoritarian Regime: Spain," and this
experience helped shape my approach to regional elites in *Rio Grande do
Sul and Brazilian Regionalism* and *São Paulo and the Brazilian Federation*. I
think it fair to say Linz's work also influenced my colleagues Robert M.
Levine and John D. Wirth, who wrote coordinated companion studies to
São Paulo on Pernambuco and Minas Gerais, respectively.[1] These and
other monographs on Brazilian regionalism made it possible to write the
following synthesis of regionalism for the first half-century of Brazil's
Republican regime.

Brazil was swimming against the centralizing tide when the
constitution of 1891, following a coup d'état creating a Republican
regime two years earlier, granted sweeping fiscal and financial powers
to the units of the federation. In Argentina and Mexico, long before the
turn of the century, de facto power, whether or not contrary to
constitutional arrangements, had begun to shift toward the central governments of those nations, and in Colombia centralization had
definitively triumphed in 1886. In Brazil, by contrast, the trend toward
recentralization was tardy and highly ambiguous. The Brazilian states
retained important powers and continued to innovate, especially in the
social sphere, after 1930. Ironically enough, fiscal federalism even

continued into the Estado Novo, the manifestly centralizing dictatorship of Getúlio Vargas (1937–1945).

Federalism should be distinguished from regionalism, a pattern of political behavior intimately associated with it. The former in this study is a system of government in which matters of national concern are reserved to the central authority—enforcement of the constitution and federal law, currency regulation, control of foreign policy, etc. But it is also is a regime in which the constituent states or provinces retain broad powers including homerule and the right to legislate on matters not in contravention of federal law, authority over the internal public domain, and control of state (provincial) fiscal and financial operations. In the Brazilian case, the last-named powers, including the power of the states to tax interstate commerce and to borrow abroad, were sources of conflict with the federal government during the era in question. But federalism in the First and Second Republics (1889–1930 and 1930–1937, respectively) also had a creative dimension as states led the way in economic and social experiments, of which coffee valorization was the best known example.

Regionalism, by contrast, is a pattern of political behavior characteristic of a federal regime. It is one in which regional actors accept the existence of the larger nation-state but seek economic favoritism and political patronage from the larger political unit, even at the risk of jeopardizing the political regime itself.[2] In Brazil during the era in question, the states were the cohesive units of political organization: Enduring parties existed only at the state level, and then only in some states. By 1910 three of the twenty units of the Federation—São Paulo, Minas Gerais, and Rio Grande do Sul—accounted for more than half the national vote totals in the all-important direct presidential elections, and they furnished a like share of gross physical product in the census of 1920. Further, the three states' wealth and fiscal powers allowed them to form disciplined paramilitary police forces capable of averting the armed intervention by the federal government that was so common in the other seventeen units of government. In effect, these three states were political regions themselves, though the term is also applied to groups of contiguous "satellite" states that occasionally attempted to act in concert. Between the relatively rich and powerful states of the Center South and the Far South and the poor and powerless units, mostly in the Northeast and North, stood three "occasional" players in presidential and federal politics, the dominant political machines of Rio de Janeiro, Pernambuco, and Bahia. Bahia, because of its large vote totals, was an important state in the elections of the 1890s, but it soon experienced a secular decline due to its weak economy. The rise of Rio Grande and the eclipse of Bahia by 1910, as well as the staying power of Minas and São Paulo, can be discerned in federal policies and patronage during the First (or Old) Republic (1889–1930).[3]

Why did Brazil diverge from the pattern of other large Latin American nations in shifting fiscal and other powers to the constituent units of the Federation in 1889–1891? The answer has to do with the shift in the dynamic center of the export economy from the Northeast (principally Pernambuco and Bahia) to the Southeast (São Paulo, Rio de Janeiro, and Minas Gerais) and the displacement of sugar by coffee. Within the coffee economy there was a shift as well: By the 1870s São Paulo's "West" on the plateau around Campinas had begun to surpass the Paraíba Valley of Rio de Janeiro Province and eastern São Paulo.

Concomitant with São Paulo's rise to a near hegemonic position in the export economy by the late 1880s was the crisis of the last slave-based economy in the Western Hemisphere. Whereas the old labor regime was clearly doomed by the mid-1880s—banks had ceased to extend credit on slaves as collateral and would not lend against land—its death was delayed as coffee planters urgently sought to devise a new labor system. For São Paulo, the labor crisis of slave-based coffee *fazendas* was solved in 1886–1887 by bringing Italian immigrants onto the plantations.

Whether the new labor regime, with its mix of wages and land use rights, was fully capitalist has been the subject of extensive debate.[4] I believe that it was.[5] It is nonetheless true that the country as a whole had a mixture of capitalist and precapitalist relations of production at the advent of the new political regime. Compromises were necessary between the political representatives of Paulista, Riograndense, and (some) Mineiro agricultural capitalists, on the one hand, and those of pre- or partially capitalist rural seigniors in most of the country, on the other. These included allowing a patronage- and clan-based control of politics to persist in the more backward areas. Meanwhile, slave-owners in other provinces were unable to attract São Paulo-bound immigrant labor because of the lesser profitability of their operations. The coffee planters of Rio de Janeiro in particular bore the brunt of abolition in 1888, as their heavy investment in slave property in the 1870s was abolished without compensation.

Part of the demand for provincial or state autonomy derived from the perception that São Paulo and other dynamic provinces could vastly increase their financial resources to support their regional economies under federalism. In 1886–1887, São Paulo contributed eight times as much to the central treasury as it received back in outlays, and a growing number of Paulistas believed its representatives were ineffective in the Imperial parliament, where the province was underrepresented.[6] When São Paulo became a state under the new regime, its representation in the new congress was increased to reflect its population gains, and São Paulo's revenues tripled with its new export tax.[7]

Paulista politicians also longed to tap new resources for development by dealing directly with foreign lenders rather than acting through a central government intermediary. Indeed, Paulistas had a foretaste of the opportunities created by foreign loans when the Imperial regime permitted the Province to assume its only foreign loan during the Empire (£749,000 in 1888), explicitly to subsidize immigration.[8] Under the Republic, borrowing by the states, led by São Paulo, would expand rapidly.

Furthermore, although Republicans in the late Empire maneuvered notoriously to sidestep taking a position on slavery, they considered themselves progressives on social matters and found the monarchy sorely lacking in achievement, notably on immigration and literacy. Though Brazil's first spurt of immigration occurred in the last three years of the Empire, averaging 84,000 persons a year, Argentina attracted 179,000 per year in the same period.[9] Brazil's literacy rate at the end of the Empire, moreover, was roughly a third that of Argentina's.[10] Awareness of, or intuitions about, the greater progress of Brazil's traditional rival in the Cuenca de la Plata helped promote the view of the old regime that "rubbish" could not be "reformed." By 15 November 1889, the Republican conspirators who gathered around Marshal Deodoro da Fonseca had convinced him to proclaim a federal republic, and his Provisional Government further separated Church from State within a year—a progressive measure in the minds of most Republican leaders, and one that was inconceivable under the Empire.

The federal constitution approved by the constituent assembly on 24 February 1891 fulfilled the promise of decentralization stressed in the Republican motto of 1870—"Centralization, Dismemberment; Decentralization, Unity." The charter provided for a wider dispersion of authority than did those of Argentina (1853, revised in 1860) and Mexico (1857 and 1917), the other two large federal republics in Latin America. Both of these countries placed greater restrictions on their states (or provinces) than did Brazil, notably in not allowing their member units to levy export taxes on goods shipped across state lines; in Brazil, taxes on products shipped out of state (including exports) were the chief source of revenue for the members of the Federation.[11] The Brazilian states could also tax imports. Although the revenue from such taxes was to revert to the federal treasury, theoretically the Brazilian state could thereby build tariff walls around their particular industries. In practice, some states unconstitutionally taxed imports under a variety of legal guises simply for revenue purposes. Thus there were fiscal and jurisdictional conflicts among the states. One of the most notable was a six year squabble between Rio Grande and Pernambuco that began when the former placed a tax on "imports" of sugarcane liquor, a leading product of Pernambuco; the government of Pernambuco retaliated by slapping a duty on Riograndense *charque* (dried beef).

Another fiscal dispute concerned Minas Gerais and São Paulo. Despite their common economic interest in coffee protection, São Paulo and Minas Gerais repeatedly found themselves at odds over interstate taxation. For most of the era of the Old Republic, São Paulo derived the bulk of its ordinary revenue from a single source—an export tax on coffee. No other state, not even Minas Gerais, had the advantage of such a huge export economy, and non-Paulista statesmen frequently resorted to the illegal taxation of interstate trade. If there were any doubt that the federal constitution of 1891 prohibited interstate import and transit taxes, there could be none after the passage of a law explicitly outlawing them in 1904. When São Paulo became a net exporter to the other states in the 1930s, its political leaders launched a more vigorous attack on such practices; but Minas Gerais and many other states depended heavily on such duties, and extralegal taxes were being collected as late as 1942 even though the Estado Novo, like previous regimes, had outlawed them.[12]

Unlike the Brazilian constitution, those of Argentina and Mexico specifically prohibited their member states from raising troops except in time of emergency. In Argentina the provinces were given no authority to set up civil, commercial, penal, or mining codes, and in Mexico the constitution of 1917 reserved all mineral rights for the nation. In Brazil, by contrast, the states could write their own procedural codes and were given authority over mineral deposits within their boundaries. The Brazilian states were also allowed to negotiate foreign loans and to sell bonds abroad, a power that the constitution of 1917 denied the states of Mexico.

By Latin American standards, then, the Brazilian constitution of 1891 permitted a high degree of decentralization. It failed, however, to make adequate provision for the poorer states. Just as the chief source of income for the states during the Old Republic was the export tax, so the major source of income for the federal government was import duties. At the constituent assembly, deputies from the depressed Northeastern states had argued for a share of import revenues, asserting that neither export levies nor property taxes would provide sufficient funds to run their governments. Time was to prove this concern justified. Thus the federalism embodied in the charter of 1891 was composed of decidedly unequal constituents. Fiscal powers reserved for the states, especially taxation of exports and later taxation of consumption, made rich states powerful and left poor ones weak and dependent on the federal government.

A noneconomic way in which the constitution tended to favor the strong states was in the relationship between the three branches of the federal government. From the earliest years it was clear that the executive branch dominated the other two. Consequently, as the Republic developed it became increasingly obvious that the selection of a president was of critical importance in controlling the political system. It was furthermore clear that the advantage lay with the stronger states since the president was chosen by a direct popular vote of literate males and the economically powerful states tended to be those with the largest populations and the best educational systems.

The state-based machines—the Republican Party of each unit—monopolized political activity in their respective bailiwicks until the 1930s. Even in the early Vargas years, self-styled "national" political organizations found the bulk of their support in single states. The most important vote deliverers were the Partido Republicano Paulista (PRP) and the Partido Republicano Mineiro (PRM); in the eleven popular presidential contests of the Old Republic, they also supplied nine of the winning candidates—São Paulo, six, and Minas, three.[13] Given the fact that less than 6 percent of the national population participated in elections during the whole period under study, politics in this era was essentially a contest between sectors of a national political elite. Nonetheless, real cleavages took place between regionally differentiated groups with conflicting demands on federal policies and patronage systems. The leaders of states with large vote totals and disciplined machines were able to translate their aspirations into demands.

At the outset of the Republic, São Paulo and Minas Gerais already led the other states in vote totals. In the first direct presidential contest in 1894, Minas Gerais and São Paulo supplied an almost equal proportion of the vote (8.8 percent each). After 1906 the Partido Republicano Riograndense (PRR) of the southernmost state, on the Argentine and Uruguayan borders, also became a major vote producer and the three big machines sometimes accounted for half the national totals. Minas Gerais held first place throughout the Old Republic, but by 1930 São Paulo and Minas Gerais were nearly even again (19.3 percent and 19.5 percent respectively). In the 1934 congressional elections (the last simultaneous national contests until 1945), São Paulo's share of the total vote was 20.9 percent compared to 19.7 percent for Minas Gerais, with Rio Grande in third place (11.1 percent).[14] Over the whole period, Minas Gerais commanded a high and, after 1902, roughly constant share of the total vote, while the shares of São Paulo and Rio Grande rose, increasing the tendency for three states to dominate national contests.

São Paulo then, as now, was the economic giant in the federation. By the time of the first economic census in 1920, it accounted for more than two-sevenths of the total agricultural and industrial output of Brazil; this figure was more than double the output of the runnerup, Minas Gerais. By 1939, the first year for which gross domestic product figures are available by state, São Paulo again accounted for more than two-sevenths of the total, a portion more than three times the size of that of the second state, now Rio Grande do Sul.[15]

São Paulo's position in the export market was preeminent. Its share of national exports, by value, consistently averaged more than half the total between 1921 and 1940. By the mid-twenties, Santos, the state's main port, was exporting three times the amount shipped abroad by Rio de Janeiro, the second most important port. Initially, coffee exports brought São Paulo its prosperity. In 1907 half the world's coffee was grown in São Paulo (and three-fourths in Brazil as a whole). By 1920 the state also led the nation in industrial output. The fact that São Paulo became a net exporter to other Brazilian states by 1931 — and remained so afterward — was an important if indirect indicator of its industrial development. By 1939 industry as a contributor to output in São Paulo had pulled abreast of agriculture.[16]

Given São Paulo's economic position, it is hardly surprising that the state government's financial resources were great in comparison to those of other states. In the years under study, São Paulo typically collected two to three times the revenue raised by either Minas Gerais or Rio Grande do Sul, the two states vying for second place.[17] São Paulo accounted for more than one-third of all state government revenues by 1937, despite persistently low coffee prices in the 1930s; and state revenues in the year of the Estado Novo coup were about one-fifth the size of that of the federal government. Of federal revenues in the 1930s, almost a third were raised in São Paulo; in that decade the federal treasury brought in six to eight times as much as in the second-ranking state, Rio Grande do Sul.[18]

As São Paulo's economy expanded, so did its population. In 1890 it still ranked third among the states, but passed Bahia by 1900. São Paulo overtook Minas Gerais in the 1930s and has been the most populous state in each decennial census since 1940, at which time its inhabitants numbered 7,180,000.[19] Until the 1930s the greatest impetus to demographic growth was foreign immigration, and during the Old Republic half the nation's immigrants settled in São Paulo. Many of these stayed in urban areas, and if Rio de Janeiro remained the national metropolis in the years under review, São Paulo city was confidently pushing toward first place. Between 1890 and 1900, the growth of the state capital exceeded that of Rio in absolute terms.[20] By 1920 São Paulo city had more than half a million inhabitants, and over 1.3 million by 1940.

For political purposes, a significant characteristic of the population was the literacy rate because only literates were enfranchised. São Paulo's literacy rate was below the national average in 1890, partly owing to its large slave population at the end of the Empire. By 1920, however, only Rio Grande do Sul had a larger proportion of literates, and the two states held their respective positions in the 1940 census, both with slightly more than 50 percent literacy among the population ages five and older.

The PRP's interest in federal politics differed from the usual concern with patronage and public works. São Paulo's minimum political program during the years 1889–1937 consisted in dominating federal policies only in issue-areas for which action at the state level was impossible or insufficient—control of monetary and exchange policy, loan guarantees, and diplomatic representation. Its leaders did not expect the public works and patronage concessions (entailing reciprocal obligations) that were central to Mineiro strategy. Only São Paulo had the option of intervening in the economy at its own initiative, and for limited periods it could point the way toward new governmental responsibilities. But state and national economic and fiscal affairs were so interdependent that São Paulo could not have long pursued a strategy of isolation in federal politics, as Rio Grande had from 1894 to 1906. The expansion of Paulista markets and investments, plus the growing military power and debt consolidation responsibilities of the Vargas government in the 1930s, directly and indirectly diminished São Paulo's liberty of action.

A closer look at the coffee economy is required to understand São Paulo's power and interests. Paulistas produced the leading export, which, during the course of the regime, became the country's monocultural mainstay. For a fleeting moment, in 1910, Amazonian rubber accounted for almost as great a share of the value of foreign earnings as coffee (40 and 41 percent, respectively) but a decade later, rubber had plummeted to 3 percent of exports, continuing to fall thereafter.[21] Meanwhile, coffee grew in importance until the end of the 1920s, rising to 70 percent of the value of Brazilian exports—a remarkable instance of monocultural dependence in a country larger than the continental United States.

Coffee meant São Paulo, and Paulista politicians eagerly sought to serve their export economy. Their leaders were ready to cooperate with other states' representatives and the federal government when they perceived shared interests; on the other hand, among state elites the Paulistas had the greatest ability to pursue economic interventionist policies from which the federal government shrank, and they sometimes did so. The most famous instances of cooperation with other states, cooperation with the federal government, and self-reliance are all provided by the valorization of coffee at different stages of its development. São Paulo initially tried to get the federal government to finance the scheme, and when it balked a tri-state plan with Rio de Janeiro and Minas Gerais was established at Taubaté, São Paulo, in 1906. Minas Gerais and Rio de Janeiro withdrew before the program was implemented, and in 1908 São Paulo shouldered the responsibility on its own—an action made possible by the fact that it produced half the world's annual output. When the first valorization loan was repaid to foreign creditors ahead of schedule, that fact was interpreted as an undiluted triumph of cartelization. The state government repeated the program in 1917 and forced the federal government to do so in 1921, arguing that coffee was a national, not a regional, asset, and that the health of the coffee industry was a federal responsibility. In 1924, the program was returned to the state of São Paulo by a budget slashing president, and during the late 1920s an interstate agreement was effected, ultimately revolving around the credit position of São Paulo. Over the years valorization inevitably brought more and more producers into the market—in São Paulo, in other states, and abroad— all of whom took advantage of artificially high international prices. With the Great Depression, valorization came to a disastrous halt, but the Depression also allowed the Paulistas permanently to shift primary responsibility for coffee protection to the federal government.

In São Paulo's demand for federal support of the state's export economy, exchange policy was at least as important as the related issue of valorization. The federal treasury and the Paulista coffee economy were thrust into a symbiotic relationship: the central government was heavily dependent on import duties for its normal operation, and imports depended in turn on exports. Coffee producers calculated costs in Brazilian milréis and received "hard" dollars, marks, francs, and pounds for their goods. It is a well-known fact that they consequently favored an ever-depreciating milréis. Although there were other interests favoring a stable or appreciating rate (including consumers and importers in São Paulo),[22] the core of the opposition to runaway depreciation came from the federal treasury itself, which had to repay its extensive loan obligations in ever-more-expensive European and North American currencies.[23] Pushed one way and pulled another, the federal government tried to compromise by holding down the rate of deterioration of the milreis. Two stabilization schemes were attempted during the Old Republic, one in 1906, which was notorious for its favoritism to exporters,[24] and a similar program in 1927. Coffee interests were adversely affected by exchange rates after 1931, though exchange policy lost some of its significance in the 1930s, when lower prices failed to expand coffee sales.

In the area of labor supply, Paulista leaders were unwilling to rely on market forces alone. Here São Paulo expected relatively little from the federal government, and was chiefly concerned with keeping Brazil's ports open to Europeans and Asians who would work the coffee fields. The labor crisis on slave-based coffee *fazendas* in 1886–1887 had been solved by bringing Italian immigrants onto the plantations, and São Paulo state subsidized immigration from that point until the late 1920s, when the subvention was temporarily suspended. Migration from other states passed foreign immigration into São Paulo in 1928, and did so consistently after 1934, when a "national origins" law restricted immigration. The magnet of the Paulista economy in the domestic labor market proved its strength, and the Paulista government did not oppose federal immigration policy, since factory and field hands—from Minas, Bahia, and the Northeast—kept pouring into São Paulo, as it moved from agriculture to manufacturing.

The other leading player in the politics of the First Republic was the establishment party of Minas Gerais, the Partido Republicano Mineiro (PRM). Minas Gerais was a state twice the size of either São Paulo or Rio Grande do Sul and it accounted for the largest share of both population and vote totals until the 1930s. But Minas Gerais had certain disadvantages—its economy was much weaker than São Paulo's, and it even lost its second place position to Rio Grande by the end of the period. Furthermore, only two of seven subregions, the Mata and the Sul, shared in the coffee-generated prosperity. Its industrial economy, focused on Juiz de Fora, was in relative decline, and cattle and dairy interests sought different kinds of policies as well. Still, the story was one of inadequate growth, rather than near-stagnation, the fate of two important Northeastern states, Pernambuco and Bahia. On a twenty-state scale, Minas Gerais's relative economic success helped save it from political fragmentation.[25] The PRM's role in national politics fulfilled the traditional stereotype of the Mineiro personality, contrasting with those of the Paulistas and Riograndenses (also called Gaúchos, because of their state's image as a land of cowboys). While the Paulista was considered enterprising, money-oriented, and sometimes arrogant, and the Riograndense something of a braggart with a vocation for arms, the Mineiro was thought of as conservative, place- and family-oriented, and politically astute.

Whereas Paulista political leaders tended to seek control over federal exchange, immigration, and monetary and fiscal policies, Mineiros looked more toward a large share of public works (especially railroads) and federal patronage for their state's inhabitants. In this endeavor, they were largely successful. Necessary but not sufficient conditions were the state's large economy, a proportionally large state budget, and high vote totals. The additional key to power was "political organization: The capacity to unite for common action," despite highly differentiated and sometimes conflicting economic and subregional interests, arising in part from strong ties to family and locality. Politically, Minas Gerais was a region; economically, it was not.[26] The ability to hold divergent interests together distinguished Minas Gerais's political leadership from that of Bahia. Abutting Minas Gerais, Bahia was a state of similar size and second in the country in population and registered voters at the outset of the period, but one in which the economy in per capita terms tended toward stasis, and in which politicians were often divided.

The political elites of Minas Gerais and São Paulo were similarly recruited from relatively wealthy, highly educated, and somewhat closed pools, though prosopographical evidence shows the Paulistas to have been much more fully integrated into the propertied classes who directed the economy.[27] The two state machines were similar in their reliance on local notables, the implicit violence associated with *coronelismo* (rural bossism), and extensive patron-client relations. The PRP, however, had a more secure financial base, with a regular dues-paying system, tending to diminish the importance of its "vertical" patron-client character.

The third powerful state machine, the Partido Republicano Riograndese (PRR), was a late contender for power, and effectively did so only from 1910. The establishment party in Rio Grande do Sul was unique in Brazil in having an explicit ideological foundation (Comtian positivism). It was also unique in facing an organized opposition with an ideological program calling for a parliamentary regime to replace the presidentialist constitution. Ideological and partisan divisions would have been less important had it not been for a bitter statewide civil war at the outset of the Republic (1893–1895), one which established the lines of political cleavage until Getúlio Vargas became governor in 1928. Partly as a result of the war, the ruling PRR was able to enforce its will at the local level, even to the extent of overthrowing powerful local *coronéis*. Thus the state machine had more power over its local chieftains than did that of São Paulo. At the opposite end of the continuum was Bahia, where one powerful colonel of the backlands, Horácio de Matos, was able to rout state police forces sent against him, prompting one student to identify "warlord" *coronéis* as a important subtype in Bahia.[28]

When the PRR became a national force after 1910, it did so in an alliance with the army, and by taking advantage of divisions between the Republican parties of Minas Gerais and São Paulo. The Riograndense Party's excellent relations with the military establishment in part derived from the large numbers of soldiers based in the state (in case of conflict with Argentina) and the Gaúchos' putative military vocation. The Republic continued the imperial practice of stationing a quarter to a third of the army in Rio Grande do Sul, and the command of the Rio Grande military district (the Third Region after 1919) was one of the most important army assignments; eight commanders of this region became ministers of war in the Old Republic. In addition, the only major professional military academy in Brazil outside of the federal capital was in Rio Grande do Sul. In 1907, the year in which two future presidents, Getúlio Vargas and Eurico Dutra, made a debut in Riograndense politics as student leaders in the law school and military academy, respectively, there were more cadets in Pôrto Alegre than in Rio de Janeiro.

The myth about the Gaúcho's military vocation had a basis in fact in the Republican era, just as it had in the Imperial era. Rio Grande had supplied more generals than any other province at the end of the Empire, and it still did so at the time of the 1930 revolution. Moreover, Rio Grande supplied more presidents of the prestigious Officers' Club (Clube Militar) and more ministers of war during the Old Republic than any other state.[29]

There were several reasons for the close ties between the PRR and the federal army, including ideological convictions (Comtian positivism, on which both the ruling party and the state constitution were based), bonds established during the struggle of 1893–1895, and regional loyalty. Another factor was the PRR's unflagging defense of military appropriations in Congress, where Riograndenses sat on key committees. Finally, the PRR was the army's only potential ally in a contest for power: The officer corps alone could not overthrow the Mineiro-Paulista alliance, which tended to control presidential succession, nor could it rely on the other state machines to stand up against the most powerful organizations. When the Gaúchos did not contend for national power, the army remained loyal to the president.

If São Paulo was the leading coffee producer, Minas Gerais was second, while Rio Grande was oriented toward the national market for its main "exports," charque and rice. The state machine of Rio Grande was more like Minas Gerais than São Paulo in seeking patronage and public works, but differed from Minas in its relatively greater interest in issues affecting the national market.[30] As Rio Grande was the destabilizing element, the politics of the Old Republic was often described as *a política do café com leite*—Minas Gerais was also a dairy state—since there was a tendency for the machines of São Paulo and Minas Gerais to alternate candidates for the presidency.

Of the seventeen lesser states, even though their fiscal situation improved in the first decade of the Republic over that of the last decade of the Empire, their revenues were woefully inadequate, and in the draught-plagued states between Rio and the Amazon Valley—a region that gained its identity as the "Northeast" precisely in this era[31]—the mass of the population experienced grinding poverty, even misery. Federalism had a different meaning there. Mainly, it meant seeking revenue transfers from the federal government. The notable instance of success for the Northeast during the period in question was a federal dam-building program, and the few reservoirs (*açudes*) actually completed were built in the three years when, as a byproduct of a split between Minas Gerais and São Paulo in a succession crisis, Rio Grande do Sul was able to make a Northeasterner president.[32] To strengthen his position, the new chief executive, Epitácio Pessoa of little Paraíba, chose six of his seven ministers from the machines of the three big states. Pessoa later revealed that his government spent almost as much on railroads alone in São Paulo, Minas Gerais, and Rio Grande do Sul, as on his entire development program for eight states in the Northeast![33] When Bernardes, the former governor of Minas Gerais, succeeded Pessoa in November 1922, the latter's cherished Northeast development program was abruptly halted, leaving many projects half-finished.[34]

Rule by family-based oligarchies in the smaller or weaker states of the Northeast and elsewhere, though present in the Empire, became a much more salient feature of politics under the Republic, because state governors were elected, and no longer appointed from Rio. The Aciolis dominated Ceará, as the Machados, and later the Pessoas, ruled Paraíba. Likewise, the Maltas in Alagoas, the Medeiros family in Rio Grande do Norte, the Nerys in Amazonas, and the Murtinhos in Mato Grosso.

At the root of this political archaism was *coronelismo* and its social foundations. The sociologist Maria Isaura Pereira de Queiroz believes *coronelismo* had its origins in the *parentela* (extended family), which was patriarchal, stratified (in part, by legitimate and bastard branches), and, within and without, suffused with patron-client networks.[35] In addition, domination required a firm economic base, and *parentela* intermarriage permitted broad alliances, enough to allow major extended families to take over the smaller or more thinly populated federal units. Control of state and local government under such circumstances was "neopatrimonial," in that modern appearances hid a renaissance conception of what government was about. Thus patronage and government-let contracts favored those of the ruling *parentela*. In the interior of these states, the *poder privado*, derived from colonial times and only modified by the Imperial state, prevailed. Thus justice and police powers, under coronel control, remained seigniorial until the revolution of 1930.

In short, while politics in the three big states of the Center South and Far South were in a transitional phase from "vertical" patron-client and *parentela* politics to a more "horizontal" form based on voluntary associations and economic interest, in the Northeast political configurations remained tied to ancient Mediterranean values and structures, of which the extended family was the spinal column. In the economically undifferentiated Northeast, the distinction between *as famílias* (the legitimate members of upper and middle class families) and *o povo* (the popular classes) was the rough equivalent of that between "classes" and "masses" in São Paulo and Rio de Janeiro in the same period.[36]

The Northeast had not only to contend with the *política do café com leite*, but also the *política dos governadores*. This arrangement enabled the president and powerful governors to make the important decisions about policies and personnel. But in a broader sense, it was the policy of all government incumbents to maintain each other in power indefinitely. In early 1900 President Manuel Campos Sales, a Paulista, had instituted the *política dos governadores* as a means of ensuring that the president would always have a majority in the Chamber of Deputies. To achieve this end, he pushed two procedural changes through the Chamber. One effectively gave the president control of the Chamber's credentials committee. The second required that a majority of county councils in each congressional district certify the winner's vote. Since the establishment party at the state level supported local politicians and vice versa, this was another safeguard against the entry of noncompliant deputies into Congress. Campos Sales had introduced the *política dos governadores* to guarantee congressional support for fiscal and monetary policies required for the Rothschild Funding Loan (1898), consolidating Brazil's external debt. These included such unpopular measures as raising taxes, decreasing both the currency in circulation and government expenditures, and placing a lien for Rothschild on customs collections. Thus the *política* was an adaptation of formal democratic structures to political conditions in a neocolonial economy.

The practice of mutual support by incumbents continued throughout the Old Republic and was associated with the domination of politics by the president and the governors of Minas Gerais and São Paulo. The inability of opposition groups to obtain office except by revolution (including those at the state level), coupled with the exclusion of urban middle and working classes from power through *coronelismo*, contributed to the demise of the 1891 constitution in 1930. Consequently the First Republic was unable to solve a problem for which the Empire did have a solution: removing incumbents from power without violence. The monarchy was able to do this by the Emperor's naming a member of the opposition party in parliament to "make" elections, the results of which, during the Second Empire, always returned the party that organized those contests.[37]

After the new federal system had stabilized under civilian control in the latter 1890s, central government intervention in the states was frequent, but the three big states and their political machines were exempted. If a president hostile to the interests of São Paulo should come to power—a rare occurrence—he would be deterred from intervention in São Paulo by the state police organization, the Força Pública. Of the twenty state police forces, São Paulo had the largest and best-equipped, with an active duty list of 14,000 men in 1925 and 1926, the peak years.[38] In fact, the Força Pública was nothing less than a state army: Its pay scale was roughly equivalent to that of the national army; it had its own military academy and a foreign military mission after 1906; and in the 1920s it added artillery, armored tanks, and an air corps. Until the 1930s the government of São Paulo had little to fear from federal military personnel.[39] Minas Gerais and Rio Grande do Sul could also count on significant state forces, though theirs were smaller than São Paulo's. The other seventeen states had much weaker forces, in terms of both size and discipline.

Federal intervention was a sure way to effect a change of government in the seventeen satellite states—the only way, in fact, short of civil war, which nonetheless occasionally erupted. Dozens of interventions against state officeholders occurred during the Old Republic, and federal intervention became the "normal" way for opposition forces to take power against corrupt state machines that controlled the ballot boxes.

Article 6 of the constitution established a set of conditions necessary for intervention. The two most easily met were the need to reestablish order and tranquillity at the request of the state government in question, and the need to preserve "federal republican" institutions and guarantees. The tactic most frequently used for intervention under the first condition was the division of the state legislature into two rump bodies, both of which then claimed legitimacy and validated only the credentials of their own adherents. If the group hostile to the governor could demonstrate a numerical majority to the satisfaction of the federal government, it could obtain federal military intervention. A legislative division of this sort occurred in the rubber exporting state of Amazonas in 1909, with the connivance of the boss of the Senate, José Pinheiro Machado of Rio Grande do Sul; but President Nilo Peçanha restored the ousted governor. In the following administration of Marshal Hermes da Fonseca (1910–1914), rump assemblies were formed in Rio de Janeiro state, Bahia, Ceará, and Amazonas, with varying results. The second method of obtaining intervention—pleading the need to guarantee republican institutions—was used to overthrow the governors of Bahia (1912) and Ceará (1914).

In 1911–1912 reformist military officers had obtained power with implicit or explicit support from the army in the Northeastern states of Ceará, Alagoas, Pernambuco, and Sergipe. In Bahia in 1912, as in Amazonas in the 1909 incident mentioned above, a military commander did not shrink from bombarding the state capital to overthrow the incumbent governor. But Senator Pinheiro and the Acioli oligarchy turned the tables on the reformers in Ceará, where the Aciolis were able to dislodge the newly-installed governor, Col. Franco Rabelo, by manipulating primitive religious sentiment in the backlands. The pilgrims of Padre Cícero in his redoubt at Juazeiro launched a kind of *jihad* against the governor in Fortaleza, Ceará's capital. Following a statewide civil war, in which the peasant "army" sacked several towns and invested the coastal capital, President Hermes and Pinheiro Machado decided that the irregularly-installed military reformer could not maintain "republican institutions," and Hermes issued an intervention decree. In the next election, the Aciolis returned to power.[40]

Amazonas perhaps exhibited the worst example of the interplay of local instability and federal intervention. There the problem was complicated by the collapse of the regional rubber economy, and consequently the tax base, of the state government during World War I. Rival governments (*duplicatas*) had persisted through the Hermes years and beyond, with the federal government supporting one faction and then another; by the 1920s the state was foundering in administrative and financial chaos. President Artur Bernardes (1922–1926) even feared U.S. intervention in Amazonas, the most notoriously insolvent and debtridden member of the Federation. According to Brazil's future ruler, Getúlio Vargas, then a member of Congress, Bernardes used the Amazonas issue to force an amendment to the federal constitution in 1926, giving the Union greater authority to intervene in the states in instances of financial mismanagement.[41] Perhaps better than any other, this case illustrates the failure of federalism in the Old Republic.

In this political system the presidency was the linchpin, and alliances at the national level revolved around the struggle to choose the chief executive. In determining presidential succession, the political parties of São Paulo and Minas Gerais usually worked together, but by

1910 Rio Grande do Sul had also entered the contest. As noted, the three machines were able to dominate national politics because of the economic and electoral strength of their states; if necessary, they could also bring paramilitary forces to bear. The three parties were in a position to rally support by subsidizing newspapers, were able to deliver half the total vote in a presidential election, and could rely on their state armies to prevent presidential intervention. The leaders of the three autonomous parties, acting in concert, could avoid the crisis inherent in every presidential succession. Disagreement among the three could sometimes be resolved by enacting compensating economic legislation: In São Paulo and Minas Gerais this usually meant the defense of coffee, in Rio Grande advantages for pastoral activities. Otherwise discord meant a contested election that imperiled the political system. This was true of all three seriously contested presidential races of the Old Republic, those of 1910, 1922, and 1930.

In those years three Gaúcho politicians attempted to gain control of the federal government when breaches occurred in the Paulista-Mineiro alliance. Senator Pinheiro Machado, already influential in the succession of 1906, had made Rio Grande a "big" state by 1910, when Rio Grande allied with Minas Gerais and the army against São Paulo and Bahia to make Marshal Hermes president. Key to Pinheiro Machado's power were the consistent backing of a "permanent" government in Rio Grande do Sul; the control of the credentials committees in Congress, as well as the control of two crucial congressional posts, those of vice president of the Senate and majority leader of the Chamber; the tool of party discipline exercised through his national coalition, the Partido Republicano Conservador; the free use of subventions to influential newspapers; and a personal ascendancy over the President. But his "system" was one of personal relationships and was therefore subject to the shifting allegiances of the political elite. When the Paulista-Mineiro alliance was reactivated in support of a strong president, Pinheiro's power began to decline, and the PRC disintegrated completely after his assassination in 1915. The Minas-São Paulo alliance was a logical outgrowth of the shared economic interests of the two coffee states; Pinheiro's coalition had no such cohesion.

Antônio Borges de Medeiros, the "perpetual" governor of Rio Grande (1898–1907; 1912–1928) did not become personally involved in the contest for control of the presidency until after Pinheiro's death. Borges's intervention in the 1919 caucus that brought about Epitácio Pessoa's election came during a deadlock between Minas Gerais and São Paulo. In 1922, the Governor initiated a unique experiment in presidential elections: He joined with former President Nilo Peçanha of Rio state to mount a campaign against Minas Gerais and São Paulo at a time when the coffee giants were united. Pinheiro had worked out an alliance with the army, and so did Borges and Nilo. Pinheiro, however, had also had the support of the Mineiro party and the "hip-pocket" votes of a delicately balanced but effective coalition of PRC satellites. In contrast, the Reação Republicana of 1922 was an attempt to unite three "semisovereign" states—Rio de Janeiro, Bahia, and Pernambuco—with Rio Grande and the military against São Paulo, Minas Gerais, and their fourteen client machines. The Reação lost, and the new President, Bernardes, intervened in Rio, Bahia, and Pernambuco. Moreover, he forced Borges de Medeiros to give up his post as governor at the end of a five year term in 1928.

By the time of Vargas's race for the presidency in 1930, a new generation of Gaúchos had risen to prominence. They threw themselves behind the first direct bid by a Riograndense politician for the presidency at a moment when Minas Gerais and São Paulo were again divided over presidential succession. Victory depended on the unreserved support of Minas Gerais. The election—as interpreted by Congress—demonstrated that an incumbent president could guide his candidate to victory even when the Mineiro-Paulista alliance was ruptured. However, 1930 was no ordinary election year, and economic stresses aggravated political discontent. The coffee market had collapsed in October, 1929, and planters began to reject PRP leadership in the persons of President Washington Luís and the President-elect, Júlio Prestes, both former governors of São Paulo. The PRR and the PRM organized a conspiracy with military officers which would bring Getúlio Vargas, the defeated presidential candidate and incumbent governor of Rio Grande, to power for fifteen years. In 1930 the Gaúchos were uniquely suited to lead a revolution against the government of Washington Luís: Of the major political groups, the Riograndenses, who had traditionally been oriented toward domestic markets, were the least dependent on the international economic system and therefore the least discredited by its collapse. The revolution of 1930 was a verdict on the viability of Brazilian federalism and the *café-com-leite* alliance on which it was predicated.

The 1930s were a period of political ferment, and Vargas' first year in office saw the ouster of the establishment Republican parties in all states except those of Rio Grande do Sul and Minas Gerais, whose machines had backed the revolution. The Partido Democrático in São Paulo, a reformist group of professionals, planters, and others who had supported the regime change, was not, however, allowed to take charge of São Paulo. The PD was frustrated because of pressures from the reformist and authoritarian faction within the army and within the Vargas coalition—the *tenentes* ("lieutenants," i.e., radical junior officers).

Continued depression and lack of "home rule" in São Paulo led to the country's only twentieth-century (interstate) civil war in 1932, as a united civilian elite—Paulista Repubicans and Democrats—unsuccessfully tried to overthrow the Provisional Government. To reconcile the defeated Paulistas, Vargas's government assumed half the coffee planters' debts, and announced elections for a constituent assembly, in which regional interests could again express themselves forcefully. The dictator further broadened the electorate, allowing women and eighteen-year-olds to vote.

A new constitution was approved in 1934 and Getúlio Vargas was elected president by the constituent assembly. Although the 1934 charter limited state powers and provided for forty corporate or "class" members in the new Congress, 212 deputies were elected from geographic constituencies, which fact inevitably meant the reappearance of state-based parties. Politics thus seemed to be tending toward the norm of the First Republic. In fact, the only parties in the Depression years having true national aspirations were the Partido Comunista Brasileiro (PCB) and Ação Integralista Brasileira (AIB), Latin America's largest fascist party. Even these, however, found the overwhelming bulk of their still modest followings in urban locales—the federal capital and São Paulo city and its industrial suburbs.

Although Vargas's skillful maneuvering in the months preceding the Estado Novo coup had split both of the two traditional liberal parties of São Paulo, the Partido Constitucionalista (which had succeeded the Partido Democrático) and the old Partido Republicano Paulista, these two strongly regionalist organizations had hardly lost power to "extremist" groups. In 1936, in São Paulo's last elections before 1945, the PC and PRP won a combined total of nineteen of twenty seats for the municipal council in São Paulo city, precisely where class-oriented parties should have done best.

All the same, power constellations were changing rapidly in the mid-1930s, in great part owing to the failed Communist putsch of 1935 and Vargas's skillful exploitation of it, enabling him to maintain a climate of crisis and introduce a state of siege. The President eliminated the last regional threat to his consolidation of power in October 1937, when the Interventor of Rio Grande do Sul, José Antônio Flores da Cunha, fled to Uruguay after Vargas nationalized the state police force. An enabling structural change was the fact that by 1937 the army disposed of double the number of active-duty troops available to all the states together, whereas twenty years earlier, the states' combined military police forces had been greater than the army's.[42] An economic dimension of the triumph of centralization was that Paulista industrialists by the latter 1930s had come to believe that a unitary regime, hostile to internal tariffs, would give rise to a more efficient national market.

In his coup of 10 November 1937, creating the Estado Novo, Vargas stridently proclaimed the end of federalism as well as that of liberal democracy. Former states were now declared to be mere administrative divisions of a unitary regime, and the President-turned-dictator replaced elected governors with appointed interventors. In a symbolic display of authoritarian centralism, Vargas had the flags of the states burned.

At the beginning and the end of the period under study, in 1889 and 1937, governing parties ceased to exist, collapsing in the former instance and being abolished in the latter. The institutionalization of a party system transcending state boundaries was a feat neither the First nor Second Republic could achieve. Beyond the questionable geographic extent of "national" parties in the 1930s, in most of the country — certainly in the more economically backward regions — party loyalties outside the AIB and PCB were based on neither program nor ideology but on patronage and clientelism.

Nonetheless, in the years 1889–1937, structural changes in the Brazilian economy were extensive: Coffee and rubber exports reached their apogees and went into sharp decline; manufacturing underwent its initial surge in a complicated set of rhythms, and expanded rapidly in the 1930s.[43] For much of the period economic growth was largely dependent on exports and foreign capital, including investments in government bonds for infrastructural development. By the 1930s, Brazil had shifted its dependence in financial and economic affairs from Great Britain to the United States. This coincided with the acceleration of industrialization by import substitution.

Brazilian society was likewise transformed. The nation received a net inflow of between two-and-a-half and three million immigrants in the years 1889–1937, more than any other comparable period in its history; half of these went to São Paulo, and 90 percent in all went to the states in the southern quarter of the nation. By the 1930s internal migration was also greater than in any previous decade. Rapid urbanization and improvements in public health accompanied these population shifts. By the census of 1940, the nation had two cities, Rio de Janeiro and São Paulo, with populations over one million, and twenty-one other cities with populations in excess of 100,000. In the cities the early labor movement was the crucible for anarchist and communist activity, only to be channeled and controlled from the top down by a government apparatus in the 1930s. In the complex interplay between federal and state units, government assumed new tasks not only in social control but also in social welfare, education at all levels, and commodity marketing inside and outside the country.

Vargas brought governmental intervention in economy and society to new levels of involvement. Some of these changes were immediate, such as his Provisional Government's acceptance of responsibility for the debts of its constituent units, including São Paulo's huge valorization debt. Others were a matter of process, such as government organization and control of the working class, beginning immediately but expanding with the size and complexity of the industrial economy. Federal government responsibility for coffee protection became permanent in 1931, and in the 1930s other agricultural products were also subsidized, e.g., sugar, yerba mate, and wheat. Federal intervention in the social sphere dates from attempts in 1918 to regulate food prices; but the 1930s was an era of vast expansion of governmental services, however paternalistic, to nonpropertied groups as indicated by the creation of the ministries of education and labor, and immigration quotas and other laws to guarantee employment to Brazilian nationals.

Yet state government intervention in economic and social matters, most notably São Paulo's, paralleled and often preceded federal activity. While primary responsibility for coffee protection lay with the central government after 1931, the state assisted the Union in this endeavor into the 1940s.[44] In the social sphere, state immigration policies were of course planter-oriented schemes, as was the creation of the State Labor Department in 1912, eighteen years before the federal Ministry of Labor was organized. Yet it appears that the São Paulo Department provided some genuine benefits for rural workers (with which it was exclusively concerned) even in the early years of its existence. In 1930 a second department was set up for urban labor; its interference in the factory routine sometimes angered employers.[45] In addition, São Paulo added a secretariat of education and public health in the same year (before the creation of its federal counterpart), and the state established Brazil's first modern university, with a faculty of arts and sciences, in 1934. By 1937 the secretariat of education was spending 22 percent of state outlays.[46]

Rio Grande do Sul provided other examples of state intervention anticipating that of the federal government. In his first year as governor in 1928, Vargas set up a state development bank, principally for charque producers. Responding to the creation of new producers' syndicates in charque and rice, the governor encouraged the formation of other corporate groups. As noted, after Vargas became ruler of Brazil, the central government intervened not only in the coffee economy, but encouraged cartelization in other commodity markets.[47]

In the Northeast, no such cooperation between state and federal governments was possible, given the poverty of the former. Though Vargas established an Institute for Sugar and Alcohol to benefit Northeastern planters and to control production levels in 1933, federal financial commitment was trifling compared to the sums spent on coffee protection. A clearer benefit for the Northeast came at the political and social levels, because *coronelismo*, in the absence of elections, became irrelevant.[48] Furthermore, the "warlord" *coronéis* and family-based oligarchies at the state level were overthrown, never to return with the same grip on power.[49]

The significance of Brazilian federalism in the years 1889–1937 can be better understood through some intertemporal and international comparisons. Nearly a century after the coup d'état creating the Republic in 1989, the historian Emília Viotti da Costa emphasized the continuity of oligarchy in the transition from Empire to Republic: "The main difference [between Empire and Republic] was that the traditional rural oligarchy had been supplanted by a new one: the coffee planters of the [Paulista] West and their allies, who, once in power, promoted only those institutional changes that were necessary to satisfy their own needs." Francisco Iglesias drew a similar conclusion in a centenary evaluation of the Republic of 1889.[50]

In my view the change of regime in 1889 was not meaningless. The shift permitted a greater realization of what modern governments are supposed to be about. Not that the Republic was so much, but that the Empire was so little.[51] Let us consider three aspects of what modern states are supposed to do: to provide educational opportunity, to improve the health of the population, and to secure the financial resources to make these things possible.

Not only did the total real (deflated) revenues and expenditures of central, state, and local governments rise with the creation of the Republic,[52] but state and local units followed the federal government in borrowing abroad. Although foreign loans increased foreign dependency, the enhanced access to hard currency meant greater access to the economic infrastructure — railroads, utilities, port facilities, etc. — necessary for export-driven growth (the model adopted by both the Empire and Republic). The value of Brazil's foreign loans (federal, state, and municipal) increased five times, in sterling terms, between the last year of the Empire and the outbreak of World War I. Partly as a result, the nation's rail network rose from 9,600 kilometers at the end of the Empire to 24,600 km in 1913.

On the expenditure side of the ledger, the Federal Government did almost nothing for the lower classes beyond public health measures, leaving the responsibility for public education to the states; but it was nevertheless highly interventionist by the laissez-faire standards of the day. Its public works, sanitation, immigration support, and coffee valorization programs are well known, but less well known are the relative dimensions of government income and outlay. Comparing the federal budgets of Brazil and Mexico between 1890 and 1910 (and omitting the larger Brazilian expenditures at the state level), Steven Topik recently discovered that Brazil's government was able to raise and spend twice the money per inhabitant (in dollar terms) attained by the autocratic regime of Porfirio Díaz. He writes: "The greater activism of the Brazilian state is perhaps surprising in light of the popular image of the Porfirian state as robust and centralized, and the Republican state in Brazil as weak and splintered into semiautonomous cantons."[53]

It was a state government, rather than the Union, that initiated programs in public health and undertook the chief responsibility for subsidizing immigration and coffee valorization. The three programs were linked: São Paulo's leaders realized that immigration was an essential element in their agricultural development model, and they quickly discovered that investment in public health was required to attract the targeted European population. In the second decade of the Republic, health measures were taken by many other states and the federal government in Rio: The campaign against yellow fever in the national capital under President Rodrigues Alves was a response to a previous campaign in the state of São Paulo. True, this would not have been possible under the Empire, since the etiology of yellow fever was not yet known, but São Paulo had already shown its ability to control an epidemic of bubonic plague early in the new regime. We do have an indication of what the Imperial regime could do regarding public health from its behavior in the great drought in Ceará and neighboring provinces in 1877–1879. The central government tried to provide relief to a peasantry in distress, but the dinosaur-like Imperial state had almost no effect at all on the problem, and 200,000 people in the Northeast starved.[54]

Other evidence further suggests that the Republican regime at state and federal levels had a greater impact on the health of the Brazilian population than did its predecessor. According to the demographer Eduardo Arriaga, between the Imperial census of 1872 and the first under the Republic, in 1890, average life expectancy improved only 1 percent; in the following decade it improved 7 percent, though still only rising to 29.4 years. General Brazilian mortality rates fell from 30.2 per thousand in 1872–1890 to 27.8 in 1891–1900, a 9 percent improvement.[55]

In education, as in public health, São Paulo state pointed the way, partly because its leaders viewed a healthy and productive labor force as dependent on basic literacy. By 1912 São Paulo alone (in constant terms) was spending almost as much on public education as the Empire as a whole—central and provincial governments together—had spent per annum in the late 1880s. At the national level, progress in education, as in public health, must be judged against the miserable situation bequeathed to the Republic by the Empire. In 1886 there was only one student in primary or secondary school for every seventy-five Brazilians (and most students were in private schools). By 1907 the ratio in Brazil was one to thirty-three, better than twice the Imperial rates just cited.[56] Moreover, the number of primary pupils in Brazil more than doubled between 1889 and 1907. As for literacy, the available census data indicate a slight decline in the last two decades of the Imperial regime—from 16 percent in 1872 to 15 percent in 1890. By 1900 the rate had risen to 26 percent.[57] Furthermore, the number of (nonmilitary) *faculdades* expanded significantly beyond the half-dozen of all sorts bequeathed by the Empire, as more states demanded institutions of higher education within their borders. By 1908 there were twenty-five such institutions in Brazil.

All in all, the monarchy did not respond adequately to the opportunities implicit in the world trade boom generated by the Second Industrial Revolution in the North Atlantic basin after 1880, nor did it address social issues that had an impact on economic performance. Powerful provincial interests consequently declared for a federal system. The feebleness of the old regime in implementing economic and social policy perhaps contributed as much to its collapse as its lack of attention to specific regional interests. The Republican regime of February 1891 did make a difference: It just wasn't enough.

Let us conclude with a consideration of developments at the end of the period under review, comparing the federal regimes of the years 1889–1937 with the Estado Novo and the contemporaneous regime in Mexico. First, in Brazil we note a continuity of government intervention in economy and society from Old to New Republics, and into the Estado Novo. For the whole period 1889–1937, the legitimate sphere of governmental activity—at state and federal levels—expanded markedly, first to assist cartelization, initially in coffee valorization and after 1930 more widely,[58] and later also to implement welfare policies, which expanded rapidly with unionization after 1937. Yet in fiscal matters the oft-noted centralization trend of the Vargas era must be qualified. Though state income as a whole diminished slightly under the Estado Novo, São Paulo increased its share of total revenues and expenditures in every decade from the beginning of the century into the military dictatorship of the 1960s.[59] The concentration of power in the national capital during the 1930s is therefore a much more clearcut process in political than in administrative decision-making.

An international comparison of state and federal revenues is even more revealing of the weakness of the centralization trend in Brazil. Although the U.S. government was less fiscally centralized than that of Brazil on the eve of World War II, Brazil's national government during the allegedly centralized Estado Novo dictatorship raised and spent less of government totals than Canada's or Argentina's federal governments in 1940.[60] Comparing Brazil and contemporary Mexico, and dividing the fifteen years of Vargas' tenure into two phases, corresponding to the revolutionary-constitutional years and the Estado Novo, we obtain the following results:[61]

	1931–1937	1938–1945
All Brazilian state revenues as a percentage of federal revenues	57.9	55.7
All Mexican state revenues as a percentage of federal revenues	22.7	17.3

Although state revenues declined slightly relative to those of Brazil's central government in 1938–1945, Mexican state revenues fell more. It is ironic that the ratio of state to central government revenues in Brazil under the allegedly centralized Estado Novo was more than three times greater than the contemporary ratio in Mexico, which had a federal, not unitary, system. Perhaps Brazil's most distinctive contribution to corporatist practice in the 1930s was its partly decentralized administration, in contrast to the more clearly unitary regimes in Italy and eastern Europe.

During the Old Republic, Brazil's statesmen failed to develop viable political institutions. They had not created political parties traversing state lines, nor could they eliminate the crisis potential in presidential succession. The lack of popular participation in politics was related to the predominantly rural distribution of the Brazilian population, its poverty, and *coronel* rule in the municipio. By the 1920s the *política dos governadores*, which tended to keep establishment groups at every level in power indefinitely, had undermined the legitimacy of the political system among new urban groups, reformist elements in the army, and nonincumbent political parties. When the Great Depression and a succession crisis coincided, the regime fell.

Broadly speaking, it was sharply skewed regional economic power combined with neopatrimonial political realities and institutional arrangements (e.g., the direct election of the president) that had given the Old Republic its oligarchic, and ultimately inflexible and illegitimate, characteristics. Yet human agency was important, since the PRM executive committee and the Gaúcho Senator Pinheiro Machado attained power and advantage disproportionate to their states' economic strength.

Despite regime weaknesses, both state and national governments intervened actively in the economy, and to a lesser degree in the social sphere. In this way, there was continuity between the First and Second Republics, despite the growing power of the central government. In instituting his dictatorship in 1937, Vargas could only blunt but not reverse the fiscal decentralization of the first two Republican regimes. His authoritarian Estado Novo still awaits systematic analysis, for which the categories and methods developed by Juan Linz will be indispensable.

Notes

1. Juan J. Linz and Amando de Miguel, "Within Nation Differences and Comparisons: The Eight Spains," in Richard L. Merritt and Stein Rokkan, eds., *Comparing Nations* (New Haven: Yale University Press, 1966), pp. 267–319; Linz, "An Authoritarian Regime: Spain," in Erik Allardt and Yrjo Littunen, eds., *Cleavages, Ideologies and Party Systems: Contributions to Comparative Political Sociology* (Helsinki: The Academic Bookstore, 1964), pp. 291–341; Love, *Rio Grande do Sul and Brazilian Regionalism, 1882–1930* (Stanford: Stanford University Press, 1971); Love, *São Paulo in the Brazilian Federation, 1889–1937* (Stanford: Stanford University Press, 1980); Robert M. Levine, *Pernambuco in the Brazilian Federation, 1889–1930* (Stanford: Stanford University Press, 1978); and John D. Wirth, *Minas Gerais in the Brazilian Federation, 1889–1937* (Stanford: Stanford University Press, 1977).

2. Beyond these bounds, of course, regionalism passes into separatism.

3. See Love, *Rio Grande* and *São Paulo*; Wirth, *Minas Gerais*; and Eul-Soo Pang, *Bahia in the First Brazilian Republic: Coronelismo and Oligarchies, 1889–1934* (Gainesville: University of Florida Press, 1979).

The relative power of these four states' machines (and, most notably, Bahia's decline and Rio Grande's rise) is roughly approximated in their tenure in cabinet posts from 1889–1930, shown in Love, *Rio Grande*, p. 123. Another important but declining Northeastern state was Pernambuco, treated in Levine, *Pernambuco*. The role of the state of Rio is treated in Marieta de Moraes Ferreira, ed., *A República na Velha Província: Oligarquias e crise no Estado do Rio de Janeiro (1889–1930)* (Rio: Rio Fundo, 1989).

4. Workers (*colonos*) and their families received wages, housing, and the right of usufruct for subsistence. Moreover, they could market their surplus. Since workers were not fully separated from the means of production and therefore not exclusively dependent on wages, some writers deny that the

arrangement was fully capitalist. For example, see José Souza Martins, *O cativeiro da terra*, 2d. ed. (São Paulo: Hucitec, 1981).

5. In that a dynamic labor market existed in the countryside, as shown by the frequency of rural strikes and *colono* movement from estate to estate, and in and out of the country. See Verena Stolcke and Michael M. Hall, "The Introduction of Free Labor on São Paulo Coffee Plantations," *Journal of Peasant Studies* 10, 2–3 (January–April 1983): 183–86. Even Souza Martins agrees the *fazendeiros* were capitalist entrepreneurs. *Cativeiro*, pp. 16, 91.

6. Love, *São Paulo*, p. 103.

7. This rise occurred in 1892, the first full year for revenues collected under the new state constitution.

8. Love, *São Paulo*, p. 108.

9. Brazil's new immigrants were attracted by subsidized passage and, of course, by the demise of slavery. For figures see Armin K. Ludwig, *Brazil: A Handbook of Historical Statistics* (Boston: G. K. Hall, 1985), p. 103; Vicente Vázquez-Presedo, *Estadísticas históricas argentinas (comparadas)*, vol. I (Buenos Aires: Macchi, 1971), p. 15. Figures are gross, not net, numbers.

10. Brazil's literacy rate was 15 percent in 1890, and Argentina's, 46 percent in 1895. See Ludwig, *Brazil*, p. 132; Vázquez-Presedo, *Estadísticas*, p. 27. However, the Brazilian figure is for all ages, including 0–4, while that of Argentina is for ages six and older.

11. João Lyra, *Cifras e Notas (Economia e Finanças do Brasil)* (Rio: Revista do Supremo Tribunal, 1925), pp. 85–88.

12. Dalmo de Abreu Dallari, "Os Estados na Federação Brasileira, de 1891 a 1937," manuscript commissioned by J. L. Love, R. M. Levine, and J. D. Wirth (1970), p. 40.

13. Owing to the interference of death and revolution, however, Paulistas served only 12 years, and Mineiros, 10.5.

14. See sources in J. L. Love, "Autonomia e Interdependência: São Paulo e a Federação Brasileira, 1889–1937," in Boris Fausto, ed., *História Geral da Civilização Brasileira*, tomo 3, vol. 1 (São Paulo: DIFEL, 1975), p. 56.

15. Estimates for 1920 computed from figures in Lyra, *Cifras e Notas*, pp. 44–45. Lyra's data are from the federal census, which unfortunately made no attempt to measure services as a contributor to national product. Data for 1939 from *Conjuntura Econômica* 24, 6 (June 1970): 95. By 1939 the Federal District had passed both Rio Grande do Sul and Minas Gerais in output.

16. On São Paulo as a net exporter, see Warren Dean, *The Industrialization of São Paulo: 1880–1945* (Austin: University of Texas Press, 1969), pp. 193–94; on industry as a contributor to state output, see *Conjuntura Econômica*, p. 95.

17. Minas Gerais's state revenues were usually larger than Rio Grande's, though during a few years of the 1920s and 1930s the latter had larger receipts. Instituto Brasileiro de Geografia e Estatística (hereafter IBGE), *Anuário Estatístico do Brasil 1939/1940* (Rio: n.d.), pp. 1412–15.

18. Ibid., p. 1271, 1409; São Paulo Secretaria do Estado dos Negócios da Fazenda, *Relatório: Exercício de 1949* (São Paulo: 1955), p. 72; Ministério da Fazenda, Contadoria Geral da República, *Balanço Geral do Exercício de 1940* (Rio:

1941), p. 365. The central government raised more revenue in the Federal District than in São Paulo, partly because of income from federally-owned enterprises in the national capital.

19. IBGE, *Anuário...1971*, p. 41.

20. Paul Singer, *Desenvolvimento Econômico e Evolução Urbana* (São Paulo: Ed. Nacional, 1968), p. 47.

21. Data in Ludwig, *Brazil*, pp. 317–18.

22. Industrialists also benefited from appreciating rates in that they could buy capital goods more cheaply. A depreciating rate tended, of course, to make foreign goods more expensive relative to national manufactures. Thus in periods of exchange rate appreciation (or stability) investment levels in manufacturing tended to be high and output low; in periods of depreciation, investment tended to decrease while output increased. See Annibal Villanova Villela and Wilson Suzigan, *Política do Governo e Crescimento da Economia Brasileira: 1889–1945* (Rio: IPEA, 1973), p. 85.

23. Of course the São Paulo state government faced the same problem, but coffee interests were more powerful on home ground. For discussions of the politics of exchange rates, see Edgard Carone, *A República Velha (Instituições e Classes Sociais)* (São Paulo: DIFEL, 1970), pp. 96–99. Coffee interests had intragroup conflicts, and it seems obvious that planters would profit less, at least directly, from exchange manipulations than would exporters.

24. According to an authority on Brazil's international finances, the rate of 15d./milréis "...was nothing more than a general reduction in the nation's financial resources for the particular interests of coffee growers"—Valentim Bouças, *História da Dívida Externa*, 2d. ed. (Rio: Edições Financeiras, 1952), p. 219.

25. Wirth, *Minas Gerais*, p. 228.

26. Ibid., p. 229.

27. See Joseph L. Love and Bert J. Barickman, "Rulers and Owners: A Brazilian Case Study in Comparative Perspective," *Hispanic American Historical Review* 66, 4 (1986): 743–65.

28. Pang, *Bahia*, p. 38 and passim; on de Matos, see also Walfrido Moraes, *Jagunços e heróis* (Rio: Civilização Brasileira, 1963).

29. Love, *Rio Grande do Sul*, p. 117.

30. For example in restricting access of lower-cost Uruguayan and Argentine charque to Brazilian markets. It was also more concerned about combating inflation, since the consumption of charque in Brazil was price-elastic. (However, because Minas Gerais was a dairy state selling its goods in Rio de Janeiro and elsewhere, the PRM also could not be oblivious to domestic economic issues).

31. Linda Lewin, *Politics and Parentela in Paraíba* (Princeton, N.J., Princeton University Press, 1987), p. 23.

32. See Love, *Rio Grande do Sul*, pp. 183–85.

33. Epitácio Pessoa, *Pela Verdade* (Rio: F. Alves, 1925), p. 374.

34. On these matters, see Albert Hirschman, *Journeys toward Progress* (New York: Twentieth Century Fund, 1963), pp. 11–50.

35. Maria Isaura Pereira de Queiroz, "O Coronelismo Numa Interpretação Sociologica," in Boris Fausto, comp., *História Geral de Civilização Brasileira*, tomo 3, vol. 1, pp. 164–71.

36. The centrality of the family as the fundamental organizing principle for middle and upper class life in Bahia is amply demonstrated in Dain Borges, *The Family in Bahia, Brazil, 1870–1945* (Stanford: Stanford University Press, 1992).

37. Richard Graham, *Patronage and Politics in Nineteenth-Century Brazil* (Stanford: Stanford University Press, 1990), pp. 79 and passim.

38. The army at the time had 30,000 active-duty troops, spread across half a continent.

39. On the militarized state police, see Heloísa Rodrigues Fernandes, *Política e Segurança* (São Paulo: Alfa-Omega, 1974), and Love, *São Paulo*, pp. 216–19 and passim.

40. On the interventions and upheavals of 1909–1914, see Love, *Rio Grande do Sul*, pp. 157–61. On Padre Cícero, see Ralph della Cava, *Miracle at Joaseiro* (New York: Columbia University Press, 1970).

41. Love, *Rio Grande do Sul*, p. 125.

42. Ibid., pp. 254–55.

43. The 1930s were a decade of unprecedented industrial expansion in São Paulo, and the number of factories in the state doubled between 1933 and 1939; the value of industrial output tripled in the same period. As noted earlier, by 1939 the value added by industry in the state pulled even with that of agriculture, and in that year São Paulo accounted for 41 percent of value added by manufacturing throughout the nation. Yet there was scarcely any consistent government policy of industrial development: Exchange policy tended to favor industry after 1931, but domestic financial policy was not aimed at industrial expansion. See Villela and Suzigan, *Política do Governo*, pp. 78–79, 368, 371.

44. Secretaria da Fazenda, *Relatório...1940* (n.p., n.d.), p. 5. "Coffee defense" in 1940 accounted for about 10 percent of total state outlays, including "extrabudgetary" items.

45. On benefits to rural and urban workers, respectively, see Thomas H. Holloway, *Immigrants on the Land* (Chapel Hill: University of North Carolina Press, 1981), pp. 108–109; and Barbara Weinstein, "The Industrialists, the State and the Issue of Worker Training and Social Services in Brazil, 1930–1950," *Hispanic American Historical Review* 70, 3 (1990): 384. The two labor departments were merged in 1933.

46. This figure is calculated on the basis of total secretariat outlays, ordinary and extraordinary, of which all retrospective tables are composed; if "extra-budgetary" items are included, the education secretariat's share falls to 14 percent. Secretaria da Fazenda, *Contas do Exercício de 1937* (n.p., n.d.), p. 7; *Relatório...1949*, p. 72.

47. See Love, *Rio Grande do Sul*, pp. 221–23, and Joan L. Bak, "Political Centralization and the Building of the Interventionist State in Brazil," *Luso-Brazilian Review* 22, 1 (Summer 1985): 9–25.

48. *Coronelismo* returned in an attenuated form after federalism and formal democracy were restored in 1945.

49. Lewin, *Politics and Parentela*, pp. 408–24; Pang, *Bahia*, pp. 186–88 (on the overthrow and assassination of "warlord" Horácio de Matos).

50. Emília Viotti da Costa, *The Brazilian Empire: Myths and Histories* (Chicago: University of Chicago Press, 1985), p. 233; Francisco Iglesias, *O Estado de S. Paulo*, November 11, 1989, "Cultura" section, pp. 1–3.

51. On the general ineffectiveness of the Imperial regime beyond the confines of the national capital, see José Murilo de Carvalho, *Teatro de sombras: A política imperial* (São Paulo: Vértice, 1988), p. 163.

52. Federal revenues temporarily declined, however, in real terms.

53. Steven Topik, "The Economic Role of the State in Liberal Regimes: Brazil and Mexico Compared, 1888–1910," in Joseph L. Love and Nils Jacobsen, eds., *Guiding the Invisible Hand: Economic Liberalism and the State in Latin American History* (New York: Praeger, 1988), p. 138.

54. Roger L. Cuniff, "The Great Drought: Northeast Brazil, 1877–1880," Ph.D. diss., University of Texas, 1970.

55. Eduardo Arriaga, *New Life Tables for Latin American Populations in the Nineteenth and Twentieth Centuries* (Berkeley: University of California Press, 1968), p. 42; IBGE, *Brasil em Números* (n.p., n.d.), p. 13.

56. Love, *São Paulo*, p. 93; IBGE, *0 Brasil em Números*, p. 5.

57. Literacy fell to 25 percent in 1920 (Ludwig, *Brazil*, p. 132) but retrospective estimates reveal that the 1920 census overstated general population by 12 percent. Thus the literacy rate may be understated, on the assumption that global census numbers are less reliable than those for the literate population. All censuses through 1920 understate literacy when compared to those in 1940 and later, in that the former included persons aged 0–4.

58. The federal government had made efforts to secure rubber valorization but it failed, not only because of the insoluble problem of blight, but also because of Brazil's smaller market share by the time of the First World War.

59. In 1968, São Paulo accounted for 50.1 percent of all state revenues, and its revenues amounted to 36.2 percent of those of the Union; 43.8 percent of federal revenues, moreover, were raised in São Paulo. Compiled from data in IBGE, *Anuário...1969*, p. 664; and *Anuário...1971*, pp. 778, 791.

60. Love, *São Paulo*, p. 266.

61. For Brazilian data, see São Paulo Secretaria da Fazenda, *Relatório...1949*, p. 72; IBGE, *Anuário...1939/1940*, p. 1409; IBGE, *O Brasil em Números*, p. 140. Similar trends are found for expenditures in the same sources. Both "ordinary" and "extraordinary" revenues and outlays are included in these data for the states and the Union.

For Mexican data, see Mexico: Secretaría de Economía: Dirección General de Estadística, *Anuario estadístico de los Estados Unidos Mexicanos: 1939* (México, D.F.: 1941), pp. 666–67; 678–79; *Anuario...1942* (México, D.F.: 1948), pp. 1234, 1238; *Anuario...1943–1945* (México, D.F.: 1950), pp. 762, 766–67. In neither case did I count the Federal District as a state, though it is grouped with the states in the Mexican data. For 1939 revenues in Mexico I used revised figures published in *Anuario...1942*.

10

Macro Comparisons without the Pitfalls: A Protocol for Comparative Research

J. Samuel Valenzuela*

Using comparative analysis to explain historical or contemporary social phenomena has a long tradition in the social sciences. Durkheim, Gramsci, Montesquieu, Smith, Tocqueville, Weber, and others whose classic works are still read for their insights into the defining forces of political, economic and social institutions, were all informed by observations regarding the similarities and differences between such institutions in various settings. Juan Linz's writings follow optimally in this social science tradition. Whether Linz focuses on the features of Spain's regions, on the breakdown of democracies, on the distinguishing components of democratic, authoritarian, or totalitarian regimes, on the social origins of fascists, on nationalism or religion and their effects on political identities, or on the defects and virtues of presidential versus parliamentary regimes—to name a few of his contributions—his approach always draws at one point or another on comparative analysis. Even when Linz is examining a phenomenon in a single setting

* My appreciation to Erika Maza Valenzuela and Robert Rishman for help in sharpening the focus of this paper. Over the years many colleagues have reacted to my presentation of the approach to comparative analysis presented here, especially Elijah Anderson, David Collier, Marta Gil-Swedberg, Jeffrey Goodwin, Peter Hedstrøm, Walter Korpi, Orlando Patterson, Allan Silver, Theda Skocpol, Richard Swedberg, Charles Tilly, and Harrison White. My gratitude as well to the John Simon Guggenheim Foundation, whose fellowship allowed me to put these ideas into article form, and to the Latin American Center at St. Antony's College, Oxford University, for its academic hospitality while writing this version.

such as local elites in Andalusía, the characteristics of the Franco regime, the party system of democratic Spain, or the latest survey results on political legitimacy in Chile, his interpretations are enriched by his knowledge of the characteristics of the phenomenon in other units or at other points in time.[1]

Linz's work over the past four decades has been an important component of an ever increasing postwar literature that uses macro comparisons, historical or contemporary, of a few cases (generally national societies) to develop concepts, to reach empirical generalizations, and to build middle range social science theory. Despite the growth in the number of studies using this approach, the methodological literature devoted to it has not developed at the same pace.[2] This contrasts sharply with the enormous development in the number and sophistication of publications devoted to other methods, especially survey research and a considerable variety of statistical approaches. Few graduate studies curricula devote a whole semester to comparative analysis, and general social science methodology courses hardly allocate one or two sessions to it if it is studied at all. In such courses, comparative analysis is usually assimilated with what Campbell and Stanley call a "quasi-experiment" (in other words, a notably unreliable method, given the absence of any controls), even if it has detailed observations of a considerable number of items within a few distinct units.[3] Moreover, the core of the comparative research design according to most presently available methodological statements is a very old one, John Stuart Mill's 1843 "method of agreement" and "method of difference."[4] Notwithstanding the importance of comparative analysis in Linz's own work, he himself has published little about the problems encountered in using this mode of research.[5]

This essay seeks to provide pointers for comparative analysis while avoiding a largely fictitious textbook version of the research process. It discusses systematically how to set up macro comparisons in ways that will avoid common error-inducing pitfalls associated with this approach to social science questions. This paper is also a homage to Juan Linz's work, not only because it draws illustrations from it, but also because his writings stand up very well to critical scrutiny from the comparative design perspective delineated here.

The protocol presented in these pages is intended for using comparative analysis to build explanations of phenomena with the ultimate aim of developing social science theory. There is a softer form of comparative analysis which aims at better analyzing or presenting certain events, settings, or epochs through a systematic comparison of two or more units. Such a descriptive use of comparisons can be very illuminating and rewarding: It may lead the analyst to recognize the importance of some aspect or aspects of the subject matter that would escape attention if the focus were only on a single unit. This mode of comparative analysis is more commonly utilized in historical studies whose aim is generally to reconstruct carefully the fullest possible view of particular settings, highlighting as a result their uniqueness.[6] As soon as systematic comparisons lead to a discussion of the sources of similarity or of variance of particular features, the comparisons come closer to the theory-building use of comparative analysis discussed here.[7] Comparative history and comparative sociology converge as an explanation for perceived commonalities and/or differences between units becomes the agenda of research.[8]

Theory-building comparative analysis may be seen, following suggestions advanced by Smelser and Lijphart in the late 1960s and early 1970s, as one of four different approaches to explain phenomena in social science—the other three being the experimental, case study and statistical methods.[9] However, while Lijphart notes that the comparative method is like the statistical one "in all respects except one," namely, "that the number of cases it deals with is too small to permit systematic control by means of partial correlations,"[10] my view is that the difference between these approaches is much greater. In arguing, by contrast, that "there are reasonably clear boundaries between the comparative method...and case study methods," Lijphart under-estimates the extent to which comparative analysis relies for its creative insights on case studies, as will be noted here.[11] Given these dis-agreements, it is best to begin with a brief prefatory comment on the differences between these methods in order to establish the dis-tinctiveness of comparative analysis. I exclude consideration of the experimental approach here because it is only remotely related to comparative analysis, and is of little use to clarify the latter's pro-cedures.[12]

Approaches to Explaining Macro Phenomena

Although comparative analysis has a unique character, it shares some aspects of both the case study and statistical methods. Hence, this discussion will begin by characterizing the latter two.

Case studies have been the poor relative of social science explana-tion. Although scholars have pointed to their virtues in building theories by helping to generate new hypotheses and by providing testing grounds for existing theories,[13] these are uses which view case studies as a tool or a stepping stone for eventually generating or sharpening explanations by means of comparative or statistical approaches. In the process, the distinctiveness of the case study method itself has been largely overlooked.

The distinctiveness of the case study is best expressed by the in-depth qualitative research that ethnographers and cultural anthropologists prefer, although it is also present, sometimes unwittingly, in the work of case study analysts from other disciplines, including history. The purpose of the research is to examine in detail a particular social phenomenon in a complex collectivity, the "case" at hand, whose boundaries make it a relatively self-enclosed system of social interaction. There is a sharp awareness that the research pertains to the "case," but conceiving it as such actually adds little if anything to the analysis. The researcher does not presume to know beforehand which are the phenomena's constituent elements (even if theories may point initially to them), but tries to discover and conceptualize them. The next step is to establish how these elements relate to each other, creating the phenomenon's configurations of social interactions. Once the constituent elements and their configurations are known, individual and collective behavior expressing the matter under research within the unit are understood to be "explained," and as such, even "predictable," as they flow under the constraints of a certain "grammar" or "logic."[14] Case study analysts have little sense of working with "variables," and they have a highly developed sense that every aspect they examine is located within a larger context. As such, individual elements of a phenomenon can be understood fully only when the workings of the whole relevant to it are clarified. For this reason the analyst must return several times to assess the significance of each element, and these operations are themselves steps to constructing piece by piece an image of the whole. The research process seeks to put into sharp relief the distinctive, essential, defining characteristics of the case at hand, those that pervade even the phenomenon's variations. Campbell likens case study research to "pattern-matching," as the analyst tests and refines a theoretically informed pattern with a broad variety of observations within the case.[15] (Naturally, some researchers may want to show a phenomenon's variations within the case, although when this becomes the basic object of the study it shifts either into the comparative or statistical method.) The ethnographic variant of case studies relies heavily on informants, and on discovering the phenomenon's elements and configurations on the basis of their visions of it.[16] Other forms of case study, for instance the analysis of a particular national political regime such as the Spanish one in many of Linz's publications, may draw on interviews, historical documents, secondary literature, newspaper accounts, survey research, electoral data, demographic trends, and so on.

Unlike case studies, the statistical method is not concerned as much with the distinctive or essential features of a social phenomenon as with measuring and explaining the extent of its variations; in fact, grasping these variations becomes from a statistical perspective a surrogate approximation to a phenomenon's distinctive characteristics. The constitutive elements of the phenomenon are not normally an object of discovery but are furnished by a preexisting theory, and they are expressed as a limited set of variables subject to quantification (sometimes by means of indicators that only capture an aspect of the element, or stand in lieu of it). There is also a clear distinction between the variables to be explained and those that do the explaining (the dependent and independent variables) in statistical procedures, although the analyst may chose to invert or combine them in various ways in the course of the research. The statistical mode requires a large number of units relative to the number of variables it uses from which to derive the latter's measurement. The notion of "case" is most often conflated with the units from which the measurements are derived, that is, the n in the sample or in the data base. When the numerical results produce, exceptionally, distinctive clusters which the analyst can treat as separate entities, statistical approaches can approximate the notion of case held in case studies or ethnographies in the sense that they become more complex units with distinctive configurations of elements or variables. However, in statistical analysis the resulting "cases" are constructed on the basis of the measurements presented by the variables, and there is no sense that the whole will affect in turn the significance of the elements, or that the cluster constitutes necessarily a collectivity of bounded social interaction.

While case studies and statistical analysis are in their starkest form polar opposites, comparative analysis, as noted previously, shares elements of both. With the case study or ethnographic approach, comparative analysis has as its object of analysis complex collectivities, viewed as the "cases." It also tries to explain the characteristics of the phenomenon it examines within the cases by looking at a large number of elements and their configurations, and by paying close attention to their context within the cases. However, by curious contrast with the case study approach, the notion of "case" lies at the very center of the intellectual enterprise in comparative analysis while it is simply a given for the former. This is due to the fact that comparative analysis does not rest with the discovery of the essential elements of the phenomenon under research and its configurations within the cases, but seeks to examine the phenomenon in more than one case, attempting to construct explanations that account for the variations of the phenomenon across the cases. Hence, as with statistical analysis, the comparative approach is interested in knowing how and why phenomena vary, acquiring either different or similar forms across the units of study. Comparative analysis also shares with the statistical approach a clear cut conception of variables, both independent and dependent. However, in contrast to the statistical approach, comparative analysis is unable to quantify its variables and expand the number of its cases to the point of satisfying the requirements of most statistical procedures.[17] As a result, comparative analysis is a very complex method to use; on the one hand it requires a deep understanding, as in case studies, of the cases it examines, and on the other it seeks to explain variations of social phenomena despite having a dearth of cases to sort out a large number of complex variables.

Given the many variables and the small as well as complex n problem, the possibility of making the wrong inferences using the comparative approach is quite high. The protocol presented in this essay is intended as a basis to generate comparative research designs that will minimize the possibility of such errors.[18] Comparative analysis should also be based on the most thorough understanding possible of the cases, so that its explanations can be supported by a base drawn from case study analysis. For this reason, while comparative analysis is at a disadvantage with respect to statistical analysis given the few cases it has to sort out its many variables, this drawback is not as debilitating as it seems at first glance because *the comparisons can be grounded on case studies to an extent that has no parallel in the statistical approach.* This occurs because the conception of "cases" in comparative analysis is much closer to that of case studies than that of statistical approaches, and therefore the difference between the comparative and statistical approaches is not simply, as Lijphart and Ragin indicate,[19] a matter of the lesser or greater number of variables relative to cases. Similarly, the fact that inferences in comparative analysis may be supported by the intensive acquaintance with the material generated by case studies points to a greater imbrication of these two approaches than analysts have envisioned.[20]

Complex research endeavors may require using more than one — even all three — approaches. However, it is usually possible to identify which form of analysis predominates in drawing the major inferences or conclusions. While case studies may use statistical methods, for example, these are often employed to better characterize the properties of the case at hand, or as an additional element in its puzzle of complex configurations. Juan Linz's work contains examples of all three approaches, although his main research mode is comparative analysis. Even when Linz writes case studies, as he has on numerous occasions focusing particularly on Spain, his material includes many comparative references. And when using a statistical approach, as he most frequently does with survey results, the numbers help him characterize aspects of a case for purposes of analyzing its similarities with or differences from others.[21]

A final prefatory point. There is a fundamental difference between crossnational analysis and comparative analysis, although they are sometimes confused given the fact that the former always draws its data from attributes of national societies, while the latter often (but not exclusively) takes them as its "cases." However, it is best to retain the term "crossnational analysis" for statistical approaches that use national societal data. As such they do not have the small *n* but many variable characteristic of comparative analysis.[22] If the analyst is interested, for instance, in determining the relationship between church attendance and socioeconomic development, obviously such a question is resolved with a statistical approach that may be crossnational if the data banks that are used draw from national censuses or surveys. But a comparative historical analysis is appropriate if the question relates, say, to the effects of Catholic, Orthodox, and Protestant variants of Christianity on the formation of party systems or national identities.

A Protocol for Comparative Research

The Question

The research question at hand determines which approach, or combination of approaches, is needed to answer it. Although this relationship between question and research procedure seems to be straightforward, there is some confusion in the literature over this matter. Stanley Lieberson, for example, in criticizing comparative analysis for drawing firm conclusions from the examination of a very small number of cases, presents a hypothetical example in which the question is what determines collisions between cars on street corners with traffic lights. He then sets up a "test" following Mill's methods of agreement and difference, with two "cases" per method, leading to absurd conclusions.[23] Although doing a "case study" — an essential tool of error minimization in comparative analysis as noted earlier — of each of these four events by interviewing the drivers would have kept Lieberson from drawing his conclusions, this is not the main problem with his simpleminded mimicry of the comparative method. The problem with this example is that the initial question calls for a statistical approach, not comparative analysis, to answer it. The "cases" are brief events (two cars approaching a street corner at the same time), not complex collectivities of social interaction with definable boundaries. Such events are easily quantifiable, and it therefore makes no sense at all to collect only two cases for analysis.[24] Whenever variables are quantifiable and the units from which their measures are derived can be expanded far beyond their number, a statistical approach should be used. An important source of error in what is sometimes billed as comparative analysis stems from the fact that another approach, usually a statistical one, is more appropriate to answer the question.

Sometimes different approaches may provide complementary answers. For instance, while Juan Linz answered his question regarding the superiority of parliamentary regimes over presidential ones with comparative analysis, the matter is also amenable to a statistical treatment that shows, albeit with a narrower set of variables, the extent to which there is a difference in terms of democratic stability and other measures between the two regimes.[25]

A question pursued with one form of analysis may eventually lead to a question pursued with another. A comparative analyst exploring the relationship between labor movements and transitions to democracy may observe that the strike rate increases in the cases under examination; however, the extent to which this is so can only be determined by adopting a statistical approach using all cases for which there is reliable data. The statistical test may show that there is only one exception to the pattern, and the analyst may wish to focus on the reasons by doing a case study of it.[26] Similarly, survey results may show considerable differences between attitudes towards democratic legitimacy across recent cases of transition to democracy, and this may lead to a comparative approach in order to find the reasons for these differences. In all of what follows here I will assume that the question at hand can only be resolved satisfactorily by using comparative analysis.

While it is almost a truism that all research should begin with a question, it is remarkable to note how many times scholars initiate comparisons not with a question but with what could be called a space. Thus, a comparison will be drawn between two or more national societies because they share common borders, they are located in the same area of the world, or they are accessible to the comparativist given reasons such as knowledge of the languages needed to study them or access to funding, family support, institutional contacts, and so on, that make the research possible. When these considerations propel the initiation of comparisons, successful ones must still formulate a question that calls for applying comparative analysis—not other methods—to cases that have been selected in this manner—and not to other cases. I will return to this latter issue below.

However, the apparent truism of beginning research with a question also has its complications. As occurs in any scientific endeavor, the initial question may not be one which is well formulated given the inadequacy of the state of knowledge over the matter to which it pertains. Consequently, the research process must often return to reformulating the question, sharpening it. With comparative analysis it is also sometimes necessary to redress the question for reasons that are unique to it, again a point to be taken up later in this essay.

After formulating the question, at least in preliminary form, the analyst should turn to the main approaches that treat the subject in order to develop a list of the causal determinants that have been suggested in the literature for the problem at hand. During the course of the research the analyst should weigh the validity of all these explanations. While in statistical approaches the hypotheses drawn from different theoretical views often must be tested sequentially, in comparative analysis the evidentiary material (historical documents, interviews, statistical series, reports, secondary literature, etc.) must be approached while keeping in mind what are many times conflicting notions—and the more the better—regarding what explains the phenomenon at hand. Sometimes there are no preexisting theoretically based explanations covering the research problem. The analyst should still try to develop some notions based on his or her intuition or experience with related questions that will explain the phenomenon. It is better to stipulate such preconceptions explicitly rather than to jump into the research material because, more often than not, they are present anyway in the back of the analyst's mind and condition his or her perceptions of the material.

In this initial stage the analyst must also pay close attention to the definitions of key concepts according to the various theoretical traditions, as they often do not agree. It is essential to generate clear definitions of the terms and to apply them consistently across all the cases. While this should be done as soon as possible, it is often not wise to adopt thoroughly fixed definitions until the empirical research has reviewed preliminarily a range of disparate cases that are relevant to the question being asked. An examination of the evidence helps to clarify the meaning of concepts, and it may even lead to creating new ones. Holding to inadequate definitions can distort considerably the interpretations of the empirical material, leading to faulty conclusions. Induction plays a central role in comparative analysis and for it to operate properly—in other words, for the evidence to contribute its part in shaping the analyst's views of it—the definitions of key concepts should be open to revision and clarification in the early stages of the research.[27] Juan Linz's work in this respect offers a model to follow given its clear and concise definitions that have been crafted after a considerable review of various historical settings. For example, Linz's careful delimitation of the notion of political legitimacy and its facets resulted from his experience in dealing with the history of the delegitimation of democracies.[28] And his definition of democracy, minimalist and procedural, has been crafted to include in its scope regimes that have considerable shortcomings, especially in terms of the extension of suffrage.[29] This is due to the fact that their overall dynamics corresponded more to democratic than to nondemocratic regimes.

The Universe

A fundamental step in comparative analysis is to determine which is the universe of cases that must be examined in order to answer properly the question at hand. Ignoring this step can lead to the well-known problem of case selection bias.[30] In statistical analysis different universes (and samples) may contain the necessary properties to test hypotheses, and each is arguably as valid as the next. Comparative analysis does not have the same latitude or flexibility. Working with few cases and many variables requires ascertaining exactly which are the cases that apply to the question. This means that a considerable amount of time must be devoted to an at least rapid review of a broad array of cases that may be suspected of having attributes of the problem under examination. And yet, comparativists often do not spend much time thinking about the universe of cases to which their question applies, and a recent methodological statement even ignores the significance of this issue entirely.[31]

A further difficulty presented here is that the universe in comparative analysis has not one but two components. The first is its core, consisting of all cases (national often, or subnational, such as city governments, parishes, firms, etc.) where the phenomenon under investigation, in whatever variant if there is more than one, has occurred. The second component can be called the ancillary one: it includes cases where the phenomenon to be explained has not occurred (even if it may nearly have occurred), but which contain the most closely parallel or kindred phenomena to the one being investigated; these are the nearest different species or subspecies of a common genus. Thus, rising up the genus-species ladder to the next generic rung and then coming down on the nearest parallel line should permit the investigator to discover which are the most kindred cases.[32] For instance, if the question pertains to the possibility of democratic outcomes from political crisis in sultanistic regimes, the core universe will include cases where the crises of such regimes have generated democratic transitions and those where they have not; it will therefore include settings with both major variations that correspond to the question. Sultanistic regimes fall under the genus of authoritarian regime as defined by Linz,[33] and the problem being researched refers to political crisis and not to other political phenomena. Therefore, the ancillary universe will be composed of cases of political crisis with and without democratic outcomes in other types of authoritarian regimes, that is other species of the same genus.

Most of the research will focus on cases in the core universe, while knowledge of the ancillary cases which may be needed as a check for the explanations drawn from the core universe—as will be elaborated below—need not be as profound. The larger the question, that is the more generic and abstract it is, the more cases will be included in the core universe, to the point that the ancillary one may be reduced to zero. Thus, if the question is how collective identities are formed, there is no use wondering where this phenomenon did not take place; but if the question is how political identities influencing voter behavior are formed in democratized postcommunist regimes—a question which is certainly much lower down on the genus-species ladder—then the ancillary universe contains a large number of cases, the most proximate ones being those of political identity formation as it affects voter choices in newly democratized regimes stemming from other nondemocratic origins.

Sometimes apparently small changes in the research question can lead to considering certain cases either as part of the core or of the ancillary universes. For example, in Linz's study of the breakdown of democracies, the core universe is composed certainly of the cases where such breakdowns occurred, but he refers as well to a case, namely France at the fall of the Fourth and inception of the Fifth Republics, in which democracy was "reequilibrated" after a crisis, generating rapidly a reassertion of the democratic regime.[34] This was a case that had the advantage for Linz's argument of having had a disruption of normal constitutional procedures, thereby eliminating the guesswork regarding the severity of its political crisis. If it is viewed for this reason as a case of democratic collapse, then it contains a variation of the phenomenon under study, that is, a breakdown that nonetheless led to a rapid reassertion of democracy instead of a long lasting nondemocratic regime, and in this sense it would belong in the core universe. However, if it is viewed (as Linz in fact saw it) as a case of survival of democracy despite having undergone a very severe crisis, then it is a "near miss" situation that belongs in the ancillary universe because it does not contain the outcome under study. Consequently, this latter qualification determines whether France in 1958 (and many other cases) are part of the core or ancillary universes. The research sometimes has to be at a relatively advanced stage before such judgments can be made and the full composition of the ancillary universe of possibly useful *non-x* cases (in a sense to be explained later) comes to light.

One of the most common of all pitfalls in comparative analysis is to try to reach conclusions for theory building purposes without examining the full range of variation of the phenomenon at hand in the core universe. It is to avoid this mistake that it is fundamental, as indicated above, to know which cases compose this universe. If such cases are not known or are simply dismissed from consideration, some variations of the phenomenon may not enter the analysis. The result may be inferences that have a high probability of being wrong or inadequate because they stem from a narrow expression of the phenomenon. Hans Daalder has noted, for example, that models of European state building have erroneously been based mainly on state building in France.[35] Similarly, for many questions it is not possible to restrict the analysis simply to a geographical area such as Scandinavia, Western Europe, the Southern Cone of Latin America, or East Asia, and yet this is done more often than not. Again, Juan Linz's work points the way in terms of its refusal to restrict its boundaries to a single area of national experiences, as shown by his taxonomic survey of the varieties on nondemocratic regimes, or his studies of fascists.[36] There is no such thing as a "theory" valid for only a limited range of cases, and yet the comparative literature in the social sciences is unfortunately full of such attempts.[37]

A second common error relating to the universe is the opposite of the first, namely, the attempt to treat too many cases. No analyst working alone, not even Juan Linz, can master with all the required nuances and contextualizations a long list of cases. Attempts to do so result not only in a cursory understanding of the cases, but also, quite inevitably, in a form of comparative analysis that is excessively deductive, consisting basically of a set of theoretical premises and their logical derivations that are then illustrated by drawing selectively from the case materials. Such analysis therefore contain little, if anything, in terms of discovery, and will simply confirm most if not all preconceived ideas. The complexity of the cases is glossed over, as the analyst's theoretical framework overpowers everything. With too many cases, comparative analysis goes too far astray from the case study approach, thereby losing the latter's contribution to error minimization through the intimate understanding of the configurations presented by the phenomenon under examination in the specific cases. It is the insider's knowledge of the material of strategic cases (given the question that is asked) that leads to the original discoveries that make comparative analysis an important tool. Consequently, it is impossible to be a good comparativist without knowing a small number of cases very, very well.

Again Juan Linz exemplifies this point. His initial studies led him to very thorough research on early to mid-twentieth century Germany, Spain, and Italy. And it was his, again, very thorough understanding of these cases that led him to develop the authoritarian regime model what we now recognize, given his writings, as a key concept in the study of politics. Franco's Spain was simply of a different species under the nondemocratic regime genus than Nazi Germany and even Fascist Italy.[38] Researchers who attempt comparative analysis without in addition being thorough students of case studies not only have little to contribute beyond their theoretically derived models, but often leave those who know particular cases well baffled by the use that they make of them. Case study students should, on the contrary, recognize the "fit" between the contributions of comparative analysis and the cases with which they are acquainted, and should derive insights for their own work from those contributions. The comparative analyst's theoretical imagination should not exceed his or her knowledge of the cases.[39]

These two common inadequacies related to the number of cases — having too few or too many of them — are like the Scylla and Charybdis of comparative analysis, and it is necessary to devise strategies to navigate safely between both dangers. These will be addressed below.

Typologizing

Comparative analysis requires abstracting or highlighting a set of attributes pertinent to the question at hand from the relevant cases — attributes which are then judged similar or different in various ways to be noted later — and as a result it is impossible to do this analysis without creating what are, in effect, ideal types. Hence, it is useful explicitly to develop what will become a typology as early as the minimal necessary knowledge of the cases permits, and to formalize the attributes of each type as clearly as possible. It may be necessary to have both types and subtypes.

The typology should be organized around *the outcomes* shown by the phenomenon under investigation (or the dependent variable or variables), and it should cover *the full range of variation of such outcomes* in the core universe. Both points are important. The latter has already been noted above: covering the full range of variation of the phenomenon is essential to reach proper theory-building generalizations. Examining briefly the ancillary cases, especially if the question leads to a very circumscribed set of core cases, may add kindred manifestations of the phenomenon to the typology for later use. Again, this will be discussed below; it is the former point that requires additional comment.

Building the typology around outcomes organizes the comparisons among the cases around the similarities and differences they contain in terms of the phenomenon to be explained. The search for what determines the phenomenon can then proceed without having the typology prejudge the results. This is what occurs if the typology is built on the other possible ways of doing so, namely, on the basis of what are understood to be, given the working hypothesis, the determinants (or independent variables) of the phenomenon under investigation, or on the basis of supposed background characteristics of the cases. The first option leads the analyst to run the risk, given the complexity of the cases, of simply confirming the hypothesized determinants as they become a powerful lens or filter that presorts the evidence. The supposed explanations organize the analysis to such an extent that it is hard to escape from them, and the research becomes unwittingly tautological or self-fulfilling because it is then difficult to examine the validity of alternative perspectives or even for new ones to emerge from reviewing the evidence.[40] This is not to say that the researcher should not have working hypotheses; the point here is that the hypotheses should be assessed by looking at material organized on the basis of what they purport to explain, that is, the outcomes of the phenomenon in question. It is possible, nonetheless, for the analyst to choose to report the research findings by presenting a typology based on the determinants of the phenomenon; but this is a matter of choice for the sake of the clarity of exposition once the conclusions of the research have been reached.[41]

The second alternative option is to organize the typology around certain background characteristics of the cases, but it is no better than the previous one. It generates the risk of skewing the analysis in ways that make the background attributes of the cases, that is, those that are unconnected to either the phenomenon to be explained or to variables the theories suggest as their causes, acquire a determinative effect, even though the analyst does not have this intention. For instance, if the question is what determines the formation of welfare regimes, and the cases are classed into Buddhist, Catholic, Confucian, Hindu, Jewish, Muslim, Orthodox, and Protestant types, it is quite likely that the answers to the question will be affected by this overarching typology of the religious and/or moral basis of national cultures. A very common source of background based typologies is the tendency to classify cases according to their levels of development, or, more crudely, into whether they are part of "advanced industrial societies" or of the "Third World," a distinction that never made much sense but is now clearly obsolete.

Having developed the typology, the relevant cases should then be listed into the various types. Obviously, there will generally be a disparate number of cases in each one. It would indeed be a very rare coincidence if each and every variation of the phenomenon were to be found in an equal number of cases, and such symmetry should not be forced into the interpretation of the material.

Coping with the Size of the Universe

If the research question calls for a manageable set of cases to be analyzed, then the size of the universe does not present any problems and the researcher can sail safely through the Scylla of having too few and the Charybdis of having too many cases. But often the question's relevant universe of cases is excessively large for any individual scholar to analyze with the required depth.[42] Moreover, the language abilities of the researcher may prevent serious consideration of all the necessary cases. In such situations (in addition to learning more languages or hiring translators), three strategies can be followed.

The first is collaborative work. A researcher who has done extensive work on a question may recruit others to discuss further cases, as exemplified with Juan Linz's model of the breakdown of democratic regimes which led to a conference and to a collective set of volumes edited with Alfred Stepan.[43] Several researchers who know their cases well may also join forces to study a common issue. This requires optimally a unified team to discuss every step of the research, and for the group's organizer or organizers to be actively engaged in studying some of the case materials in depth, otherwise the latter will be too detached intellectually to be able to pull the various strands together effectively in concluding observations. Perhaps the best example of this model is the group directed by Charles Tilly for the Social Science Research Committee which examined the issue of the formation of national states in Europe.[44] But in most situations this form of collaborative research will be impossible to organize, as its funding is hard to secure and a compatible team is rarely assembled.

A second strategy is to reformulate the question by dropping to a lower level of abstraction along the genus-species ladder. This will necessarily reduce the size of the universe, particularly the core universe. For example, if the general question is, What are the effects of religion on the formation of political parties in democracies? it calls for an examination of all cases where democracies have been established. Reducing the question to "what are the effects of religion on the formation of political parties in those democracies that developed before 1920?" would, of course, drastically cut down the size of the core universe only to those cases that were earliest in developing democratic regimes; how much so would depend on the definition of democracy. It is also possible to reduce the relevant universe by following the genus-species line along the religious dimension, and investigating, for instance, only the impact of Catholicism on the formation of political parties in democracies. In this case the core universe would be composed of countries with democratic regimes and a significant percentage (to be defined) of Catholics in the population.[45] Or the universe can be reduced even further by focusing on what the effects of Catholicism are on the formation of political parties in well established democracies (according to a clear cut definition) where only a minority (again, definition required) of the national population is of Catholic background or tradition. In this case the core universe would be composed of Germany, The Netherlands, Switzerland, the United States, the United Kingdom, and perhaps some other cases depending on the definitions.

While this strategy is highly effective in reducing the size of the core universe, it has two drawbacks. The first is that every additional qualification to an initially grand question also reduces the breadth and, possibly, the theoretical payoff of the conclusions. Although all of these questions fall into the domain of middle range theorizing, their scope becomes smaller and smaller with each reduction. Although it is better to have solid research on more limited questions than poorly grounded work on larger ones, at an extreme the question and the resulting theoretical payoff may become trivial or insignificant. Hence, in doing this type of reduction of the universe, it is important not to eliminate the case or cases that present the most theoretically meaningful variations of the problem at hand, those that stand out in the literature given, for instance, their "deviant" nature. For example, with the last reduction to the question in the previous paragraph the universe of cases no longer contains any where Catholicism is or was the established Church, or where Catholics were the main state-builders. Eliminating such cases means that the phenomenon of the effects of Catholicism on the formation of political parties in a democracy can no longer be examined, because an important variation to this phenomenon has been lost. However, a researcher may well be interested in looking specifically at the effects of sizable Catholic minorities on party formation in countries where Protestants were the main state or democracy builders, given that this matter has received less attention in the literature.

The second drawback is that such reductions of the core universe increase the size and potential significance of the ancillary one, and hence beyond a certain point the number of cases ceases to become much smaller. While the research need not go into depth with ancillary cases, if the core universe becomes so narrow that it does not contain a sufficient number of cases for the analyst to undertake a proper check of the inferences he or she draws from its comparisons, then the ancillary ones will become important to the research. I will return to this point in the discussion of the process of drawing inferences from comparisons.

The third strategy to cope with the excessive size of the universe is to take a cue from statistical analysis and to draw a sample from it. This is the preferable procedure to navigate between the problem of having too many or too few cases when the analyst does not want to limit the theoretical scope of the question. Naturally, the results depend on having an adequate sample, and this kind of sampling cannot be done at random. The cases the analyst already knows best, or those in which the phenomenon under study first came to his or her attention, can of course be included in the sample. But the sample has to follow strictly the typology (which in turn has to be correctly designed), and it should include at least one case, but preferably two or three, in each type. The aim is to have a manageable number of cases, but for that number to contain all the significant manifestations of the phenomenon being researched, thereby preventing the common mistake of trying to reach generalizations on less than their full range of variation. Cases from the ancillary universe, which need not reflect all possible kindred variations, should also be selected into separate types if need be.

As noted above, every question points to a set of variables pertinent to it, a set that can be determined preliminarily by examining the theories that address it. These independent variables, together with the dependent one or ones, from part of the "active" variables the analyst focuses on during comparisons. There are also many "background" variables, that is, those that are known to the analyst but which express attributes of the cases that are considered to be irrelevant to researching the question at hand. The "background" variables do play a part, however, during the sampling phase of the research, for it is best to select cases for each type in the sample that have overall affinities in terms of such background variables. This is preferable because the research process may uncover that the active variables which were originally considered to be determinative, given the theoretical perspectives, cannot account adequately for the phenomenon at hand. In such circumstances the researcher may want to bring background variables to the foreground (making them part of the active ones) in an effort to discover new explanations, and this operation will be easier with cases that are, by and large, closer to each other in ways that were originally considered irrelevant. Hence, if the choice is, for example, between including material from France or from Zambia in a certain type, it is best to opt for the case that has greater affinities with the one or more cases already included in the type in terms of the seemingly irrelevant political, economic, cultural, demographic, and so on, background variables.

Setting up the Comparisons

The literature on comparative analysis still presents, as indicated previously, Mill's methods of "agreement" and "difference" as its main tools to work towards research conclusions. Figure 10.1 exemplifies these methods in a simple form with two cases and three variables to explain phenomenon x. With Method I, to be used when x is present in both cases, the researcher tries to find a few similar attributes among the many differences between the cases with the presumption that such similarities account for the similar outcome. With Method II, to be applied when x is present in only one case, the researcher seeks to match the attributes of what are presumed to be similar cases in a search for those that are different, as the latter would then explain the x and *non-x* outcomes.

There is no reason why a researcher should use only one of the methods in Figure 10.1, as both can be used by comparing more than two cases, and in fact it is best to do so. Berins Collier and Collier even apply both schemes at the same time: After constructing a typology of labor "incorporation" outcomes in Latin America, they analyze pairs of cases that presumably share the basic similarity of belonging to a single type but are as different as possible within that framework.[46]

However, the methods in Figure 10.1 contain very simple minded renditions of comparative research designs. First, they do not contemplate all the possibilities that present themselves in comparisons. Cases that have the outcome to be explained may have arrived there by more than one route, contrary to what is implied in Method I. There may be, in other words, coincidental determinants for similar outcomes. Moreover, Method II assumes that cases that do not show similar outcomes are nonetheless matched in every other respect! This is a tall order in comparative social science, because the cases are of such complexity that it is impossible for them to be so extensively similar that the only differences will be those that explain the different outcomes. This points to the second deficiency in this rendition of comparative designs, namely, that it is insufficiently complex in its depiction of the variables in so far as it makes no distinction between the "active" and "background" ones, as defined above. Thus, Method II depicts a possible comparison between two cases if and only if all the variables, from a to w, are part of the *active set* of variables, while in Method I, for all

Figure 10.1 Standard Methods of Comparison Based on Mill

Method I Of Agreement (Mill) or of Difference (Przeworski and Teune)		Method II Of Difference (Mill), of Similarity (Przeworski and and Teune), or of Comparable Cases (Lijphart)	
Case 1	Case 2	Case 3	Case 4
x present	x present	x present	x absent
Other variables:		Other variables:	
a	b	a	a
c	d	b	b
e	f	c	c
g	h	d	d
i	j	e	e
k	l	f	f
Explanatory variables:		Explanatory variables:	
o	o	r	s
p	p	t	u
q	q	v	w
x results from o, p, q variables that are matched in both cases		x results from $r, t, v,$ variables contained in case 3 but not in case 4	

intents and purposes, the variables from *a* to *l* are part of the irrelevant *background set*.

Figure 10.2 presents the missing possibilities in comparisons by placing determinants and outcomes into a fourfold table, and by adding to its visual scheme the distinction between active and background variables.

The foreground boxes in Figure 10.2, which contain only the active variables, illustrate the varieties of possible comparisons. The first box pertains to those cases that are seen as generating *similar cases comparisons* because they have the same outcomes in terms of the phenomenon to be explained, and matching determinants can be located to explain them. It is like Method I in the previous figure, except that box 1 in Figure 10.2 would contain only variables *x, o, p, q* of Figure 10.1 (that is, the active ones) while the rest (including some similar variables not contemplated in Method I) would fall in the background variable space behind box 1.

The second box corresponds to *coincidental similarities*. The outcomes are similar, but the determinants for them are different. There is no way to know a priori if a comparison is of a similar case or of a coincidental variety, and yet in the course of the research the analyst may well discover that there are different routes to the phenomenon under investigation. (Such results can lead the analyst to prefer creating a typology of determinants in order to report them.)

The third box represents comparisons in which the outcomes are different, but the determinants are very nearly similar; these are *intervening variable comparisons*, for a particular variable (or a very limited set of them) can be clearly identified as having created the difference.[47] Box 3 is, therefore, like Method II in Figure 10.1 if all the latter's variables from *a* to *w* are considered active ones.

Finally, the fourth box pertains to *different cases comparisons*. The outcomes are different and so are the determinants. Box 4 is like Method 2 in Figure 10.1 if the explanatory variables *r* through *w* are considered (in addition to *x*) to be the active ones, with the rest (*a* to *f*) being background variables.

The cases placed within each type of the typology created for the research establish similar cases comparisons (box 1), though on further examination they may turn out to be of a coincidental nature (box 2). Comparing cases from different types generates different cases comparisons (box 4), although a deeper analysis may reveal that they are in fact intervening variable comparisons (box 3).

Figure 10.2 Beyond the "Methods of Similarity and Difference":
Active and Background Variables in Comparative Situations

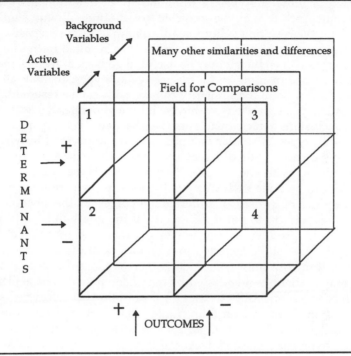

Drawing Inferences

Similar cases comparisons are the best anchor for drawing inferences from comparisons, and the research should always begin with them if at all possible, that is, if there is more than one case per type. It is much better to search for the determinants of a phenomenon by studying cases where it is commonly present. It is riskier to do so with different cases comparisons because so many differences are bound to be present even within the active set of variables that it is much more difficult to determine which ones actually explain the phenomenon under examination; in such circumstances, the analyst will be tempted to simply choose as explanatory variables those that correspond most closely to his or her theoretical preferences or preconceptions.

The similar cases comparisons may lead to the discovery that there are coincidental similarities at work. This conclusion should be reached only after considering the possibility that some of the background variables may provide a common explanation. If the type under examination does indeed have coincidental similarities, this means that it contains two or more subtypes of different causal determinants leading the same outcome. It may be possible to continue doing similarity comparisons if the resulting subtypes still contain at least two cases. If no two such cases are found and the cases in the type resulted from sampling out of a larger universe, then it may be useful to go back to the original list of cases to add one or more to the respective subtypes, thereby altering the sample. At that point the similarity comparisons can be resumed.

The similarity comparisons within each type generate, however, only tentative conclusions which then must be checked by comparing cases across different types. If similar determinants are uncovered in what are supposed to be cases with different outcomes, then there is obviously something wrong with the original conclusions. These different cases comparisons can be done exclusively with cases in the core universe if it contains a sufficient variety of different outcomes to the phenomenon under investigation (or, to put it differently, if the question is sufficiently general so as to produce a core universe containing several—at least three—species that can be included in a typology). If the question leads, for example, to a core universe which is then organized into four types given the main variations manifested by the phenomenon to be explained, and if each type has at least two cases (or if sampling has left two cases in each type), then there will be four similar cases comparisons (one per type) and six different cases comparisons as a check for the conclusions drawn from the former ones. However, if the core universe contains only cases with similar outcomes given a highly focused question, or even if it contains only two types (which would only permit one different cases comparison), it will be necessary to draw on cases in the ancillary universe to check with different cases the solidity of the explanations developed with the similar cases comparison. As the purpose of the different cases comparisons is to verify the solidity of the explanations derived from those that are similar, it is not necessary to do extensive research on the ancillary cases; it suffices to examine them enough to ascertain that they indeed do not have the same configuration of causal variables that have been seen to operate in the similar cases within the core universe. After all, the research question focuses on the core universe of cases, and does not aim to explain the characteristics of the ancillary ones. If the analyst is driven to do so, then the research question in fact changes, and the previous steps of the research as noted above would have to be retraced.

The best support for the similarity analysis comes from difference comparisons of the intervening variable form (box 3 in Figure 10.2). Such box 3 comparisons may occur both with core as well as with ancillary cases. However, they are especially useful when trying to answer a question that is sufficiently generic so as to produce several outcomes in the core universe. With the intervening variable form of comparison the research is able not only to check the solidity of the similar cases analysis (for example, by ascertaining that the causal variables do not appear in the same form), but it is also able to pinpoint much more specifically the likely reason or reasons for the difference. With a different cases contrast (box 4 in Figure 10.2), this latter conclusion does not go beyond showing that the cases are different indeed, and hence the similarity analysis internal to each type still bears the full weight of the explanation.

When there is only one case within a type, there is no alternative but to rely, in addition to the conclusions of the case study analysis, on different cases comparisons. Again, in such circumstances it is best if these comparisons prove to be of an intervening variable or variables kind (box 3 in Figure 10.2).

In conducting the comparisons, the analyst should not consider each variable as having only binary values, as if they could be coded simply yes/no or 0/1. Such treatment steers the researcher towards viewing variables as having absolute values and one-to-one relations among them, rather than seeing them as having variously weak or strong expressions, as operating in contexts where they may acquire different significance, and as forming part of complex sequences. Thus, in comparing party systems, the terms "Conservative," "Liberal," and "Socialist" parties do not mean the same thing in different countries, nor across time in the same country. Similarly, large landowners since the 1850s cannot be presumed to have everywhere the same political and economic interests. Land ownership can be used not only to produce a very broad variety of products from milk and wine to wood, but also to secure credit for investment elsewhere in the national or international economy, to block other people's access to potential mineral deposits or to water, to have the necessary local influence to build a political career, and so on. Hence, Ragin's suggestion of using Boolean algebra as a shorthand mechanism to help annotate the effects of the variables can be useful,[48] as long as the researcher assigns the 0/1 values to variables after assessing their strength, placing them in their context, and viewing whether they operate as part of a sequence of variables when they exert their effects only through peculiar interactions among them.

Conclusion

The protocol contained in these pages is designed to steer the scholar who wishes to use comparative analysis for causal and theory-building purposes away from the most common pitfalls that are associated with this method. To restate these pitfalls in a nutshell, they are the following: (1) beginning comparative analysis focusing on a "space" rather than with a clearcut question; (2) seeking to answer questions with comparative analysis which should be addressed by using other approaches, particularly a statistical one; (3) not anchoring the analysis on clear definitions that are applied consistently across all cases; (4) not spending any time thinking about the universe of cases containing manifestations of the phenomenon under research; (5) not creating a typology explicitly, or devising it on a basis other than the variants shown by the phenomenon that is being investigated; (6) comparing fewer cases than the number of variations shown by the phenomenon, or sampling the universe without including at least two cases per variant, if at all possible, or at least one, if not; (7) trying to examine too many cases, thereby losing the ability to ground comparative analysis explanations on thorough case studies; (8) adopting a research design that leads only to examining different cases when it is possible to do similar cases comparisons; (9) neglecting to check the conclusions derived from the analysis of similar cases by looking at those that have different outcomes, referring, if necessary, to the ancillary universe.

Comparative analysis is not an easy method to use properly. In addition to containing many possible sources of error, it often demands careful historical research, linguistic abilities, and the capacity to sift through a great deal of information. Juan Linz's work over several decades provides an excellent model to emulate. With his erudition, his knowledge of languages, his limpid questions and definitions, his attention to the universe of settings to which his questions apply, his in-depth studies of specific cases which can be seen as his "sample" from the larger set of cases, and his careful judgments of the evidence without losing sight of its contextual configurations, Linz has basically followed, *avant la lettre*, the protocol presented here.

Notes

1. I will refrain from providing extensive citations to Linz's work here. The reader is strongly advised to examine the impressive list of his publications in Houchang E. Chehabi, ed., *Politics, Society, and Democracy: Juan J. Linz —*

Untranslated Writings and Complete Annotated Bibliography (forthcoming), a companion volume of *Essays in Honor of Juan J. Linz* to this one

2. A large number of publications use the term "comparative" in their titles, but few among them are specifically devoted to the problem of how to draw inferences from research that requires considering many complex variables within a far smaller number of cases. In this essay, the term "comparative analysis" refers only to this situation. Defining comparative analysis as "the study of dissimilar social units," as Neil J. Smelser does in his *Comparative Methods in the Social Sciences* (Englewood Cliffs, N.J.: Prentice-Hall, 1976), p. 2, is inadequate because it makes "comparative analysis" virtually indistinguishable from social scientific investigation—as Smelser notes himself, pp. 2–3. It also places the accent on the study of differences among units, while much of comparative analysis should rest, when possible (as will be noted below), on examining their similarities. It is the use of Smelser's and other such definitions that has led to the apparently very large number of works on comparative analysis since the 1950s.

3. Donald T. Campbell and Julian Stanley, *Experimental and Quasi-Experimental Designs for Research* (Chicago: Rand McNally, 1966). Campbell himself reiterates that he and Stanley viewed "cross cultural comparison as a weak form of quasi-experimental design," in Donald T. Campbell, "'Degrees of Freedom' and the Case Study," *Comparative Political Studies* 8, 2 (July 1975): 179.

4. See for example Adam Przeworski and Henry Teune, *The Logic of Comparative Social Inquiry* (New York: Wiley-Interscience, 1970); Arend Lijphart, "The Comparable Cases Strategy in Comparative Research," *Comparative Political Studies* 8, 2 (July 1975): 178–93; Smelser, *Comparative Methods*; Theda Skocpol and Margaret Sommers, "The Uses of Comparative History in Macrosocial Inquiry," *Comparative Studies in Society and History* 22, 2 (April 1980): 174–97; and Charles C. Ragin, *The Comparative Method. Moving Beyond Qualitative and Quantitative Strategies* (Berkeley: University of California Press, 1987). Mill's terms are contained in his *A System of Logic: Ratiocinative and Inductive* (London: Longmans, Green, Reader, and Dyer, 1875), book 3.

For a review essay discussing developments in comparative analysis (although it also discusses statistical and case study approaches) since the early 1970s see David Collier, "The Comparative Method: Two Decades of Change," in Dankwart A. Rustow and Kenneth Paul Erickson, eds., *Comparative Political Dynamics: Global Research Perspectives* (New York: Harper Collins, 1991), chapter 2.

5. An exception within his voluminous writings is Juan J. Linz and Amando de Miguel, "Within-Nation Differences and Comparisons: The Eight Spains," in Richard L. Merritt and Stein Rokkan, eds., *Comparing Nations: The Use of Quantitative Data in Cross-National Research* (New Haven: Yale University Press, 1966). This paper stresses the convenience of using within country comparisons, and not only cross-country ones, given that many variables are held constant by the presence of overarching national institutions as well as important historical and cultural commonalities.

6. Marc Bloch, for instance, asserted that the purpose of comparisons was to "analyze and isolate the 'originality' of different societies," cited in Stefan Berger, *The British Labour Party and the German Social Democrats, 1900-1931: A Comparative Study* (Oxford: Clarendon Press, 1994), p. 3. In an inaugural lecture delivered at Oxford University in 1991, John H. Elliot noted that "the value of comparative history lies not so much in discovering the similarities as in identifying the differences," cited in Eduardo Posada-Carbó, "Elections before Democracy: Some Considerations on Electoral History from a Comparative Approach," in Posada-Carbó, *Elections before Democracy: The History of Elections in Europe and Latin America* (London: Institute of Latin American Studies Series, University of London, MacMillan Press, 1996), p. 4.

7. Charles Tilly, *Big Structures, Large Processes, Huge Comparisons* (New York: Russell Sage Foundation, 1984) distinguishes "individualizing comparisons," in which the uniqueness of each case is emphasized, from "encompassing comparisons," "universalizing comparisons," and "variation finding comparisons," all of which posit some element of commonality—in addition to their individual features—between the units that fall within the scope of the comparisons. The first pertains to the contrasting-descriptive approach often used by historians, and the latter to the more theory-building use of comparisons. An excellent example of an "individualizing comparison" is the classic work of Sir John Clapham, *The Economic Development of France and Germany, 1815–1914* (Cambridge: Cambridge University Press, 1936).

8. This convergence can be seen in Berger, who is a historian. His work focuses on the similarities between British and German labor movements and their related parties, and criticizes the often expressed view that they are polar opposites given their ideological differences.

9. See Arend Lijphart, "Comparative Politics and the Comparative Method," *American Political Science Review* 65, 3 (September 1971): 682–93, who acknowledges in a footnote, p. 684, his debt on this point to a paper presented by Neil Smelser at the Sixth World Congress of Sociology (1966).

10. Lijphart, "Comparative Politics," p. 684.

11. Lijphart, "Comparable Cases," p. 160. Lijphart does note that the analysis of "deviant cases" can be a form of comparative analysis, p. 160. In "Comparative Politics," pp. 691–93, Lijphart has a useful discussion of six varieties of case studies, deviant cases among them.

12. With experimental designs researchers introduce scientific controls by manipulating variables and by repeating the experiments. This can hardly be done with the macrophenomena which are the object of comparative analysis. Naturally, all scientific explanation requires some form of control over variables, and in this sense there is a remote relationship between comparative analysis and experimental designs. The protocol presented here shows how controls can be introduced in comparative studies.

13. See Collier for a brief review of the literature assessing case studies, pp. 23–24.

14. In his generally informative discussion of the differences between case study, comparative, and statistical approaches, Charles Ragin, *Constructing Social Research: The Unity and Diversity of Method* (Thousand Oaks, London,

New Delhi: Pine Forge Press, 1994), ch. 2, does not consider this form of predicting social phenomena by using case or ethnographic studies; see especially pp. 37–39, and 51.

15. Campbell, p. 182. Given the many different observational points in case studies, Campbell argues convincingly that they in fact have an *n* which is much larger than one, and that they do not have, therefore, the negative degrees of freedom problem that is usually associated with them.

16. See for an example of this type of work Elijah Anderson, *Streetwise: Race, Class, and Change in an Urban Community* (Chicago: University of Chicago Press, 1990).

17. Ragin, *The Comparative Method*, advocates the use of Boolean algebra for drawing inferences in comparative analysis. Obviously, this is a very different form of quantification of variables from that used in conventional statistical analysis.

18. Lijphart, "Comparative Politics," pp. 685–86, and "Comparable Cases," pp. 159–63, has suggested four strategies to deal with the small *n*-many variable problem. However, the first one, increasing the number of cases, is often not a realistic option unless the variables permit quantification, and if that is possible, a statistical approach was often preferable from the very beginning. I am skeptical of the other strategies for reasons that will become apparent in reading this paper.

19. Lijphart, "Comparative Politics," p. 684; Ragin, *Constructing Social Research*, p. 49.

20. Ibid., p. 160.

21. For an example that illustrates both of these observations, see Juan J. Linz, "La sociedad española: presente, pasado y futuro," in Juan J. Linz, ed., *España: Un presente para el futuro* (Madrid: Instituto de Estudios Económicos, 1984), pp. 63–64, and 73–95.

22. The confusion in question appears most clearly in Przeworski and Teune. Their preferred approach to comparison, which they label as "most different systems" (to be discussed below), generally assumes a statistical mode, and should be assimilated to "cross national analysis," not the comparative method. Lijphart also makes this criticism of these authors when he notes that their most different system "should be assigned to the category of statistical analysis." Lijphart, "Comparable Cases," p. 164. Much of the discussion in Smelser, *Comparative Methods*, chaps. 6 and 7, refers also to cross national statistical approaches rather than to comparative analysis.

23. Stanley Lieberson, "Small N's and Big Conclusions: An Examination of the Reasoning in Comparative Studies Based on a Small Number of Cases," in Charles C. Ragin and Howard S. Becker, eds., *What Is a Case? Exploring the Foundations of Social Inquiry* (Cambridge: Cambridge University Press, 1992), pp. 105–18.

24. Lieberson also argues that conclusions in the social sciences should take the form of probabilistic statements, while comparative analysis draws deterministic ones, pp. 106–109, 117–18. It is indeed very hard to state conclusions in a probabilistic manner without using a statistical approach. This

does not mean that comparativists are not aware of the tentative nature of their conclusions. They hold only in so far as another analyst, after making the great effort required to understand the pertinent cases in all their complexity, is able to point to their deficiency and to generate a different, more convincing set of conclusions. In the last analysis, this difference between statistical and comparative analysis is more of form than of substance.

25. A statistical approach to the question can be seen in Arend Lijphart, "The Virtues of Parliamentarism: But Which Kind of Parliamentarism?" in H. E. Chehabi and Alfred Stepan, eds., *Politics, Society, Democracy. Comparative Studies* (Boulder: Westview Press, 1995). Juan Linz's basic articles on this question are "The Perils of Presidentialism," *Journal of Democracy* 1 (Winter 1990): 51–69; and "The Virtues of Parliamentarism," *Journal of Democracy* 1 (Fall 1990): 84–91.

26. My appreciation to Nancy Bermeo for her talk on this topic at Nuffield College, Oxford University, 14 May 1996, in which she noted that strike data from Ecuador constituted such an exception.

27. These considerations are applicable whether one subscribes to an essentialist or a monimalist view of definitions.

28. See Juan J. Linz, *The Breakdown of Democratic Regimes: Crisis, Breakdown, and Reequilibration* (Baltimore: Johns Hopkins University Press, 1978), pp. 16–23.

29. Linz, *Breakdown*, p. 5, where even regimes with *suffrage censitaire* are included among democracies.

30. See Smelser, *Comparative Methods*, pp. 211–20; and Barbara Geddes, "How the Cases You Choose Affect the Answers You Get: Selection Bias in Comparative Politics," *Political Analysis* 2 (1990), pp. 131–50.

31. Ragin, *Constructing Social Research*, p. 113. Ragin simply notes that the cases selected for comparison are those the analysts or their intended audiences find interesting, and that they should be "comparable," that is, they should "belong to the same category."

Geddes, p. 134, does realize the importance of searching for the proper universe. However, she does not discuss the specific problems confronted in determining the universe when there are many variables but far fewer cases. In fact, her definition of the universe as "the cases to which the hypothesis should apply," and her discussion of sampling procedures that should be "correlated with the placement of cases on the dependent variable," simply apply the standard procedures suited to statistical approaches; pp. 134–35.

32. This procedure borrows from Giovanni Sartori's classic article on the use of concepts in comparative research, "Concept Misformation in Comparative Politics," *American Political Science Review* 54, 4 (December 1970): 1033–53.

33. Juan J. Linz, "Totalitarian and Authoritarian Regimes," in Fred I. Greenstein and Nelson W. Polsby, eds., *Handbook of Political Science, Volume 3, Macro Political Theory* (Reading, MA.: Addison-Wesley, 1975), p. 179 and passim.

34. Linz, *Breakdown*, especially pp. 87–88.

35. Hans Daalder, "Paths Toward State Formation in Europe: Democratization, Bureaucratization, and Politicization," in Chehabi and Stepan.

In Daalder's words, p. 115: "[W]ritings on European political development in general, but most notably writings on the development of the state, are generally couched in terms of a dominant paradigm that on closer look is clearly derived from a stylized analysis of the French case."

36. Juan J. Linz, "Totalitarian and Authoritarian Regimes"; Juan J. Linz, "Some Notes toward a Comparative Study of Fascism in Sociological Historical Perspective," in Walter Lacqueur, ed., *Fascism: A Reader's Guide* (Berkeley and Los Angeles: University of California Press, 1976); and Juan J. Linz, "Political Space and Fascism as a Late-Comer," in Stein Ugelvik Larsen, Bernt Hagtvet, and Jan Petter Myklebust, eds., *Who were the Fascists?* (Oslo: Universitetsforlaget, 1980).

37. It may be argued that it is possible to draw empirical generalizations from comparing cases that do not contain the full range of variation of the phenomenon at hand. But the conclusions of most such studies do not make such a limited claim. And these generalizations would be of little use in any event. What sense would it make to conclude, after studying the origins of social security systems in Brazil and in Italy, that such systems originate with fascist or protofascist authoritarian regimes?

38. The authoritarian regime model was presented initially in Juan J. Linz, "An Authoritarian Regime: The Case of Spain," in Erik Allard and Yrjo Littunen, eds., *Cleavages, Ideologies and Party Systems* (Helsinki: Westmark Society, 1964).

39. What I have called here the deductivist and illustrative approach to comparative analysis does have its advocates. One of the most extreme is Angelo Panebianco, *Political Parties: Organization and Power* (New York: Cambridge University Press, 1988), who writes that in comparative analysis "*one's research is based on a predetermined analytic picture,* [and] an investigation of this type will inevitably do an injustice to...historiographic interpretations (filtering them through different theoretical lenses) and to historiographic material in general. Comparative historical research almost always leaves historians (specialists in individual case studies) perplexed and unsatisfied. And this is virtually inevitable because the comparativist...can only be highly selective in his choice of historical literature, *having to discard those aspects of the historiographical debate which are not compatible with his theoretical perspective.*...An ever present risk is that of doing an overly superficial analysis of the different case studies. But the alternative is even riskier; in fear of doing an injustice to history, the researcher...loses sight of his goal: to isolate the similarities and differences between the various cases (which, in turn, is possible *only if the predetermined theoretical perspective is not abandoned in the process*)." pp. xiv–xv, my emphasis. Needless to say, I reject the substance of the comment categorically. It makes a virtue out of forcing the case study material into a preconceived conceptual and analytical straightjacket!

Lijphart's fourth suggestion to deal with the small *n* many variable problem, that of "restricting the analysis to the key variables and omitting those of marginal importance," ("Comparable Cases," p. 159) also can lead to this problem. The analyst may restrict him or herself too much to a predetermined conceptual scheme and minimize the possibility of discovery from cases studies.

40. This procedure is, again, similar to the deductive and illustrative form of comparative analysis which does not open itself to discovery. For an example of this inadequate form of typologyzing in comparative analysis see Clark Kerr, John T. Dunlop, Frederich Harbison, and Charles A. Myers, *Industrialism and Industrial Man. The Problems of Labor and Management in Economic Growth* (New York: Oxford University Press, 1964), chapter 2, in which the typology of industrializing elites also explains the course of industrialization and labor management.

41. In my "Labor Movements in Transitions to Democracy: A Framework for Analysis," in *Comparative Politics* 21, 4 (July 1989): 445–72, I chose to organize the presentation of comparative research findings with a typology based on the determinants of the phenomenon I analyzed. In my "Labor Movements and Political Systems: Some Variations," in Marino Regini, ed., *The Future of Labor Movements* (London: Sage Publications, 1992), I chose to retain the working typology based on outcomes.

42. Having too few cases, even one, in the core universe is not a problem as long as it is indeed true that there are no other cases with the phenomenon under investigation. It is also possible to do the comparative analysis equivalent of computer simulations, that is, to invent cases on the basis of speculation of the "what if" sort. While historians rightly shy away from such exercises, they can be fruitful from a conceptual and theoretical point of view.

43. Juan J. Linz and Alfred Stepan, eds., *The Breakdown of Democratic Regimes* (Baltimore: Johns Hopkins University Press, 1978).

44. Charles Tilly, ed., *The Formation of National States in Western Europe* (Princeton: Princeton University Press, 1975).

45. For an important recent contribution to the study of the varieties of Catholic political party formation in Europe see Jean-Dominique Durand, *L'Europe de la Démocratie Chrétienne* (Brussels: Editions Complèxe, 1995).

46. Ruth Berins Collier and David Collier, *Shaping the Political Arena. Critical Junctures, the Labor Movement, and Regime Dynamics in Latin America* (Princeton, N. J.: Princeton University Press, 1991), pp. 16–18.

47. Smelser uses the term "near cases" to refer to these comparisons; Smelser, *Comparative Methods*, pp. 215-20. Linz and de Miguel's paper refers to them as well.

48. Ragin, *The Comparative Method*, chapters 6–8.